INDEPENDENT
CONSULTING
FOR
EVALUATORS

OTHER RECENT VOLUMES IN THE
SAGE FOCUS EDITIONS

8. **Controversy (Third Edition)**
Dorothy Nelkin
41. **Black Families (Second Edition)**
Harriette Pipes McAdoo
64. **Family Relationships in Later Life (Second Edition)**
Timothy H. Brubaker
89. **Popular Music and Communication (Second Edition)**
James Lull
119. **The Home Care Experience**
Jaber F. Gubrium and Andrea Sankar
120. **Black Aged**
Zev Harel, Edward A. McKinney, and Michael Williams
121. **Mass Communication and Public Health**
Charles Atkin and Lawrence Wallack
122. **Changes in the State**
Edward S. Greenberg and Thomas F. Mayer
123. **Participatory Action Research**
William Foote Whyte
124. **Experiencing Fieldwork**
William B. Shaffir and Robert A. Stebbins
125. **Gender, Family, and Economy**
Rae Lesser Blumberg
126. **Enterprise Zones**
Roy E. Green
127. **Polling and Presidential Election Coverage**
Paul J. Lavrakas and Jack K. Holley
128. **Sharing Social Science Data**
Joan E. Sieber
129. **Family Preservation Services**
Kathleen Wells and David E. Biegel
130. **Media Coverage of Terrorism**
A. Odasuo Alali and Kenoye Kelvin Eke
131. **Saving Children at Risk**
Travis Thompson and Susan C. Hupp
132. **Text in Context**
Graham Watson and Robert M. Seiler
133. **Social Research on Children and Adolescents**
Barbara Stanley and Joan E. Sieber
134. **The Politics of Life in Schools**
Joseph Blase

135. **Applied Impression Management**
Robert A. Giacalone and Paul Rosenfeld
136. **The Sense of Justice**
Roger D. Masters and Margaret Gruter
137. **Families and Retirement**
Maximiliane Szinovacz, David J. Ekerdt, and Barbara H. Vinick
138. **Gender, Families and Elder Care**
Jeffrey W. Dwyer and Raymond T. Coward
139. **Investigating Subjectivity**
Carolyn Ellis and Michael G. Flaherty
140. **Preventing Adolescent Pregnancy**
Brent C. Miller, Josefina J. Card, Roberta L. Paikoff, and James L. Peterson.
141. **Hidden Conflict in Organizations**
Deborah M. Kolb and Jean M. Bartunek
142. **Hispanics in the Workplace**
Stephen B. Knouse, Paul Rosenfeld, and Amy Culbertson
143. **Psychotherapy Process Research**
Shaké G. Toukmanian and David L. Rennie
144. **Educating Homeless Children and Adolescents**
James H. Stronge
145. **Family Care of the Elderly**
Jordan I. Kosberg
146. **Growth Management**
Jay M. Stein
147. **Substance Abuse and Gang Violence**
Richard C. Cervantes
148. **Third World Cities**
John D. Kasarda and Allan M. Parnell
149. **Independent Consulting for Evaluators**
Alan Vaux, Margaret S. Stockdale, and Michael J. Schwerin
150. **Advancing Family Perservation Practice**
E. Susan Morton and R. Kevin Grigsby
151. **A Future for Religion?**
William H. Swatos, Jr.
152. **Researching Sensitive Topics**
Claire M. Renzetti and Raymond M. Lee

INDEPENDENT CONSULTING FOR EVALUATORS

Alan Vaux
Margaret S. Stockdale
Michael J. Schwerin

editors

SAGE PUBLICATIONS
International Educational and Professional Publisher
Newbury Park   London   New Delhi

For information address:

SAGE Publications, Inc.
2455 Teller Road
Newbury Park, California 91320

SAGE Publications Ltd.
6 Bonhill Street
London EC2A 4PU
United Kingdom

SAGE Publications India Pvt. Ltd.
M-32 Market
Greater Kailash I
New Delhi 110 048 India

Printed in the United States of America

Library of Congress Cataloguing-in-Publication Data

Main entry under title:

Independent consulting for evaluators / Alan Vaux, Margaret S.
    Stockdale, Michael J. Schwerin, editors.
        p.   cm.
    Includes bibliographical references and index.
    ISBN 0–8039–4667–8 (hard). — ISBN 0–8039–4668–6 (pbk.)
    1. Psychological consultation. 2. Psychology, Applied—Practice.
3. Psychology, Industrial—Practice. I. Vaux, Alan.
II. Stockdale, Margaret S.   III. Schwerin Michael J.
BF637.C56I53   1992
158'.023—dc20   92–20201

92 93 94 95   10 9 8 7 6 5 4 3 2 1

Sage Production Editor: Astrid Virding

Contents

Foreword
ROSS F. CONNER   vii

Preface
ALAN VAUX, MARGARET S. STOCKDALE,
and *MICHAEL J. SCHWERIN*   x

PART I: Laying the Foundation: Training and Roles

1. Applied Research Training: A Guide for Faculty,
   Students, and Practitioners
   RONALD G. DOWNEY and *KARL W. KUHNERT*   3

2. Finding Room on the Rack for More Than One Hat:
   Combining Multiple Professional Roles
   FRANK E. SAAL   21

3. Combining Research and Consultation: Advantages,
   Pitfalls, and Recommendations
   FREDERICK T. L. LEONG   33

PART II: Getting It Right: Working With People, Building Relationships

4. Creating Challenging Client-Consultant Relationships
   MICHAEL F. CRISTIANI   51

5. Evaluation Skills Nobody Taught Me
   GAIL V. BARRINGTON   69

6. The Growing Importance of Multiculturalism for
   Independent Consulting
   CARL L. JENNINGS   85

PART III: Making It Better: Tools, Techniques, and Advice for Improving Applied Psychological Consulting

7. Ethical and Professional Guidelines for Construction
   and Use of Contracts
   KARL W. KUHNERT and *BARBARA A. GORE*   107

8. Using Government Information and Other Archives
   JACK McKILLIP and *HUGH STEPHENSON*   127

9. Using Graphical Displays to Empower Evaluation
   Audiences
   GARY T. HENRY   141

10. Preparing Reports and Presentations That Strengthen
    the Link Between Research and Action
    CYNTHIA ROBERTS-GRAY   161

PART IV: Showing You How: Case Studies of Small Consulting Practices

11. Being Values Driven: A Challenging Way to Do
    Business
    KASS LARSON and *ARLENE BROWNELL*   183

12. Applied Research Consultants (ARC): A Service
    and Training Model
    ALAN VAUX and *MARGARET S. STOCKDALE*   196

    Index   212

    About the Authors   217

Foreword

I am completing this Foreword on an airplane, going to a national grant review session. I began to write this earlier this week, on another airplane returning from a meeting to consult with program planners and policymakers from a national AIDS prevention program. And, tomorrow I leave for yet another meeting, this time to lobby for a change in policy related to state-level AIDS research activities. In and around these trips and meetings, I met with students, other faculty, university administration officials, and representatives of a foundation. I also attended the monthly board meeting of a local community organization, the focus of which is related to my current teaching and research. Such is the life of a professor-applied researcher-independent consultant-community member. The book you are about to read describes this life in detail, with instructive examples, suggestions and advice, as well as with insights into the excitement and opportunities that this life entails.

More and more, academics in many fields, including psychology but extending well beyond, are involved in many more roles than the usual ones of campus-based teacher and researcher. Alan Vaux, Margaret Stockdale, and Michael Schwerin have edited a volume that will be useful to academics who are just entering—whether by choice or chance—this new multirole environment, to academics who have been in this environment already and to students who are sampling various environments for their futures. There are lessons here for all these readers. The chapters are written by people who are living and thriving in multiple professional role positions, and they provide many useful examples and insights. Because of the authors' candidness about the challenges of having multiple roles, the reader will develop a good understanding of the stresses and strains that incongruent role demands can generate. At the same time, however, the authors also convey the intellectual and pedagogical benefits which can result from congruence among the roles. In some cases, the multiple role demands produce a synergy, resulting in even better performance in all of the roles.

The idea that academics should undertake multiple roles is not new. Many universities expect their faculty to conduct research, teach classes, perform administrative duties, undertake professional activities, and play a role in the community. The reason often given for this expectation is that there is a useful interaction that takes place among the roles. Active researchers are better teachers because they are involved in their disciplines at the active cutting edge, and community-involved college professors are better university citizens because they understand how to relate interests off campus with those on campus, whether related to teaching or research. In certain disciplines, psychology among them, it is easier to undertake these multiple roles. The challenge, however, is not simply to undertake these roles but to succeed in combining them productively and to capitalize on the opportunities which are present. This book advances past discussion by addressing this challenge and providing examples and illustrations of how others have met the challenge.

The editors and all the authors agree that, useful as examples are, there is no substitute for hands-on experience. They and I encourage the reader who is new to this multiple-role environment to take the next step: begin to undertake new roles and pay close attention to the experiences. Academic training can provide the skills, but only field experience can provide the sensitivities toward and sensibilities about juggling multiple role demands. The realities of field experience are important for another reason: the excitement of the synergy that results from combining roles can only be felt, not described. Once experienced, this excitement is hard to avoid. It has another benefit as well: it provides the extra energy when you have to make one more airplane trip to consult with program or policy personnel, when you have to stay up several hours later to finish a proposal or report, when you take the extra time to revise your lecture to include the field work you have been doing, or when you are sitting in a frustrating faculty meeting. Multiple roles provide multiple perspectives which can help us keep our busy lives in balance. Vaux, Stockdale, and Schwerin have done all of us a service in providing a forum for the discussion of the benefits and costs of multiple professional roles and advancing our understanding of how to maximize the benefits and minimize the costs.

—Ross F. Conner
University of California-Irvine

Preface

Graduate programs in experimental psychology and related fields have upheld a long tradition of training students in the rigors of theory and science, preparing them for productive research and teaching careers. The incorporation of practical training in graduate programs often proved an uneasy accommodation. The scientist-practitioner model, established in the Boulder Conference of 1949, set the stage for turning the tide toward greater emphasis on developing practitioner-related skills in graduate programs while upholding the virtues of theoretical and research competencies. Although implemented most directly by clinical psychology programs, other applied psychology programs adopted the Boulder model as their own—notably, industrial and organizational (I/O) psychology. Psychology graduate programs for helping professions (e.g., clinical, counseling and school psychology) institutionalized scientist-practitioner curricula requiring APA accreditation not only for the graduate program itself but also for the internship programs as well.

Applied psychology programs in other specialty areas have resisted attempts to develop strict accreditation-type guidelines to develop these skills (see Schmitt, 1991, for a review of the accreditation/licensing debate among I/O psychologists). What remains is a wide variety of programs, loosely and broadly categorized as "applied psychology," that allows students opportunities to mold unique and interesting career paths. The lack of clear definition and structure in training experiences to develop applied skills, however, is frustrating for students and new professionals trying to establish careers as practicing applied research psychologists.

Consulting in applied psychology, whether it be program evaluation, industrial-organizational, organizational development, career development, survey research, and so forth, is a popular career choice. Howard (1990) reported that 29% of I/O psychologists responding to her survey held primary positions in consulting. This was second only to academic positions. Furthermore, the independent consulting topical interest group (TIG) of the American Evaluation Association maintains a roster of well over 2,000 members—one of the largest TIGs in this organization. But how do students learn to become consultants? Books and seminars abound on how to start and market a consulting practice, but the skills of learning to work in effective consultant-client partnerships, for example, or to manage multiple role demands and political realities are skills not routinely and explicitly transferred. Moreover, unlike methodological and statistical skills, these are difficult to teach in the classroom. Graduate training in the scientist-practitioner model, however, is incomplete without attention to developing these skills.

In this book, the editors have attempted to gather a collection of papers from a wide variety of experts in applied psychological consulting in order that they could share their experiences about effective consulting. Our goal has been to bring together in a single volume views on training experiences to develop consulting competencies; hard-hitting advice on the "soft" skills needed to survive as well as thrive as a consultant; practical, detailed information for improving an applied psychological consulting practice; and case-study descriptions of two small consulting organizations—one as a profit-minded but values-driven company, the other as a training program for graduate students in an applied experimental psychology program.

The intended audience is reflected by our authors (and editors). Contributing authors include program evaluators, I/O psychologists, and organizational development consultants with years of practical experience, consultants from academic institutions with the latest innovations in data procurement and presentation, new professionals who are learning to bridge their academic expertise with their professional experience, and graduate students who bring an often untold perspective.

We hope to reach, therefore, a wide and varied audience including beginning professionals, graduate students, and faculty in applied psychology-related programs. For example, students in I/O, applied social/applied experimental, program evaluation, organizational development, as well as human factors, and consumer/marketing psychology should find guidance. In addition, we believe that the novice (or even seasoned) professional, and the academic consultant will find a few pearls herein. No matter at what career stage you find yourself, or in what particular specialty you claim marketable expertise, some rudimentary questions will be common to all: (a) What kind of training experiences might I seek as a complement to formal coursework during graduate school? (b) What kinds of work do applied research consultants conduct? (c) How can I combine consulting with an academic or research career? (d) Aside from technical expertise, what professional skills do I need in order to deal with clients? (e) How does one go about negotiating projects, formalizing agreements, and so forth? (f) How might traditional methodologies—data collection and analyses, presentation of findings, and so forth—be altered for the applied context? (g) How have applied research groups conducted projects in light of these concerns? These are some of the questions that we hope to address in this book.

The first section describes some of the issues one might face in laying the foundation for a professional applied research career and in negotiating the often-competing demands in such a career. Ronald G. Downey and Karl W. Kuhnert ("Applied Research Training: A Guide for Faculty, Students, and Practitioners") show us ways to enhance applied research training. Included in their chapter are the results and a discussion of a national survey of the training practices of I/O academic programs. Practical applications of the findings are also discussed.

Frank (Skip) E. Saal produces a discussion of the difficulties of having multiple professional roles ("Finding Room on the Rack for More Than One Hat: Combining Multiple Professional Roles"). The varied responsibilities of academic professor, academic department chair, and independent consultant are brought out as examples of role conflict and role ambiguity, and role congruence. Suggestions for training are also forwarded from this chapter.

Frederick T. L. Leong ("Combining Research and Consultation: Advantages, Pitfalls, and Recommendations") chronicles the ways that consultants might be able to turn a consulting venture into a research opportunity, which gets at the heart of the philosophy of the scientist-practitioner model. Leong reveals some of his experiences integrating research and consultation.

In the second section, the mysteries of intra- and interpersonal consulting competencies involved in consulting are revealed. Michael F. Cristiani ("Creating Challenging Client-Consultant Relationships") delineates and discusses the roles involved in client-consultant relationships and ways of protecting and enhancing those relationships. Gail V. Barrington ("Evaluation Skills Nobody Taught Me") shares with us some of her secrets to success and the skills that helped her survive. Barrington gives us suggestions that could help lessen the daily turmoil of a professional life. Carl L. Jennings ("The Growing Importance of Multiculturalism for Independent Consulting") brings a very important discussion of cultural diversity and the opportunities this presents for organizational consultants. The benefits of the cultural heritage and traditions of various racial and ethnic groups in the workplace are becoming more evident as the work force becomes more culturally diverse.

The third section is a presentation of skills and practices that can improve the quality of one's work, including some interesting variations on traditional methods of data collection, data presentation, and reporting findings. Karl W. Kuhnert and Barbara A. Gore begin this section with a chapter on the utility and function of contracts ("Ethical and Professional Guidelines for Construction and Use of Contracts"). Also included in the discussion is a sample contract to help point out some of the purposes that the contract serves.

Jack McKillip and Hugh Stephenson follow with a discussion of various methods of procuring and using databases ("Using Government Information and Other Archives"). This chapter identifies sources of databases, outlines how such data might be used by evaluators and consultants, and illustrates such use in a variety of projects.

Gary T. Henry discusses methods of presenting data in graphical formats ("Using Graphical Displays to Empower Evaluation Audiences"). Henry describes a novel application of graphical displays of univariate and multivariate data. For example, he employs a geometric star diagram as an alternative to tables and scatterplots. These methods are designed not only to make data more accessible but also to empower clients to both examine the data and propose alternative explanations for themselves.

Cynthia Roberts-Gray ("Preparing Reports and Presentations That Strengthen the Link Between Research and Action") discusses methods of improving client-consultant communication by delving into the written report and methods for enhancing and clarifying the evaluator's or consultant's findings. This chapter highlights the special demands of the applied context and the limitations of traditional approaches.

The fourth and final section is an application of philosophical principles to independent consulting. Specifically, case studies of two small but very different consulting organizations are described in order to synthesize the information presented earlier. Kass Larson and Arlene Brownell ("Being Values Driven: A Challenging Way to Do Business") describe a small training organization that maintains a collective company value structure. This case-study is an examination of the possibility of not just being "ethics driven" but "values driven."

This section concludes with a chapter by Alan Vaux and Margaret (Peggy) S. Stockdale ("Applied Research Consultants (ARC): A Service and Training Model") describing a graduate training model. The centerpiece of the graduate program is Applied Research Consultants (ARC), a faculty-supervised consulting firm that is staffed by graduate students within the program. The inner workings and daily challenges that are encountered in such a program are discussed.

The editors, in fact, owe a personal debt of gratitude to ARC and its associates: William Deniston, Fred Detwiler, Elke Geisler-Brenstein, Kris Glade-Wiebusch, Michelle Hall, Tamra Kinkner, Brenda Klostermann, Hugh Stephenson, John Wallace, and Joseph Watkins (Michael Schwerin, another ARC associate, lead the project for the group and became a co-editor). Many of these bright and energetic graduate students worked with us in conceptualizing the purpose of the book, procuring chapter authors, and providing editorial feedback on preliminary drafts.

We hope that this compilation of soft skills and hard skills concluded with a series of case-study applications can help you improve features of your professional and personal career. It is the intent of the editors (and authors) that the information presented here be applicable to students, their faculty, and practicing professionals in the broad and exciting field of applied psychological research consulting.

References

Howard, A. (1990). *The multiple facets of industrial-organizational psychology: Membership survey results.* Arlington Heights, IL: Society for Industrial and Organizational Psychology.

Schmitt, N. (1991). Report on efforts to revise SIOP's licensure position. *Industrial-Organizational Psychologist, 29*(1), 33-58.

—Alan Vaux
Margaret S. Stockdale
Michael J. Schwerin

PART I

Laying the Foundation: Training and Roles

1

Applied Research Training

A Guide for Faculty, Students, and Practitioners

RONALD G. DOWNEY
KARL W. KUHNERT

Increasingly, students from a wide range of research-based psychology graduate programs are being trained to work in applied (nonacademic) settings. The development and implementation of such training programs often requires the use of a wide range of activities identified as internships (also, practicums, field training, etc.). Though models, standards, and methods for such activities have existed for many years in the health-care areas (e.g., clinical), the applied research areas have yet to develop such models and procedures. This chapter first provides a review of some efforts in industrial/organizational (I/O) psychology to understand internships and second it outlines general issues and procedures for the stakeholders of the internship process.

I/O psychology, although it has been divergent from the health-care areas in how it implements its training model, has continued to affirm a scientist-practitioner model (Society for Industrial and Organizational Psychology, 1985). The models and approaches developed by I/O psychology are, in general, consistent with other applied research programs such as evaluation training, applied social, and so forth.

Since World War II the most widely adopted model for professional training in psychology (clinical, counseling, school, and industrial/organizational) has been the scientist-practitioner model established during the Boulder Conference in 1949 (Rainey, 1950). The Boulder model was an educational experiment designed to blend the theoretical, applied, and research aspects of clinical psychology into a single training program. The training goal was a scientist-professional with "the combination of the skilled acquisition of reality-based psychological understanding and the attitude of constant inquiry toward this knowledge" (Shakow, 1976, p. 554). Later conferences dealing with graduate training in psychology have reaffirmed this approach; the Thayer Conference in 1954 (Cutts, 1955), the Miami Conference in 1958 (Roe, Gustad, Moore, Ross, & Skodak, 1959), Graystone Conference in 1964 (Thompson & Super, 1964), Chicago Conference in 1965 (Hoch, Ross, & Winter, 1966), and the Vail Conference in 1973 (Korman, 1973).

The typical educational program for psychology graduate (Ph.D.) students in the professional areas is primarily geared to the development of scientific skills and knowledge as represented by a set of methodological and core content courses (e.g., statistics, design, testing, social, personality, etc.). The primary difference in training between applied research programs and the health-care professional groups has occurred in programs to develop practitioner skills. Standards for graduate programs, accredited practicum and internship experiences for clinical, counseling, and school programs have been developed (APA Committee on Accreditation and Accreditation Office, 1986). For other areas, however, the growth of formal training procedures and programs for the development of practitioner skills has been a more recent development and is, perhaps, even more varied over the different subareas (e.g., I/O, applied social, evaluation training, and so on).

Applied research internship programs are not structured and in general are loosely organized and managed. Increasingly, we are seeing such programs using internships as an approach to aid students in the development of skills, knowledge, and abilities relevant to performance in applied settings. There are no universal standards as to what an internship should be (see, for example, Society for Industrial and Organizational Psychology, 1985) and thus one is often left with the impression that they are anything we want them to be. The following section summarizes some recent efforts to better understand internship experiences in I/O psychology.

The I/O Internship Experience

In a three-part series in the *Industrial-Organizational Psychologist* (TIP) on I/O internships, Klimoski (1983a; 1983b) and Hinrichs (1983a; 1983b) sketched the role of internships from three perspectives: corporate, student, and faculty. In the first part of the series, Klimoski outlined five major areas in which students may be deficient in practitioner skills: interactions with lay people, ability to conduct applied research, oral and written communication skills, time management, and supervision of others. Klimoski notes that, though the requirements and conditions surrounding an internship program for the subspecialities of School, Clinical and Counseling are well developed, the situation is much less consistent in I/O psychology. In the remaining materials Klimoski and Hinrichs outline the pros and cons associated with the current concepts and practices connected with internships from the various perspectives involved.

In response to a growing interest in and concern about internship programs, Kuhnert and Downey (1989; 1991) conducted two national surveys. The first study was designed to determine what directors of I/O programs are doing in the internship area. The second was to learn about student perceptions of the internships and whether they converge with those of I/O program directors. Their major findings are summarized here.

First, the major goals for both program directors and graduate students associated with an internship are experience in organizations and the development of business skills and language. Making an informed career choice was also deemed an important goal for students. Developing research skills and strengthening of the student's vita, résumé, or general marketability were seen as minor goals.

Second, in articulating the standards for selecting an internship site, the modal response was related to the nature of the work—that is, professional and/or relevant work in I/O psychology or human resource management. A second standard included supervision, either by an I/O psychologist or another professional.

Third, when asked about the types of internships in which students were placed, no clear consensus emerged. Interns were sent to small-, medium-, and large-sized companies, both with and without professional supervision, although there was a trend for students placed in larger companies to receive professional supervision. Research facilities were the least-used internship sites.

Fourth, faculty members tended to take an active role in identifying, approving, and contacting internship sites, as well as referring students to specific locations. Few program directors and students indicated that faculty played no role in the internship process.

Fifth, as a general rule student evaluations were conducted by the internship site supervisors and were either informal oral or written reports (23.5%) or formal written evaluations (25.5%). Seventeen percent of the institutions indicated that they did not evaluate students' performance on internships. Both students and program directors lamented the lack of general supervision and evaluation in the internship process.

Sixth, in describing the disadvantages of an internship, program directors and students agreed that the major disadvantage was that an internship delayed students' progress toward graduation. The major advantages were that students gained practical job experiences and had the opportunity to obtain a realistic job preview.

Finally, when asked what needed to be done to improve the internship process, no clear reaction appeared. The most common suggestions were for the development of a national listing/clearinghouse of internship sites and opportunities and the development of standards for internships. The general impression of both students and program directors was that something needed to be done by the profession, but they were not sure what.

What is very clear from the Kuhnert and Downey (1989) survey of I/O program directors is the degree to which I/O programs treat internships differently than clinical, counseling, and school psychology programs. From the second survey, it is also clear from students' internship experiences that there are two major differences from APA accredited standards: the general lack of requirements that a doctoral-level psychologist provide on-site supervision, and the variability in the length of the internship for I/O internships, both of which are prescribed by the other three professional programs (APA Committee, 1986). Only a limited number of the I/O internship programs described by the respondents would be approved under current APA standards for the other three groups. Clearly the use of the term *internship* for I/O programs has a vastly different meaning than that for other organizations.

Although there was a great deal of variability in programs, 70% of the I/O program directors who responded said they did have some form of an internship, either as a formal requirement of the department curriculum or requirement for graduation from the I/O program. The results clearly show that internships are seen as a principal mechanism for the education and training of I/O students. It is also clear that I/O psychology does not have full control of the process in that 65% of the programs are willing to send students to a non-I/O supervised site.

Another conclusion of the study was that a great deal of diversity exists in how I/O internships are defined and implemented. There is no prototypical internship; rather, there appear to be at least four different kinds of internship models that I/O programs use. These are: the "mini-job," "practicum," "supervised," and the "professional" internship. The characteristics of each are described as follows:

The Mini-Job Internship. In this model there is little professional supervision, the work tends to be practical (e.g., conducting job analyses) and students tend to find internship sites on their own and operate independent of any professional oversight.

The Practicum Internship. In this model, faculty supervise general professional issues, but students are on their own for the technical and professional issues that face them on a day-to-day basis. Faculty are likely to obtain the internship but are not actively involved in the evaluation of students' progress.

The Supervised Internship. This model is characterized by on-site professional (human resource management professional or non-I/O psychologist) and faculty supervision. The nature of the interns' work is agreed upon by the supervisor and the faculty member. Faculty usually obtain the internship and closely monitor the interns' progress.

The Professional Internship. This model emphasizes on-site I/O supervision (as distinct from another profession as in the supervised internship) with I/O issues studied. Faculty usually obtain the internship and the nature of the work is agreed upon jointly by the student, faculty, and corporate sponsor.

It was also concluded that there is no "typical" internship site. In general, the four most frequent employers of I/O interns are service industries, manufacturing, government, and public utilities. Notable industries that appeared to have low usage rates are transportation, agriculture, retail trade, and finance/insurance.

Given that about one third of the doctorate and one quarter of the master's students were part-time, much of the determination of an internship site was driven by the types of nearby opportunities. For the full-time interns, the selection of a site was most likely a mixture of local, regional, and national locations. Given that the majority of the advertisements in the *Industrial and Organizational Psychologist* for internships are for Ph.D level individuals, it is also likely that more doctorate students obtained internships at a national level and on a competitive basis.

Functionally, interns appeared to engage in four types of activities: (a) selection and placement, (b) training and development, (c) organizational development, and (d) performance measurement. A limited number appear to carry out activities related to quality of work life and consumer psychology. Many of the interns reported performing more than one activity in their internship. These functions are consistent with the types of skills that interns are expected to acquire on their internship. These functions are very consistent with the specialties listed in *The Multiple Facets of Industrial-Organizational Psychology* (Howard, 1990, p. 20, Figure 10). The two notable exceptions for interns are organizational behavior and management.

Questions concerning the compensation received by interns yielded a wide range of responses. The majority of the interns were paid in the $10,000 to $30,000 range per annum. Much of this variability may be due to the part-time employees. Though slightly more than 25% of the master's students were serving in an unpaid internship site, none of the doctoral students reported being unpaid. Perhaps the most telling information about the pay status of the internship was related to the benefits received. Though 88% of the doctoral students received benefits, *none* of the master's students did. This suggests that the master's-level interns were being treated as temporary employees and most likely paid on an hourly basis. Doctoral students, however, were being treated as regular salaried employees. This also supports the notion that Ph.D. students were being recruited into their positions. In a majority of cases for both M.S. and Ph.D. interns the programs were willing to send them to a site where they would be unsupervised.

In summary, it would appear that I/O interns are being employed in a broad spectrum of the economy and being asked to perform a wide range of activities. Although the results would be expected to vary for a wider population of applied research students, these results do provide an insight into what can be expected in general. The next section provides detailed procedures for developing a program, selecting students and sites, and running a program.

Developing and Running an Internship Program

Developing, maintaining, and running an internship program is a labor-intensive activity for faculty. Identifying potential internship sites and engaging in activities that lead to being selected for an internship are also time consuming activities for students. The work load of the internship site is highly dependent upon the type of internship program the faculty has developed. Although the procedures provided below are intended for general use, they can and will vary given the special needs of the programs, students, and sites. Before discussing the procedures it is necessary to outline some of the broad parameters that may require modifying the procedures.

Program Parameters

Each internship program will be driven by four major factors and their interactions: (a) the goals and objectives of the internship program, (b) the number and type of faculty, (c) the types of students in the program, and (d) the location of the educational institution. Internship programs that fail to attend to these issues will have major problems in establishing and maintaining a viable program.

The typical goals and objectives for applied research programs have already been discussed in detail. It is important to note that, if an internship is established as a requirement of the program, this places greater strain on the faculty in the development and selection of internship sites and the evaluation of students. If internship experiences are encouraged as part of the development of students' skills and training, but *not* required, the burden on the faculty may be diminished. The more specific the program objectives are for the internship program the greater the control and effort required by the faculty.

Effective internship programs do not run themselves: faculty direction and supervision are required. Applied programs with a limited number of faculty and/or faculty with limited industry contacts will likely have more problems. As was noted, running a program is labor intensive and requires certain experiences and skills by the faculty coordinator of the internship program. Limited faculty resources will drive the program to be more student-initiated.

The types of students in the program are also a major factor in determining the nature of the program. A program with terminal master's students will be different from those with doctoral students, and a combined program will be different from both. The types of students will both alter the goals and objectives of the program and the types of internship sites that are available.

Finally, the location of the educational institution will be a major contributor to the type of program established. Institutions that are in large urban areas can do things that rural institutions cannot, because internship sites are likely to be some distance from rural educational institutions. Urban programs can establish part-time internship programs in which the student simultaneously attends classes and serves an internship. Under these conditions, programs are more likely to be able to require an internship in that sites are likely to be available and do not place an undue hardship on students (e.g., married students who may not be able to move, students who can not pay moving expenses, etc.). Urban institutions are also more likely to have faculty who engage in consulting activities on a frequent basis. Institutions in small towns may need to be much more flexible in their requirements for students. Thus, the procedures should be considered in light of the aforementioned issues and modified as necessary to fit the situations and conditions of each program.

Developing a Program

One of the first (and most frequently ignored) steps in the development of an internship program description is the formulation of a formal statement of the goals and objectives of the program. This statement could include a wide range of activities that would classify as an internship. The statement should declare if the internship is a required part of the program, if students are to sign up for course credit, when students are generally expected to serve on an internship, the minimum time for an internship, the types of activities and settings that are allowed, the role of faculty, the role of students, and the responsibilities of the internship site. Appendix A provides a sample goals and objectives statement for an applied research internship program that can be used to develop a formal statement.

The next step in developing an internship program is to identify a faculty member to coordinate the program. Though it is possible for each faculty member to handle her/his students, this may lead to inequities. One faculty member may have greater contacts or experience and thus give her/his students a greater advantage. The more formal the program, the greater the need for a single coordinator. A list of job duties for a coordinator can range from developing a statement of goals to providing reviews of the internship sites. Appendix B contains a sample list of responsibilities for a faculty coordinator. The specific requirements will be determined by the type of program developed. Though the coordinator may serve as the person who provides supervision from the educational institution (including obtaining site evaluations and assigning grades) this can also be a shared responsibility with other faculty.

One of the most important responsibilities of the faculty coordinator is the development of procedures and methods for determining a list of potential internship sites. Although there are some internships that are advertised on a national basis, the majority of doctoral internships (and to a greater degree master's students) are identified from personal contacts (of faculty, students, and alumni). Established programs are in a better position in that many times an internship site that has had a positive experience with an intern will return for placement of another intern.

A related issue is how to make the students aware of the internship opportunities identified by the faculty and alumni. There may be no expectations that potential sites identified by a student be shared with other students, though other internship opportunities should be shared with all students (e.g., posted on a bulletin board, etc.). A failure to deal with this issue can breed discontent between students and between students and faculty. Once potential sites are identified a system needs to be developed for students' applications.

Selecting Students

There are a variety of methods that faculty may wish to consider in helping students apply for an internship site. The two extremes would be to allow all students to apply to a site if they wish versus the faculty making all assignments. There are factors that favor the inclusion of a mixed system. To the degree that a long-term relationship has developed between the faculty/program and an internship site, the greater the expectation on the part of the site that the program will "send" them qualified individuals. Conversely, internships that advertise a position generally would not expect any "help" in selecting an intern (other than references). A compromise position would be for the faculty to *inform* all students who plan on applying for an internship to submit their résumés for review by the faculty. The faculty would review the résumés and make recommendation as to who they feel are qualified for the internship. For positions in which there were no expectations that the program would provide a pre-review, students would still be free to send their résumés, but with the understanding that the faculty would *not* respond if asked to provide a recommendation. This type of system would have a uniform set of procedures and most students would respect the opinions of the faculty. A sample set of guidelines, consistent with the above concerns, is shown in Appendix C.

This set of procedures also ensures that students will provide the faculty a copy of their résumé for review and comment. The résumé is an important part of the selection process for the student and the internship site. Faculty should provide a review of both form and content and try to ensure that students are acting in an ethical fashion. For the faculty who may not feel qualified to review the form of a résumé, they can often receive help from a campus career planning or placement center who have qualified individuals.

For programs requiring an internship, one issue is whether students can apply for multiple internships (over time). Given the limited numbers of internships, supporting students who have had an internship to apply may limit the opportunities of others. This will be the greatest problem for internships that are done over the summer months.

Other issues can rise in the selection process and need to be addressed. Some internship sites may want to conduct interviews of students (and sometimes faculty) on campus. Programs need to decide if they are willing to support this type of effort with their time and resources. Sometimes programs want a representative from the program to visit the site before they will make a final selection. Again, faculty need to have a clear policy on their willingness to support this type of activity.

Discussions of the selection process should also consider issues from the students' point of view. In many ways obtaining an internship is like a mini-job search. Many on-campus career planning and placement organizations provide support to students in finding an internship just like finding a job. Finding an internship requires a great deal of time and energy on the part of the student. Although some opportunities are identified by the faculty, the majority of internship opportunities are likely to be found by the students themselves.

Selecting a Site

The site selection process is a joint effort between the student and the faculty. The process used to make this determination is driven by several factors. If the program has formal requirements, these must be determined and followed: for example, the type of on-site supervision, number of hours, type of work and so forth. Just as important are the students' needs: location of the site, pay, type of work, and expected outcomes are determinations that each student must make.

Applied research programs are different from the traditional health-care fields in our requirements for an internship site. The "clinical" model has incorporated a formal review process that accredits intern-ship sites and is very specific in its requirements. The other applied areas are much more diverse in the types of work and setting in which they operate. A sample checklist of potential factors to be considered, both by the students and by the program, in selecting an internship site are illustrated in Appendix D. To aid new programs, a sample agreement among the program, the student, and the site is shown in Appendix E.

Running an Internship Program

Programs in applied psychology vary in their approach to internship supervision. Policies can range from a full hands-off policy in super-vision to a full partnership in the process. The policies adopted by a program should be consistent with its goals and objectives. As a rule, programs requiring an internship will have a greater degree of involve-ment in the conduct of the internship. There are four major areas in which the program can be involved: (a) on-site visits, (b) interactions with the intern during the internship, (c) interactions with the intern after the internship, and (d) interactions with the internship supervisor. The on-site visit has two major purposes. First, it provides the faculty an opportunity to evaluate the student's progress during the conduct of the internship. Second, and more frequently, it provides the faculty an opportunity to evaluate the site itself. To the degree that the faculty are heavily involved in the process of selecting sites for potential intern-ships, it is recommended that regular visits be made to sites. In some cases, due to distance and cost, the best that can be done is a telephone contact on some prearranged schedule with the on-site supervisor. This has an added advantage of increasing the likelihood that the site will select future interns from your program.

No matter what the goals of the internship program, it is strongly encouraged that student interns keep in close contact with their pro-grams. This provides the faculty an opportunity to correct problems before they become unmanageable and further insights into how the internship is progressing. It also provides the students a sounding board for their difficulties, both technical and professional. Faculty should ensure that students feel free to contact them with any questions and concerns that they encounter while in the internship program.

Many programs also institute a process in which students are required to provide a formal report on their internship experience. This report is provided shortly after completion of the internship. It is normally either a written log and evaluation of the internship experience submitted to the advisor or an oral report provided to faculty and students. (In some special cases students provide interim reports of this nature while they are still serving the internship.) Reports of this nature serve several purposes. They force the students to focus on the internship process and evaluate what happened. They also provide further information to the faculty in evaluating an internship site. More importantly, they are used to aid the faculty in evaluating the students' performance. Finally, they are a rich source of information to future interns who gain a better understanding of the process by this type of report.

Finally, the most frequent type of interaction is a report from the on-site supervisor of the intern's performance. These types of reports vary and can include an unstructured letter of evaluation, a formal evaluation using the companies' own evaluation form, a formal evaluation using a form developed by the faculty, and so forth. Once again, the process used by the faculty should match their goals and needs. To the degree that an internship is required, a more formal evaluation process may be desirable. One advantage of a faculty-developed form is that it can be used to improve the nature of the internship process and to prepare interns. It can also include factors that the faculty feel are an important part of the internship outcomes (see Appendix F for a sample evaluation form).

Summary

The first part of this chapter has shown how internship experiences in the applied research area differ from the health-care programs and how that has had an effect on the nature of graduate training programs for applied research psychology students. The results from a series of studies of I/O psychology internships do not appear to be inconsistent with the concerns for applied research training programs in general. Also, the four internship models found in I/O psychology (the mini-job, practicum, supervised, and professional) would seem to have the potential to generalize to all areas in applied research.

The second part of this chapter summarizes important issues in the development, maintenance, and running of an internship program. Formal internship programs do *not* just happen, they are planned. The exact parameters of any internship program are determined by a complex interaction of factors. Graduate programs that fail to attend to the issues that are detailed in this section are setting themselves up for potential failure.

It should be clear that the internship models and procedures articulated above differ from those in the health-care areas. Developing procedures for a program is a delicate balancing act. A rigid set of rules can stifle creative solutions and will fail to deal with the varying needs and concerns of programs and subareas. Conversely, having no rules leads to anarchy. Many of the applied research areas are in the first stages of developing training programs and procedures and given the diversity of the applied research programs, they also have differing goals. The materials provided here were developed with the intent of providing a structure that will promote: good training practices, consistent definitions, and flexibility for differing needs and conditions in graduate training programs.

Appendix 1. A

Goals and Objectives of the Internship Program

The education and training of an applied research psychologist includes a wide variety of experiences. One of these experiences is an internship. An internship is a practice experience in an operating environment outside of the academic department and provides the student with skills and knowledge that cannot be acquired in the classroom or in faculty research programs.

The psychology department at State University requires all students in its applied research program to serve an approved internship. Major requirements of this program include:

1. All sites must be approved by the faculty prior to the student serving an internship.
2. Internships will be the equivalent of 3 months full-time duration.
3. Students must sign up for 6 hours of practicum credit.
4. Internships will not be approved unless they provide professional supervision by a graduate level supervisor and appropriate types of applied experiences.
5. Internships must be served after the completion of the second year of the program.

Appendix 1. B

Job Description-Faculty Coordinator

The Internship Coordinator is responsible for the following activities:

1. Will develop and maintain (with the concurrence of the faculty) a statement of goals and objectives of the internship program.
2. Will identify appropriate internship sites.
3. Will provide announcements to all students of internship opportunities.
4. Will, where appropriate, coordinate the review and selection of interns.
5. Will serve as the instructor of record for all interns, or agree to appropriate alternatives.
6. Will coordinate reviews of internship sites.
7. Will coordinate the evaluations of all interns.
8. Will coordinate student presentations on their internship experiences.

Appendix 1. C

Guidelines for Announcing Internships

The following are the procedures to be followed in the announcement and endorsement of internship opportunities once they are identified:

1. All students will be informed by memorandum of these opportunities and be provided a deadline for indicating an interest in the internship.
2. All students who are interested in an internship will indicate their interest by submitting their résumé and a letter of interest.
3. The program faculty will review the credentials of all interested students. Based on the needs of the company and our evaluation of each student's record, we will indicate those students we are willing to support for that position. A letter will be sent to the company indicating our support for the student(s) for that internship position.

Internships that are not approved by this process are in grave danger of not receiving approval by the faculty and therefore will not satisfy the internship requirements of the department. The faculty encourages open competition for all internship opportunities.

Appendix 1. D

Site Selection Checklist

This check list is intended for use by both faculty and students, but the weight provided to each item may differ for faculty and students and by specific program.

YES NO

___ ___ The work is appropriate? Comment:

___ ___ Professional supervision is provided? Comment:

___ ___ The pay/benefits are adequate? Comment:

___ ___ The length is appropriate? Comment:

___ ___ Good match with student's skills? Comment:

___ ___ Experience builds student's résumé? Comment:

___ ___ The location is appropriate? Comment:

___ ___ Good potential for learning? Comment:

___ ___ Good potential for data collection? Comment:

Appendix 1. E

Sample Internship Agreement

A short statement of the history and purpose of the program.

I. Objectives

1. Provide students with supervised experience appropriate to their level of training and experience.

2. Provide students with a general orientation to the range of activities carried out in an applied research environment.
3. Provide students with an opportunity to work at a professional level in their chosen field.
4. Provide students with an opportunity to develop professional attitudes, values, and ethics in a business setting.
5. Provide students with detailed feedback on their activities during the internship.

II. Responsibilities

State University:

1. SU will, upon request, provide a reference for students in the program and certify that they have completed the necessary course work and are prepared to serve in the internship.
2. SU will be available for periodic consultation with the intern concerning questions and issues they may encounter during the internship.
3. SU will correspond with the internship site concerning questions, problems, and concerns related to the intern and their functions.
4. SU will, in consultation with the internship supervisor, assign the student a grade for the internship experience.

Student:

1. The student will at all times behave in a professional manner that reflects positively on the internship site, SU, and themselves.
2. The student will abide by the rules of conduct and performance established by the internship site.
3. The student will, unless specifically released by the internship site and SU, serve out the term of the internship as originally determined by the student and the internship site.

Internship Site:

1. The site will provide students with a general orientation to the organization, and to directly related office activities.
2. The site will provide students with an appropriate level of supervision during their internship activities.
3. The site will assign the student job responsibilities consistent with their background, skills, and abilities.

4. The site will allow students to participate in in-service seminars and other informal/formal educational activities.

5. The site supervisor will provide the student and the faculty at SU with evaluation feedback concerning the intern's performance during the placement. The student should receive this information on at least a monthly basis, and the faculty at the end of the internship (in writing). This evaluation will be part of the process used to assign internship grades.

Appendix 1. F

Internship Evaluation Form (sample dimensions)

Communications

1. Ability to communicate verbally with technical staff.
2. Ability to communicate verbally with non-technical staff.
3. Ability to write technical materials.
4. Ability to write non-technical materials.
5. Ability to handle briefings for management.

Knowledge Base

1. Knowledge of field.
2. Ability to acquire information from other sources.
3. Ability to acquire knowledge of company.

Technical Skills

1. Ability to apply appropriate designs.
2. Ability to use appropriate statistics.
3. Ability to develop appropriate measures.
4. Computer skills.

Management and Social Skills

1. Ability to get along with other staff.
2. Contributions as a team member.
3. Ability to provide group leadership when required.
4. Ability to provide supervision when required.

References

American Psychological Association Committee on Accreditation and Accreditation Office. (1986). *Accreditation handbook.* Washington, DC: Author.

Cutts, N. (Ed.). (1955). *School psychologists in midcentury: A report of the Thayer Conference on the functions, qualifications, and training of school psychologists.* Washington, DC: American Psychological Association.

Hinrichs, J. R. (1983a). The corporate view of internships in I/O psychology. *Industrial-Organizational Psychologist, 20*(2), 25-29.

Hinrichs, J. R. (1983b). Internships in I/O psychology: The faculty perspective. *Industrial-Organizational Psychologist, 20*(4), 26-30.

Hoch, E. L., Ross, A. O., & Winder, C. L. (Eds.). (1966). *Professional preparation of clinical psychologists* (Chicago Conference). Washington, DC: American Psychological Association.

Howard, A. (1990). *The multiple facets of industrial-organizational psychology: Membership survey results.* Arlington Heights, IL: Society for Industrial and Organizational Psychology.

Klimoski, R. (1983a). The making of an I/O psychologist: The role of internships. *Industrial-Organizational Psychologist, 20*(2), 22-24.

Klimoski, R. (1983b). Internships in I/O psychology: The student's perspective. *Industrial-Organizational Psychologist, 20*(3), 26-29.

Korman, M. (Ed.). (1973). *Levels and patterns of professional training in psychology* (Vail Conference). Washington, DC: American Psychological Association.

Kuhnert, K. W., & Downey, R. G. (1989). Internships and I/O psychology: A national sample. *The Industrial Psychologist, 27,* 45-50

Kuhnert, K. W., & Downey, R.G. (1991). *Internships and I/O psychology: A student's perspective.* Paper presented at the Sixth Annual Conference of the Society for Industrial and Organizational Psychology, St. Louis, MO.

Rainey, V. C. (Ed.). (1950). *Training in clinical psychology.* Englewood Cliffs, NJ: Prentice-Hall.

Roe, A., Gustad, J. W., Moore, B. V., Ross, S., & Skodak, M. (Eds). (1959). *Graduate education in psychology* (Miami Conference). Washington, DC: American Psychological Association.

Shakow, D. (1976). What is clinical psychology? *American Psychologist, 31,* 553-560.

Society for Industrial and Organizational Psychology. (1985). *Guidelines for education and training at the doctoral level in industrial/organizational psychology.* College Park: University of Maryland.

Society for Industrial and Organizational Psychology. (1986). *Graduate training programs in industrial/organizational psychology and organizational behavior.* College Park: University of Maryland.

Thompson, A. S., & Super, D. E. (Eds.). (1964). *The professional preparation of counseling psychologists* (Graystone Conference). New York: Columbia University, Teachers College, Bureau of Publications.

2

Finding Room on the Rack for More Than One Hat

Combining Multiple Professional Roles

FRANK E. SAAL

The challenges of combining multiple professional roles are all too familiar to many independent organizational consultants. This chapter examines the benefits to be derived from combining several different roles, as well as the dangers that lurk in the dark closets of independent consultants who "wear more than one hat." Before examining these benefits and blights in more detail, however, let us clarify who these consultants are.

Most organizational and evaluation consultants operate in one of three basic sets of professional circumstances. Many are associated with professional consulting firms that employ as few as two or three individuals or as many as hundreds of professional staff. Because these consultants act on behalf of their employing firms, however, their activities are *not* independent. Further, because most consulting firms frown on independent moonlighting or freelancing on the part of their professional employees, this first group falls outside the focus of this chapter. A second contingent of consultants are undeniably independent. In business for and by themselves, these professionals maintain wardrobes uncluttered by any headgear other than their "independent-consultant hats." Because they contend exclusively with only *one* professional role, however, these consultants also lie beyond the pale of this discussion.

A third group of organizational and evaluation consultants includes women and men whose consulting activities are, like the second group's, independent in that those activities do *not* take place within the context or confines of formal or institutionalized professional relationships (e.g., partnerships or consulting firms). Unlike the second group, these individuals pursue their consulting activities in conjunction with other formalized, professional endeavors. More often than not, they hold positions as instructors or professors on college and university campuses. It is this group of organizational and evaluation consultants, and the challenges they confront as they presume to wear more than one hat, that is the focus of this chapter.

The discussion is divided into three major sections. The first section examines some of the obstacles that typically litter the paths of independent organizational and evaluation consultants who try to combine more than one professional role (e.g., consultant and professor), paying particular attention to such classic organizational topics as role conflict and role ambiguity. The next section looks at several ways in which multiple professional roles can complement each other; instances of role congruence can provide strong incentives to those willing to battle role conflict and ambiguity. The final section addresses the issue of training. How can we best prepare students who wish to pursue careers as independent organizational or evaluation consultants in addition to their roles as teachers and researchers (and administrators) on college and university campuses?[1]

Role Conflict and Ambiguity

Social or organizational roles are typically defined as sets of expected activities and behaviors that are deemed appropriate or necessary for those who occupy specific positions within social (including "industrial") organizations. Role *conflict* refers to a situation in which expectations associated with two or more roles are either antagonistic (compliance with one necessarily renders compliance with another increasingly difficult) or mutually exclusive (compliance with one renders compliance with another impossible). Role *overload* occurs when the sum of all the expectations associated with one's role(s) exceeds the capabilities of the role occupant. Because role overload boils down to a role occupant's inability to be in more than one place at the same time, or do more than one thing with limited resources (money, energy, etc.), it will be treated in this chapter as a special case of role conflict. How should one expend resources that are insufficient to address all of the demands associated with one or more roles? The barrier here is not so much logical as it is logistical. Role *ambiguity* refers to uncertainty or lack of clarity concerning the expectations associated with one's role(s). Independent consultants who attempt to accommodate multiple sets of expectations are vulnerable to each of these role-related sources of dissatisfaction and stress.

Role Conflict and Overload

My efforts to combine the roles of independent consultant, university professor, and (more recently) academic department head have generated role conflict or overload in three basic domains. First and, without doubt, most oppressive are the *time demands* associated with these three roles. Because many professionals enjoy rich and busy careers occupying only one of these roles, it is hardly profound to acknowledge that each of them could devour every waking moment of every day, even assuming competent time-management skills. Those who try to combine multiple roles do not and cannot enjoy this luxury, however.

For example, as I rummaged through the three in-boxes on my desk one morning, each held several major items that clamored for immediate attention. The "University Professor" found: (a) three books and one chapter (this one) under contract, the deadlines for which were long passed; (b) two manuscripts to review as consulting editor or ad hoc reviewer for professional journals, the deadline for one of which was ancient history; (c) one manuscript that was tentatively accepted for publication pending a few relatively minor revisions—8 months previous(!); and (d) a variety of other miscellaneous but important tasks (class preparations, stacks of professional literature to ward off professional obsolescence, meetings with faculty and students, etc.) The "Department Head" confronted: (a) documents and tasks pertaining to the proposed promotion of a faculty member to the rank of Professor; (b) documents and tasks pertaining to another faculty member's recertification to continue supervising doctoral dissertations; (c) documents and tasks pertaining to recruitment of an entry-level, tenure-track assistant professor for fall 1992; (d) a report required by the dean describing the department's efforts to confront dramatically increasing class enrollments and inflated numbers of undergraduate majors and graduate students at the master's and doctoral levels; and (e) a variety of other miscellaneous but important tasks (reports to the faculty concerning use of departmental computer equipment and faculty performance evaluation, scheduled meetings of various committees and task forces, etc.). The Department Head is generally better at meeting deadlines than the University Professor, but this is almost entirely attributable to the relative costs and aversive consequences of tardiness in the two roles.

This is the context in which the "Independent Consultant" currently operates. At the time, my "To Do" list in this role was mercifully limited to: (a) completing a final report of a comparable-worth study conducted for a public agency; and (b) assembling requisite continuing-education documentation to qualify for relicensure in the state of Kansas. Nevertheless, combined with the numerous tasks confronting the University Professor and the Department Head (or academic administrator) these consulting commitments compound my sense of role overload.

It is worth noting that I (we? the three of us?) did not purposefully make multiple commitments to major projects with approximately concurrent deadlines. That is, I did not knowingly invite role overload/conflict. Unfortunately, many obligations and opportunities that confront professors, administrators, and independent organizational and evaluation consultants involve relatively long-term commitments. Spread out over many months and sometimes years (e.g., book contracts), such commitments often frustrate one's efforts to predict with any precision when major investments of time will be required. At rates that seem to defy chance distributions, multiple long-term commitments and associated deadlines often conspire to demand major investments of time and energy at more-or-less the same time. Short of refusing to undertake second and third major projects until a first is essentially completed—a strategy often deemed unacceptable even by professionals who luxuriate in only a single professional role—this dilemma may simply defy solution. Role overload may, therefore, constitute an unavoidable occupational hazard for consultants with other hats in their closets.

A second example of role conflict directly attributable to my own forays into multiple professional roles involves the *use of specific facilities and equipment*. Although the university in which I teach, conduct research, and administer an academic department encourages faculty to engage in consulting activities, provided those activities do not interfere with their responsibilities and commitments to the university, faculty are expressly forbidden to transact personal business from a university office. This would not constitute a serious restriction if all my independent consulting activities took place within the physical confines of my organizational clients. Typically, however, this is not the case.

Far more common are situations in which on-site times are interspersed with off-site consulting activities. Such off-site activities include computer analyses of organizational and evaluation data and composition of reports and presentations that summarize empirical findings and attendant recommendations. Because my university denies the use of its equipment to facilitate these necessary off-site consulting activities, I am left with two alternatives. I can choose to honor those policies and refrain completely from using university facilities and equipment (my office, its furniture and everyday supplies, my computer/ word processor, my telephone, etc.). However, unless I am prepared to devote an entire workday to these off-site consulting activities, a luxury my other roles rarely afford, this alternative necessitates additional travel between home and university offices. Extra travel consumes additional time, of course, which adds to role overload/conflict. Alternatively, I can choose to disregard the university's policies. After all, if I am careful, who will know that I used my university office and word processor to prepare a report for a client organization? Unfortunately, unless I can dismiss those policies as absurd or irrelevant, and thereby rationalize that behavior (at least in my own mind), the role (and ethical) conflicts inherent in this alternative are obvious.

A third manifestation of role conflict commonly experienced by independent consultants who also hold research-oriented academic positions involves the *trade-off between efficiency and thoroughness.* Academicians are trained to conduct careful, meticulous research in response to problems or unanswered questions in their disciplines. Designing rigorous experimental procedures or administering large-scale surveys typically consumes substantial amounts of time, a relatively plentiful commodity for most academicians (especially those who enjoy tenured positions). For organizational and evaluation consultants, however—independent or otherwise—time is usually an extremely scarce resource. Organizational problems usually translate (directly or indirectly) into reduced productivity and less profit. Clients are typically anxious to receive evaluation results as soon as possible (or even quicker!). It is therefore quite predictable that organizational representatives who contract with consultants reliably stress the urgency of the consultant's

task. "We need it yesterday!" is a plea all too familiar to many independent organizational and evaluation consultants.

Balancing these two antagonistic sets of needs and values can generate tremendous frustration and debilitating role conflict. The University
Professor is loath to abandon the tenets of scientific research with its
emphasis on proper sampling procedures, highly controlled data-collection
techniques and sophisticated statistical analyses. The Independent Consultant, however, is all too aware that the organization will not and
cannot tolerate the disruptions necessary to effect proper sampling
procedures, that data must be collected "on the run" while organization
members try to satisfy the demands of their jobs, and that nothing is
more likely to cause managers' eyes to glaze over than reams of
computer printouts overflowing with the intricacies of unpronounce-
able multivariate statistical procedures. All too often the necessary
compromises satisfy no one, and the role conflict persists.

Role Ambiguity

As if role conflict and overload were not sufficient punishments for
those who dare to don two or more professional hats, independent
consultants with academic appointments must also contend with various levels of role ambiguity. Consider the following two examples of
unclear role expectations.

Cognizant of a professor's expertise in the areas of job analysis and
job evaluation, a government agency invites the professor to serve on
a task force charged with the responsibility of conducting a comparable-worth study of several official public positions, both elected and
appointed. The study will obviously require substantial time commitments, but task force members will be expected to serve without
compensation.

For the University Professor whose sole hat is the mortar-board, this
invitation represents nothing more than an opportunity to perform a
valuable community service, and it can be accepted or declined in that
relatively unambiguous context. The academician who also pursues a
career as a paid independent consultant, however, is in something more
of a quandary. Although the invitation presents the same community-
service opportunity to the University Professor, the Independent Consultant is being asked to donate generous amounts of professional time
and service that would normally result in substantial consulting fees. Is
this a reasonable expectation?

Let us take this a step further and "add some insult to injury." Suppose the task force identifies a need for subsequent professional work in a related area in which the Independent Consultant also claims expertise. Should he recommend that someone else be hired to do that work, thereby further undermining his efforts to acquire financially profitable consulting contracts? Or, should he point out that the needed work is also within his area of expertise and express a willingness to complete it in the context of his normal fee structure? Would this constitute unethical abuse of either his access to the governmental agency that requested the original study or his participation on the task force that conducted it? Exactly what are reasonable expectations in this situation?

A second example of role ambiguity emerges when the University Professor-Independent Consultant is contacted by a local business organization in search of professional expertise and assistance. After listening to the organizational representative's description of the perceived problem, it becomes clear that the necessary work could be performed either by the Independent Consultant (in return for professional experience and a handsome consulting fee) or by some of the students involved in university-sanctioned practicum exercises under the University Professor's supervision. Which of this professional's multiple roles should take charge of this situation? This lack of role clarity can easily lead to the reluctant acceptance of an additional role—"insomniac."

Fortunately, professionals who try to combine their roles as independent organizational and evaluation consultants with other roles (such as university professor or department head) can also derive numerous benefits from the complementarity of those multiple roles. All is not *Sturm und Drang*. Let us turn now to several of the advantages associated with combining one's role as an independent consultant with other professional roles.

Role Congruence

Perhaps as a reward for tolerating the frustrations and anxieties that accompany role conflict and ambiguity, one's efforts to combine the roles of independent consultant and university professor will predictably illuminate these roles' symbiotic relationship. Although I believe the academician benefits more than the consultant, each role is strengthened through the actions of the other.

The university professor, who comes to the classroom armed not only with notes and theories, but also with an ample supply of anecdotes and war stories about his efforts to apply the course material out in the real world, is usually far more credible and entertaining than a colleague who restricts his classroom remarks to abstract models and theories found in textbooks. Many students in higher education are very concerned with the relevance of their courses to their future careers. The instructor who also consults can appeal to her students' real-world interests far more convincingly than can her colleague who has not confronted course-related challenges off campus. In the process, of course, the former instructor might also make stronger contributions to her students' broad, liberal educations.

The university professor with experience as an independent consultant is also better situated than her purely academic colleagues to obtain necessary cooperation from organizations when searching for suitable sites in which students can conduct research and/or benefit from practicum or internship experiences. Organizational representatives are more likely to respond favorably to requests from professionals whom they know and trust through prior consulting relationships. Of course, these contacts can also work to the direct advantage of the academician herself when she requires access to samples of men and women in order to pursue her own research agenda. Clearly, the role of university professor is enhanced when it is complemented by the role of independent organizational or evaluation consultant.

Finally, I would be remiss to ignore the potential of independent consulting activities to provide lucrative financial compensation far exceeding that within the grasp of all but the brightest academic stars. To the extent that this extra income frees the professor to devote summer months to pursuits instrumental to obtaining academic tenure and/or promotion (writing grant proposals, conducting research, obtaining further continuing education, etc.), his consulting activities will surely contribute to greater success in the academy.

In return, one's consulting activities can benefit from an academic affiliation. I have found on numerous occasions that organizational representatives ascribe greater credibility to my work and recommendations because of my affiliation with a respected institution of higher education. It is important to note, however, that this typically occurs only *after* they have been disabused of any stereotypical perceptions concerning ivory tower academics who lack common sense and an appreciation for real-world issues and problems. In a sense, then, one must often *initially* gain organizational representatives' trust and respect *in spite of* one's academic credentials and affiliation. Once accepted, however, those credentials can become an asset.

One's role as a university professor also improves one's consulting skills because the academician must remain conversant with the research literature in order to avoid professional obsolescence. Recent theoretical and empirical advances described in that literature can strengthen one's consulting efforts. If the professor attends academic conferences, she can gain even quicker access to new ideas that can facilitate her independent consulting.

Given this synergy between the roles of independent organizational or evaluation consultant and university professor, there is every reason to encourage graduate students pursuing degrees in industrial/organizational psychology, program evaluation, or other related disciplines (organizational behavior, etc.) to entertain the possibility of combining multiple professional roles. Can we construct their graduate training programs so as to minimize the negative effects of role conflict and ambiguity? The final section of this chapter addresses this question.

Training for Multiple Professional Roles

Beyond providing graduate students with solid backgrounds in the traditional subject matters of their disciplines and initiating them into the mysteries of sound research methodologies and statistical analyses, I believe there are several constructive strategies for preparing them to cope with the rigors of combining the independent-consultant role with other professional roles. These tactics might best be incorporated into a graduate curriculum in the following order.

First, students can participate in an on-campus seminar designed to orient them to the pleasures and pitfalls of assuming multiple professional roles. Following discussions of classic and contemporary research in the areas of role conflict, overload and ambiguity, students can explore these phenomena with experienced professionals who have developed successful coping strategies. First-hand advice based on personal successes and failures can then be supplemented with carefully prepared case studies that prompt students to wrestle with some of the dilemmas and vagaries inherent in the opportunities and oppression associated with multiple roles. Yes, such a seminar will further burden many students already wrestling with demanding graduate curricula.

And yes, the success of such a seminar will depend heavily on the availability of articulate, candid and experienced professionals, as well as a skillful leader capable of maximizing the pedagogical advantages of case studies. Fortunately, neither of these obstacles is necessarily prohibitive.

Second, students can engage in closely supervised practicum exercises, in which they have opportunities to work on real evaluation projects or other organizational problems in small groups, under the close scrutiny of one or more faculty members and, perhaps, senior graduate students. Such practica depend upon the availability of one or more local organizations, representatives of which are willing to work with students and faculty members in a predictable win-win situation. The organization benefits by gaining access to qualified professional expertise at minimal cost (e.g., the project may be drawn out over longer time intervals). In addition to invaluable practical experience with the tools and methods of their own discipline(s), the students begin to appreciate first-hand some of the role-related challenges discussed in this chapter as they go about integrating their academic responsibilities with their obligations to the participating organization. If successive groups of students progress through the practicum component of a graduate training program, it will not be necessary for each group to restrict itself to a project with a beginning and end that correspond to the onset and conclusion of the academic term. One group can simply pick up where the preceding group left off. The project is eventually completed, and all participants benefit from the experience.

Third, more advanced graduate students can accompany and collaborate with faculty members who complement their academic activities with off-campus excursions as independent consultants. Having gained first-hand experience with some of the trials of role conflict, overload, and ambiguity during their practicum experiences, students can benefit from close working relationships with senior mentors as they strive to overcome those tribulations. Of course, this training component requires potential mentors who are experienced in combining multiple professional roles and willing to share their weaknesses as well as their strengths with graduate proteges. Mentors must also be able to transform predictable negative encounters into valuable educational experiences. This last requirement became very clear to me several years ago when a young, female graduate student accompanied me to a meeting with several representatives of municipal police and fire departments in the process of exploring possibilities for improving their personnel-selection procedures. Upon being introduced to my female protege, one of those representatives asked, "So tell me, Sweetie, what's a pretty little thing like you doing here?" Although appalled by this remark, this probably was an eye-opening lesson for this young woman in the sexist attitudes she could expect to encounter in certain organizational settings. I only hope I was able to help her transform that insult into a learning experience.

Finally, the advanced student should pursue an internship with an off-campus organization. On one's own in a strange organizational environment, buffeted by politics and norms that are sometimes diametrically opposed to those assimilated in graduate school, budding professionals can begin their solo struggles with the sources of role conflict, overload and ambiguity. On the brighter side, they can also begin to experience the satisfactions to be derived from coping with the pressures and realizing the benefits of successfully combining multiple professional perspectives and roles. (The chapter by Downey and Kuhnert in this volume deals more extensively with the challenges and frustrations inherent in internship experiences.)

Summary

We have examined some of the role-related perils and possibilities experienced by those who try to combine the role of independent consultant with one (and sometimes two or more) other professional role(s). Although the specifics vary from professional to professional, those who accept multiple sets of social expectations can confidently anticipate debilitating bouts of role conflict, overload, and ambiguity. If they are willing to battle these demons, however, they can also expect to benefit from the synergy that characterizes relationships among various components of multiple professional roles. Those fortunate enough to emerge from graduate programs that specifically prepare students to assume multiple professional roles will be more likely to avoid the pitfalls and embrace the possibilities than will those whose initial exposure to combining two or more roles comes in the form of on-the-job training. Whether we decide that our wardrobes have room for only one hat, or we embrace the challenges of coordinating complex and varied collections of chapeaus, our decisions can and should be well informed. Since the day we were old enough to choose (and later purchase) our own apparel, few of us have been content to select a hat without first trying it on. The occasion of career choice or change is no time to start.

Note

1. The reader deserves fair warning that the following paragraphs are either enlightened or beclouded (depending on whether you agree with the contents and conclusions) by the author's 16 years of experience trying to combine the roles of independent organizational consultant and university professor, and by 3 years of experience trying to incorporate the blessing or curse (depending on which day you ask) of a third role—academic administrator/department head.

3

Combining Research and Consultation

Advantages, Pitfalls, and Recommendations

FREDERICK T. L. LEONG

The mission of the consultant is to assess and resolve the problems presented by the client through the use of special expertise. One area of expertise that the social scientist brings to the consultative relationship is his or her knowledge and skills in research design and methodology. Within the field of psychology, the value of scientific research to practice, whether in the industrial or clinical setting, is explicitly recognized. Hence, the majority of training programs within applied areas of psychology (e.g., clinical psychology, industrial/organizational psychology) subscribe to the scientist-practitioner model, which attempts to produce psychologists trained to integrate the science and practice aspects of their fields. By implication, organizational consultants who seek to use both their professional and scientific training are assumed to be more effective than those who do not. Although many consultants subscribe to the scientist-practitioner model, a major problem concerns the process of integrating science and practice. The present chapter discusses this process by reviewing some of the advantages and pitfalls of combining research and consultation and concludes with some recommendations for their integration. *Consultation* may be interpreted broadly as any effort to utilize behavioral science knowledge to facilitate the resolution of a problem. Most examples reflect my own experience in industrial/organizational (I/O) consultation.

For the purposes of the present chapter, the typology of research provided by Cherns, as cited in Rothman (1980), will be adopted. According to Cherns, there are four different forms of research: (a) pure basic research—theoretical and knowledge producing in nature, (b) basic objective research—research arising out of some field of application of the discipline but not aimed at prescribing a solution to a problem, (c) operations research—research aimed at solving ongoing problems within organizational settings, and (d) action research—research that incorporates a strategy for the introduction of planned change. (Cited by Rothman, 1980, p. 17).

Although the research that consultants utilize in their settings will most probably fall into the last two categories (i.e., operations and action research), it is conceivable that a consultant will either recommend basic research to the client or collect data that could later be used for basic research. Given this possibility, I would like to define research broadly to include any project that involves the collection of empirical data whether for basic or applied purposes. However, it is probably safe to assume that most of the research that consultants will conduct will be applied in nature.

The types of research that a consultant can conduct are a function of the nature of the presenting problem as well as the type of organization that is involved. However, there are several categories of research that could be quite easily conducted by consultants given the common problems for which consultants are brought into organizations. First, many problems can be addressed by needs assessment. For example, the client may be concerned with the extent of alcoholism among the delivery drivers. Second, program evaluation is a common research approach for consultants. For example, the sponsor wants to know if the $500,000 a year for the Employee Assistance Program is effective. Another common consulting problem that is amenable to research concerns work attitudes and performance. For example, is there a morale problem among our downtown bank staff? What is the job satisfaction levels of research and development (R&D) staff given the high turnover the last three years? Selection, training, and development issues in organizations are also quite amenable to research approaches. For example, how can we select and train the next group of management trainees so that they will stay with the organization for more than just a few years?

Another common strategy for combining research and consulting is to test a new construct or concept. For example, if the organization that has brought you in as a consultant is concerned with high turnover among its new personnel, you may have realized from previous consultations that much of the problem centered on the recruitment approach. Being an astute consultant and a good researcher, you formulate a concept of the *realistic job previews* (RJP), which you believe, unlike traditional recruitment procedures, will reduce the high turnover rates among new entrants into the organization. You proceed to operationalize and test this concept of RJP in the organization and obtain data to support your concept. Chances are this scenario is not too different from what happened to John Wanous, developer of the concept of realistic job previews. Another example of this research strategy, which will be discussed later, concerns Benjamin Schneider's concept of organizational climates.

Consultants can use established or newly developed instruments to test the utility of theoretical models for solving organizational problems (see Cook, Hepworth, Wall, & Warr, 1981, for measures). For example, Gottfredson and Holland's (1990) Position Classification Inventory can be used to test the person-environment model for predicting job satisfaction among factory workers. Relatedly, consultants may use the research opportunity to compare two or more instruments to assess their relative utility and validity. For example, a study concerned with job satisfaction may compare Brayfield and Rothe's (1951) Overall Job Satisfaction measure with the recently developed Jobs in General scale from the JDI. Consulting contracts provide very good opportunity for testing and evaluating new instruments in that there is a strong need to determine how well the new instrument will work with different samples in different settings during the early stages of an instrument's life span. In addition, consultants may use consulting contracts to assess the "population validity" of instruments. An instrument may have considerable amounts of reliability and validity data in its support, but this body of data may be limited to college students, a common research study would be to assess its validity with developmentally more advanced samples (e.g., will this instrument work equally well with a group of business executives at mid-life?).

Advantages

Opportunities for consulting depend on an individual's expertise, reputation, and marketing. Expertise, and the reputation which goes with it, is often built on a program of publication. That is where research comes in to play. One of the best ways to establish one's reputation and to increase one's opportunities for consulting is to engage in a program of research in an area in which one wishes to provide consulting services.

Anecdotal information from well-known consultants has often indicated that these individuals were consulted because of their expertise in a particular area. Their expertise was noticed by clients via publication in high visibility outlets such as the *Harvard Business Review* or an in-depth article in the *New York Times* concerning the author's theories and findings. The commodity or product possessed by the consultant that is needed by the client is expertise. Hence, a successful consultant must have an area of expertise, and his or her clients need to be aware of that expertise.

Doing and publishing research help establish one's reputation as an expert. However, getting published is only part of the process. A professor of mine once made an important distinction regarding research that is relevant to the current issue of reputation and expertise. He pointed out that the important goal is "not just getting published but getting read" (Schneider, 1985). Of course the latter depends on the former but the former by itself may not be sufficient. Therefore, what one publishes and where one publishes is also very important to the establishment of a reputation. However, without that expertise and reputation, one's consulting will probably be limited to opportunistic engagements (i.e., being in the right place at the right time). With an established reputation in your field, the clients will seek you out.

Besides gaining a reputation via publications, an alternative or supplemental strategy is marketing. Some consultants would maintain that publishing in high visibility or trade journals is a marketing strategy in itself. Others would argue that publications alone are not sufficient. Giving pro bono presentations to various groups and associations is another highly recommended strategy for increasing your reputation and visibility as an expert. Milton Hakel (1991) in a recent practical chapter for the "consulting academician" has pointed out the importance of marketing and how academicians tend to avoid this aspect of their consulting practice: "Marketing is a touchy subject for academicians. The stereotypical academician likes to believe that the truth will win out, that logic and rigor will prevail, and that 'good ideas will sell themselves.' Wrong!" (p. 165).

Depending on personal preference, marketing and advertising are definitely essential strategies for those desiring to increase their consulting practice. For academicians, professional networking is an important component of this marketing plan. Many consulting contracts are established by referrals, and colleagues are invaluable in directing business to each other. However, that will happen only if one is a member of the "network" and many colleagues know about one's expertise.

Returning to the advantages, an example of the artful combination of research and consultation is provided by Benjamin Schneider, a former professor of mine at the University of Maryland. As one the early pioneers in the area of organizational climates, most of his research involved applying the concept of organizational climates to his client's problems and providing some useful suggestions for change. A review of his research articles on organizational climates will indicate that he carefully planned ground-breaking studies and collected data from organizational clients to demonstrate the important role of climates to organizational functioning. His work on "service climates" in banks serves as an excellent example of the type of research-consulting integration that I am describing (Schneider, Parkington, & Buxton, 1980). Not only did he help his client "get a handle on an important problem" but he also convinced them of the value of research while advancing his own program of research.

The ability to combine research and consultation tends to set up a success cycle. Conducting research in one's consulting practice will produce relevant publications that will be read, which in turn increases one's visibility and consulting opportunities. More consulting then leads back to more research and the cycle repeats itself—provided that the consultant has the motivation and skills to execute the needed combination of research and consultation. An edited book by Cummings and Frost (1985) serves as an excellent guide and resource for consultants interested in getting their research published.

Another advantage of combining research with consulting is that it is ideal for faculty members who consult and who are trained as scientist-practitioners. Making use of their consulting activities to obtain empirical data not only helps them with their research program (and promotion and tenure) but also provides a useful role model of scientist-practitioner integration for graduate students. It also encourages faculty members to have hands-on consulting experience rather than just book knowledge.

Making a habit of combining research and consulting results in a cross-fertilization effect. Your consultation improves in that it is based on research. Similarly, your research is more relevant and usable in that it is based on your observations/experience in organizations and the research questions spring from real-world problems. Ideally, such a synergistic effect of integrating research and consulting is the primary purpose of advocating a scientist-practitioner model in the different fields of applied psychology.

Entry into organizations solely for research purposes often meets with considerable resistance. However, if you have been brought in as a consultant to solve a problem, you have greater leverage in convincing your clients of the importance of research to either understanding or solving the problem. Of course you are bound by ethical standards not to abuse such uses of a consultant-client relationship. Ethical issues will be discussed in more details under the section "Pitfalls."

If you are successful in using research to help your client solve his or her problem, you have also succeeded in convincing managers and practitioners of the value of appropriate research. This imparting of an "empirical attitude" to clients is quite important given the general attitude maintained by practitioners that much of the research undertaken by academicians is so theoretical and irrelevant to be of use for the real-world problems practitioners encounter. There are some valuable resources available to the consultant-researcher for increasing his or her understanding of doing practical research and doing research in the real world (e.g., Hakel, Sorcher, Beer, & Moses, 1982; Lawler, Mohrman, Mohrman, Ledford, & Cummings, 1985).

As scientists we are interested in assessing what factors lead to which outcomes and in increasing our ability to predict those relationships. As consultant we want to be able to demonstrate to our future and potential clients that our interventions work. Program evaluations allow us to achieve this dual purpose. Hence program evaluation research conducted as part of our consultation often can help us increase our scientific knowledge-base and provide evidence for the effectiveness of our interventions that in turn will increase our client's confidence that his or her company's money has been well spent.

George Miller, a past president of APA, is well-known for his presidential address in which he pointed out to the profession that one of our greatest contributions would be to "give psychology away" rather than hide our knowledge in our scientific journals. Integrating research and consultation can be an important part of the "giving away" process, to educate our clientele concerning the importance of using research to monitor, evaluate, and redesign our work. By actively conducting and depending on research, we teach our clients to recognize the limits of common sense and habit and to recognize the value of relevant research.

Doing research during consultations also provides opportunities for one's graduate students to experience research on applied problems rather than continuing to add to "Psychology as the science of the college sophomore." Additionally, it is good training for applied psychology students who are interested in applied positions when they complete their training. Many of these applied research opportunities can also help fund the graduate student's education.

Another advantage of combining research and consultation is that it contributes to the scientific and professional communities in the long run. Collecting data on various samples in a variety of settings with different measures eventually accumulates into very valuable baseline datasets that can be utilized by future researchers to address important problems (e.g., have the value orientations or intellectual capabilities of our work force changed in the last four decades?). These baseline datasets could also form the basis for longitudinal research programs (e.g., how has the career aspirations of entry level managers changed as they have aged and how can information about these developmental changes be used to help future generations of managers?). At first blush, it may seem that this particular advantage is more relevant to researchers; however, the indirect benefits of cumulative research data can be easily conveyed to managers and professionals. Such research contributions are really long-term national R&D investment into human resources development. More and more managers are beginning to see the need for a competitive work force in the global market (e.g., business and school partnerships to provide remedial education to workers).

To take full advantage of this opportunity, what is needed is some form of a clearinghouse of such datasets. The datasets would be made available to both researchers and consultants. Organizations already exist to execute this function in the social sciences (e.g., the Inter-University Consortium for Political and Social Research, University of

Michigan and the Henry Murray Research Center at Radcliffe College; See also McKillip and Stephenson, this volume). An organization that collects and archives research datasets on organizational studies or program evaluations will add considerably to this function and be an invaluable resource to researchers and consultants alike. At present, information about such datasets are typically only available through informal networks that are not at all centralized.

Pitfalls

Although there are many advantages to combining research and consultation, some of which I have discussed, there are also some pitfalls that need to be kept in mind. Very often, a key problem concerns the question of, Who owns the data? Ownership of the research data is a particularly tricky situation and needs to be negotiated carefully and at the outset of the project. See, for example, the November 1991 issue of the *APA Monitor* (Adler, "Confidentiality clause struck down by judge: HHS had restricted data release," p. 11) which described a lawsuit filed by Stanford University against the National Institutes of Health, a government agency, concerning the disposition of data collected under a grant from that agency. NIH requires that grant recipients clear their research reports with them prior to publication, a procedure with which Stanford disagrees.

Many organizations will want to have some control over the data collected if not actually housed there. Other organizations will release the data but with the provision that they are provided a preview of the reports based on the data. Such conditions create a grey area if the organization disagrees with your interpretations of the data or if the organization feels that your report contains information that would be detrimental to their operations (e.g., your report contains information about the organization's strengths and weaknesses which can be used by competitors). The balance between academic freedom and the organization's veto power needs to be thoroughly negotiated, preferably at the outset.

In addition, because all problems cannot be anticipated, the researcher-consultant needs to be very flexible in balancing his or her role as consultant and as researcher. The latter role's loyalty is to the scientific community, whereas the former role's commitment is to the client. It is not possible in the present context to discuss all the potential conflicts created by this dual role but the consultant-researcher will need to be guided by his or her profession's ethical guidelines as well as the responsibilities inherent in the consultant role.

Support from the organization's higher levels of administration for the research-collaboration is very important. Otherwise, the cord could be yanked on a project in midstream after considerable investment of time and energy. Alternatively, longitudinal studies could be terminated and follow-up studies prevented from occurring. A related problem is change in administration during the project. Based on my expertise in career psychology, I had been consulted by the assistant dean of Academic Affairs at a medical school to help address the career development concerns of some of their students. Given the number of students involved and the lack of established procedures in doing career specialty interventions—much of the career literature is limited to initial career choice and little attention is usually paid to specialty choice—I decided that a series of exploratory career workshops should be conducted and their impact evaluated. (See Leong, Gaylor, & Ford, 1991, for a full description of these workshops.) We also decided that the value of the selected career instruments should be evaluated longitudinally. Unfortunately, a new dean of the medical school was hired in the interim and the workshops were discontinued. Fortunately, however, three classes of medical students were assessed and provided assistance via the workshops. They form a small but sufficient baseline group on which to conduct longitudinal follow-up studies.

In a book exploring factors believed to be responsible for the under-utilization of research, Rothman (1980) provides some very useful insights about doing research in organizations. For example, he reviews different articles that point to the "two-worlds" model: "the notion that the world of research and the world of administrative practice have essential differences in language, values, methods, and points of view" (Havelock, 1980, pp. 11-12). Rothman (1980) goes on to cite some of the studies demonstrating this two-world perspective: "Caplan (1977: 194-195) has presented statistical evidence to show that the 'two communities' theory best accounts for distance between researchers and policy makers (as compared with theories that place blame on inappropriate behavior by researchers or the constraints under which operational people work)" (Rothman, 1980, p. 95).

As a function of these two opposing communities, Rothman (1980) provides an excellent discussion of some of the factors responsible for practitioners' resistance to research. The consultant, in the process of integrating research and consultation, should be alert to these factors. For example, one factor is *forces of custom.* "It was said that a certain inertia and unthinking conservatism exists in agency situations. As one director put it: 'Things get repeated based on custom. The system runs itself, but it doesn't criticize itself'" (p. 99). Another factor is *Defensiveness against criticism.* "One of the major blocks to serious attention to research, it was said, is the tendency of operational people to feel threatened by information that implies a criticism of their practices" (p. 100). Other factors discussed by Rothman, that are well worth careful study by the research-consultant, include: *attachment to particular services, loss of autonomy, loss of status or role, climate of pressure, intuitive intellectual style, misunderstanding of research, and anti-intellectual radicalism.* In summary, research-oriented consultants who are not careful may then be viewed by their clients as either irrelevant and too ivory-towered to be of any use or too threatening because he or she is using theories and methodology with which the client is uncomfortable.

There are also political realities that all external consultants need to monitor and manage. For example, some clients may view research as intrinsically problematic in that it may damage the organization (e.g., discovery of a tobacco organization's shift in marketing strategies, targeting groups in developing countries that have less stringent government regulations). Other clients may sense an inherent conflict between research and business. The goal of research is to discover knowledge whereas the goal of business is to make profits by competing. Information discovered in research may become available to their competitors that would diminish their competitiveness. This brings us back to the issue of the ownership of the data, but some clients may not even be willing to allow the collection of data by external consultants. Another political reality is that a client may not care about the underlying causes but only the outcomes (e.g., a manager not interested in morale and job satisfaction as underlying causes but instead just wants the consultant to improve work performance).

Another major pitfall involved in combining research and consultation involves ethical issues and dilemmas. As a consultant-researcher, one has two separate relationships that have ethical implications: the first relationship is with your sponsor, the second relationship is with the members of the organization who will be the subjects in your research study. As a psychologist, all of the ethical principles that apply to research with human subjects will apply to the second relationship (e.g., obtaining informed consent and respecting subjects' rights to withdraw from participation at any time).

The ethical issues involved in the first relationship are somewhat more complicated. However, Lowman (1991), in a discussion of some of the ethical issues involved in human resources practice, has pointed out that there are some common parameters. The consultant-researcher, in his or her relationship with the sponsor, needs to be aware of and stay within these parameters: that is, to avoid deception, coercion, and invasion of privacy, and to carefully monitor potential risk and the validity of the approach (Lowman, 1991, p. 198). The use of these parameters may help in resolving ethical issues. For example, deception is clearly unethical; hence, adding research questions to the study that are not directly related to your client's problem without informing your sponsor would be unethical. Yet, is such a practice clearly ethical, once the sponsor has been informed about the "piggy-backing" process? What if the sponsor also serves as a research collaborator and will eventually be a co-author in the publication. Given the sponsor's dual role, who will protect the "subjects"?

A common ethical concern with combining research and consultation is the potential abuse of the consulting relationship. It is very tempting to use the consultation to advance one's research without regards to one's obligations as a consultant given the difficulty in obtaining research samples. One way to avoid this practice would be to assess the degree of relevance of the research attached to consulting. Research that is very relevant to the organization's problem and the consultant's interests is ideal. On the other hand, research that is very relevant to the consultant's interests but not the organization's problem would be unethical. It would be akin to a psychotherapist using most of the time in session to talk about his personal concerns rather than those of the client's. Some organizations, like some clients, lack the resources and resilience to confront such abusive practices. As with most ethical practices, self-monitoring is the primary mechanism for ensuring this balance of interests. With each research project, it would be prudent to ask oneself, how much of this research addresses the organization's needs and how much it addresses one's research needs? However, most universities and organizations will have human subjects committees to provide safeguards and independent assessment of such practices. Nevertheless, checking one's practices against the principles and parameters outlined by Lowman (1991) as well as consulting more experienced peers is certainly a worthwhile strategy.

Recommendations

Sometimes the problem for which a consultant has been called in may not be amenable to research. However, given the broad definition of research that I have adopted in this chapter, I believe that those instances would be quite rare. Whether one can execute a research project during the consultation is another matter and one subject to all the pitfalls I have discussed above. A more important determinant would be one's own comfort level with research and feelings and attitudes about research. If one does not believe in the value of research, one is not likely to conduct it or make use of it. For example, if an individual believes that common sense is sufficient or that his or her intuitive judgments have seldom failed, then they will likely believe that research is superfluous. On the other hand, once a person has adopted an empirical attitude, then they will be more likely to use research in their consultation. The rest of my remarks will assume such an attitude.

One way to deal with the resistance to research and the question of the ownership of data is to collaborate with a member of the organization. Of course, all of the caveats concerning research collaboration apply here. Nevertheless, collaboration with an insider offers numerous advantages such as information about political realities which impact the research project, and greater acceptance of the research in that a colleague is involved. The insider can also provide a certain amount of reassurance to the higher administration concerning potential dangers of the project (e.g., release of important information to the competitors). Because the insider is also invested in the project, you have someone running interference on a regular basis until the completion of the project. The insider also knows more about the organization than you do. The combination of this insider information and your outsider's perspective can also provide a creative and integrative aspect to the research that neither alone could do.

The ideal would be to have someone from the highest level of administration be the collaborator. Failing that, it would be useful to cultivate support of the project from the higher administration with the help of your collaborator. Besides obtaining support from higher-level administration during the beginning of the project, maintaining and building on that support with regular meetings and progress reports are worthwhile investments of time.

Both cultivating and maintaining support for the project requires that you assess your clients' attitudes towards research. Such attitudes can range from wholehearted support to lip service to outright hostile reactions. You can assess those attitudes during the initial contact (e.g., what information has been gathered on this problem and by whom?) as well as during your proposal (e.g., embed the idea of the research into the proposal but have a backup plan). Your assessment will need to cover not only the client's attitude toward research but also his or her openness to change and innovation. Generally, the more open-minded your client is, the more he or she will be willing to allow and to use the resulting research information.

One efficient way to assess your client's attitudes toward research would be to use Myers Briggs Type Indicator (MBTI) data. The MBTI is quite widely used in management training and may be available on your client. As a means of understanding the management team's problem-solving style, you may request access to the managers' MBTI profiles. This should not be a very threatening request in that the MBTI does not assess deficits or weaknesses. For example, you may anticipate some resistance to research if the client has a very high preference for an intuitive style (N) of data-collection. Such an individual may not initially see the value of collecting quantitative data in that he or she prefers to make decisions based on personal intuition.

At times, it may be useful to bring in examples of how research has helped an organization with a similar problem. Such examples, if linked directly to positive outcomes for the organization, will go a long way toward convincing your client of the value of research (e.g., Company X also had a problem with absenteeism related to alcohol abuse, but a research study found that an employee assistance program reduced that problem and eventually saved the company money). The popularity of books such as *In Search of Excellence* (Peters & Waterman, 1982) is due to the concrete illustration of successful cases and the identification of the ingredients supposedly responsible for the success. This in turn requires that you have access to relevant examples of the successful use of research.[1]

Besides having an insider as a collaborator, an alternative strategy would be to identify allies within the organization. In the initial assessment, try to find out the attitudes toward research of different players. If there are individuals who are more supportive of research than others, it would be advantageous to gain their support. Sometimes these individuals can be found in the research and development units within the organization. At other times, these individuals may resent your status as an outside researcher and withhold their support until they can trust you.

A key ingredient in presenting the research-consultation combination is to use problem-oriented terms and a direct link to the outcomes with which the client is concerned (e.g., Schneider et al.'s, 1980, work on service climates—"creating a service climate is very important to your bank's attractiveness to customers"). This is especially true for professors who serve as consultants. They work in an environment which emphasizes scientific rigor so much that often relevance is sacrificed. Your proposal is doomed if it is perceived as irrelevant and not problem-oriented. For example, Hakel (1991) has observed that "Research is hard to sell. . . . Managers want answers, now. If a consultant is not prepared to shoot from the hip, they will find someone who is" (p. 163). Yet, with experience and perseverance, a consultant should be able to convince the organization of the advantages and value of a more systematic solution over the typical "band-aid" approaches.

One approach would be to have an "action research plan" that is akin to the ubiquitous "business plan." This action research plan would outline specifically what problem is being addressed by the research and how the research will be used to solve the identified problem(s). Consultant-researchers should be expected to be accountable for their interventions, and having to formulate the action research plan will encourage them to be problem-oriented and to think through the links between research and practice. The action research plan will also provide the sponsor and his or her organization a concrete plan with which to evaluate the consultant's proposal.

There are as many ways to translate an organizational problem into a research question as there are different types of organizations. One way to reduce this complexity is to use a two-stage diagnostic process. Let us assume that the presenting problem is a bank president's concern with the high level of risk-taking behaviors among her vice-presidents at different branches across the country. The first stage involves problem definition and formulation: the consultant must diagnose the problem and decide which "toolkit"—intervention or research—is needed. The second stage involves using the selected toolkit: that is, implementing the intervention or research program.

Sometimes, an appropriate intervention tool already exists and research is unnecessary. For example, Bank X had an identical problem a few years ago. Consulting Company Y did the necessary research, solved the problem, and is willing to help us implement the same intervention for our client for a fee. Often, however, some degree of new knowledge is needed and the research toolkit must be selected. This kit includes tools such as computerized literature searches and literature reviews. For example, what knowledge is there about bankers and risk-taking behaviors, and what is the quality and practical utility of such knowledge? Researching the literature may yield ideas for interventions or change techniques that can be adapted to the present problem. Alternatively, the literature may reveal how little is known about the problem. In either case, the collection of new data will be necessary, either to evaluate the intervention, or to answer more fundamental questions about the nature of the problem. Once it is determined that research is needed, the second diagnostic stage involves identifying research aims and implementing appropriate strategies. Thus the research toolkit includes strategies such as program evaluation, action research, and true experimentation, as well as specific techniques such as using particular instruments, conducting statistical analyses, and so forth.

Certainly, consultants often are too quick to choose their intervention toolkit. Even when intervention precedents exist, they often lack a solid foundation in research. Even when research-based interventions exist, their adaptation to a new context needs to be empirically evaluated. Often, our understanding of problems is incomplete. In every case, some research would be useful. There are a number of resources for the consultant-researcher to utilize in developing his or her research toolkit (e.g., Hakel, Sorcher, Beer, & Moses, 1982; Lawler, Mohrman, Mohrman, Ledford, & Cummings, 1985).

Here are some final suggestions on how to combine research and consultation for the beginning consultant. Start small, do not be picky, do not go for big bucks (you need to get research done in order to develop a "product" and to build a reputation), and be proactive (look for opportunities). Just as research is a cumulative enterprise, so also is the development of a consulting practice. In the beginning, the opportunity to consult and conduct research will be more important than the amount of the contract or the prestige of the organization. As you do more research and increase your reputation and visibility, there will come a time when you can be more selective about which contract to accept. Consider some form of marketing but maintain control over it so that it does not become more form than substance. Follow ethical guidelines and avoid short-cuts (see Lowman, 1991, for discussion of ethical principles).

To conclude, the advantages of combining research and consultation and the value of functioning as a scientist-practitioner in applied psychology is very aptly summarized by Hakel (1991) in his chapter on the consulting academician. Of the scientist-practitioner model, he writes, "It's essence is simple, elegant, and unitary: The best practice is based on scientific research, and the best science is useful for solving practical problems. Scientific practice and practical science. What could be better?" (p. 170).

Note

1. I have been accumulating a casebook of such examples. Readers interested in the collection may contact the author of this chapter directly.

References

Adler, T. (1991, November). Confidentiality clause struck down by judge: HHS had restricted data release. *APA Monitor*, p. 11.

Brayfield, A. H., & Rothe, H. F. (1951). An index of job satisfaction. *Journal of Applied Psychology, 35*, 307-311.

Cook, J. D., Hepworth, S. J., Wall, T. B., & Warr, P. B. (1981). *The experience of work: A compendium and review of 249 measures and their use.* New York: Academic Press.

Cummings, L. L., & Frost, P. J. (1985). *Publishing in the organizational sciences.* Homewood, IL: Richard D. Irwin.

Gottfredson, G. D., & Holland, J. L. (1990). *The position classification inventory (PCI).* Odessa, FL: Psychological Assessment Resources.

Hakel, M. D. (1991). The consulting academician. In D. W. Bray & Associates, *Working with organizations and their people: A guide to human resources practice* (pp. 151-171). New York: Guilford.

Hakel, M. D., Sorcher, M., Beer, M., & Moses, J. L. (1982). *Making it happen: Designing research with implementation in mind.* Beverly Hills, CA: Sage.

Havelock, R. (1980). Foreword. In J. Rothman, *Using research in organizations.* Beverly Hills, CA: Sage.

Lawler, E. E., Mohrman, A. M., Jr., Mohrman, S. A., Ledford, G. E., Jr., & Cummings, T. G. (1985). *Doing research that is useful for theory and practice.* San Francisco: Jossey-Bass.

Leong, F. T. L., Gaylor, M., & Ford, S. (1991). *Career specialty workshops for medical students.* Special Research Report, Counseling and Human Development, Dartmouth College Health Service, Hanover, NH.

Lowman, R. L. (1991). Ethical human resources practice in organizational settings. In D. W. Bray and Associates, *Working with organizations and their people: A guide to human resources practice* (pp. 194-218). New York: Guilford.

Peters, T. J., & Waterman, R. H. (1982). *In search of excellence: Lessons from America's best-run companies.* New York: Harper & Row.

Rothman, J. (1980). *Using research in organizations: A guide to successful application.* Beverly Hills, CA: Sage.

Schneider, B. (1985). Some propositions about getting published. In L. L. Cummings & P. J. Frost (Eds.), *Publishing in the organizational sciences* (pp. 238-247). Homewood, IL: Richard D. Irwin.

Schneider, B., Parkington, J. J., & Buxton, V. M. (1980). Employee and customer perceptions of service in banks. *Administrative Science Quarterly, 25*, 252-267.

PART II

Getting It Right: Working With People, Building Relationships

4

Creating Challenging Client-Consultant Relationships

MICHAEL F. CRISTIANI

An accounting manager asks for a film on communications to use in his department. His people are not getting along with each other. There's a lot of bickering back and forth. He wants your help. . . .

A salesperson on a major key account wants to know if you can assist her in addressing some customer issues. Actually, there is not just one issue. The customer, who is her main client, heads up the entire planning and material distribution operation and is not happy. He does not like the way he and his team are being handled by her company and its key account team. Although fulfilling the letter of the contract agreement, he wants more. And of course, her company, including her superiors, thinks everything is going along smoothly. . . .

A three-thousand person high-tech division of a major company has been experimenting with total quality management and has embarked on using high-performance teams of employees to generate quality improvements. The time has come to assess progress of this divisionwide effort. How should they

AUTHOR'S NOTE: I want to extend my personal appreciation to Phil Grosnick and Jim Maselko of Designed Learning, Plainfield, NJ. Their continuous support enabled me to be of value to my clients while I practiced being a consultant! Michael Cristiani, 4 Arbor Road, St. Louis, MO 63132.

make a valid assessment? Who should they ask? What should they ask? What methodology should they use? What would be statistically sound? Should they hire outside consultants to help as well as internal ones?

The above three examples are real ones taken from recent experience. And although they vary greatly in complexity—time required for successful resolution and in type of customer—all require the use of both technical skills and something less tangible we can call *consulting skills* in order to achieve customer satisfaction. This chapter is about developing and using these consulting skills.

Let us discuss these two distinct competencies. As in the examples, the technical competence required could be knowledge of training films, salesmanship and negotiations, or evaluation expertise. Being technically competent obviously is important both to you and to your client. In many cases we have spent years of schooling, experience, and hard work to get that way! When a problem or opportunity presents itself, we often define the problem based on our competencies. We look for opportunities to demonstrate what we can do and we have grown comfortable in exercising our abilities. What we do is important! There are also, less obviously, other skills needed to make sure that those competencies are actually brought to bear on the client's situation. Although these interpersonal relations and interactional consulting skills are less tangible and harder to define, all the expertise in the world will seldom be used without these skill competencies as well. Successful consultants are able to connect with their clients on many levels, not just task and technology but on a personal level that ensures client commitment and success to the project. There is no magic. What there is is hard work and attention to the needs of the customer. Some people call it the "soft stuff." The reason it is soft is that it is very hard to get a hold of and do it right—not that it is so easy anybody can do it (although we think we can). As a famous quote from Fred Smith, CEO of Federal Express goes, "The hard stuff is the easy stuff. The soft stuff is the hard stuff." Although he was referring to the implementation of total quality management, the sense of his statement certainly applies to our discussion here. So in this chapter we will concentrate on some of the more subtle "stuff" that makes a significant difference in how you consult and consequently in how successful you are in getting your expertise and your technical skills used.

Here's an outline of what we will cover in this chapter:

1. *The what*—we will define terms and the roles consultants play. We will discuss consequences of these roles and share a profile of successful consultants.
2. *The how*—we will cover the importance of first impressions and stress contracting, reaching an agreement to proceed, as a key phase in getting started on a solid footing with our clients. Part of contracting is effectively negotiating what both client and consultant want.
3. *A perspective*—we will provide a context of the client organization and discuss the consultant's personal stress and strain.
4. *The end*—we close with a discussion of partnerships and choosing clients.

The What

Terms Defined

Before we go further, we need to define our terms.

Consultant. There are lawn consultants, financial consultants, hairstyle consultants, shopping consultants, legal and tax consultants, computer consultants, consultant consultants. Sometimes it seems as though the world is full of consultants, although I have yet to run into any fast food consultants. (Now there is an opportunity!) In fact, by some estimates, 250,000 people a year in the United States start consulting practices. But according to Hubert Bermont, executive director of the American Consultants League, a little more than 90% do not make it (Solomon, 1991, p. 17). So what is the consultant? A working definition is a person who is hired by the client to provide value by improving processes or obtaining the client's desired results. The client may or may not pay for the consultant, as in the case of an internal consultant who does not charge for services or time, but may be "hired" nonetheless. So *hired* here is agreement to use the services of. *Value* is in the eye of the beholder, namely, the customer. The customer must perceive that the consultant can add value and that hiring the consultant is preferable to not hiring one. Of course there are things a consultant can do to increase—or on the other hand destroy—that perception. Finally, the nature of the work you do as a consultant improves the way things are done by the client or the client's organization (processes) or achieves the desired results (ends), again defined by the customer.

Client/Customer. I use these two terms interchangeably whether the client/customer is internal or external to consultant's organization. So, simply put, the client (or customer) is the person or persons who want and/or need the added value the consultant provides. This definition leaves room for situations in which as the consultant, one would like to have a client who does not know they ought to be a client. The consultant may perceive them to have needs they may not fully understand or realize. In order to have an effective management force, for example, they may need to screen management candidates using psychological batteries as well as assessing technical or functional skills. In these instances, the consultant's immediate objective might be to get them to be a prospective client.

Working Relationship. In this context, it is defined as the operating mode between the client and the consultant, whether it be by explicit agreement or implicit action.

Expertise. Expertise is what the consultant brings to the party, or more scientifically, the skill sets, knowledge, and experience brought to bear by the consultant that adds value for the client.

Consulting Skills. These are the behaviors exhibited by the consultant that address the nature of the client-consultant relationship—that is, how they work together. This includes but is not limited to reaching agreement on how to proceed (called contracting), giving support, and working collaboratively with the client.

Roles Consultants Play

As consultants we often relate to our clients in one of three ways: an expert role, a pair-of-hands role, or a collaborative role. Even with one client these roles may change. First, there is the element of power. Oftentimes when consultants and our clients use the word *consultant* what is meant is a person who has and uses their real or perceived power to make a difference in the organization and achieve results. Sometimes, because the consultant comes from somewhere else, there is the presumption of powerful input. The consultant also has the power of his or her abilities. Perhaps the consultant is one who knows how to do a regression analysis or statistical sampling or knows about the current tax laws. In these cases, the consultant has the power of skills and tools, what we call expertise. Sometimes a retired executive officer, CEO or CFO, becomes a consultant bringing with him or her the power of past experience and business practice. This could be termed the power of knowledge or experience. Other times consultants have the power of authority and are known for their position. All these are examples of the *expert* consultant role. The consultant does most of the deciding because of the power of the position, knowledge, authority, or expertise. How consultants exercise that power can be productive or counterproductive. Bellman (1990) speaks of the darker side of consultants' power. Creating a dependency on the consultant for the answers infrequently leads to the client taking responsibility within his or her own organization. On the other hand, there is a time and place for experts.

Another quite different role consultants play can be called the pair-of-hands role. When I moved from a management development and consulting company to a Fortune 100 company, one of the first responsibilities I undertook was to collate training materials and put them in the appropriate binders. Then I did it some more. I went from an outside expert consultant role to an inside pair-of-hands role. The work was important even though not particularly challenging. In this line of work few decisions are made by the consultant. Power resides with the client. Many of us have experienced this loss of power that seems to go with an internal employee status even though the particular expertise may actually reside in-house. Of course, outside consultants can also operate in a pair-of-hands mode. For example, designing a new performance appraisal evaluation form could be a discrete task independent of any needs analysis or implementation considerations. The pair-of-hands role does not bother with whether the solution is the right solution. On the other hand, there is a time and place for a pair-of-hands.

A third option for consultants is the *collaborative* role. Both the client and consultant share responsibility and work out how they will operate together. This is not to be confused with sharing the technical competency. The client may not know how to do a work redesign or job analysis but can still operate collaboratively with the consultant who does bring that particular expertise. In this kind of role, the consultant shares the decision-making responsibility with the client. That is different from the client's (e.g., line manager's) power to make the decision in the first place and to implement the program. The consultant, by definition, cannot authorize the program, otherwise the consultant is actually managing the intervention. That power—or illusion of it—resides with the manager. To form a collaborative role with a client, however, does takes time. On the positive side, to do so can help engender genuine client commitment for change. As in the others, there is a time and place for the collaborative role of consultants.

Knowingly or not, all of us operate in one of these three orientations, be it by design, desire, happenstance, habit, or culture. Peter Block

(1981), in his book *Flawless Consulting*, describes these roles in more depth. As indicated in the pair-of-hands example, all have their appropriate place as well as their advantages and disadvantages. We are most familiar with the expert role and the power it entails. What we do not consider is that we do have choices. We have the informal power to choose to work with our clients in a collaborative fashion. Though we want to please the client, we might well be more effective in achieving the client's objectives by operating in a collaborative rather than an expert or pair-of-hands role. Ultimately achieving the client's objectives will result in customer satisfaction.

Think back to the first example at the beginning of this chapter. The accounting manager wants a film on communications. Does he? What he really wants is the accountants and analysts to stop their bickering and get on with completing their work on time and without mistakes. The client was asking that I be a pair-of-hands and provide the communications film. He did not want me to get my own sense of the problem. I determined that providing a film on communications would not only not stop the bickering it might well inflame the situation by insinuating that the real problem was his people's inability to communicate with each other. I did not provide the film. Although customer satisfaction is the aim, in this case the prospective client would not make a good customer! The objective is not to accept all customer engagements but to have successful ones. One option in contracting is saying no!

Working with clients, then, means not only using our particular expertise, whatever it is, but also in reality to achieve results. This may mean fixing a problem, raising a problem, or assessing results. It could mean preventing future problems from recurring. It could be coming up with the data to justify a decision already made or determining a future business course of action. It could mean getting the client to take on the responsibility he or she has been successfully avoiding. It may mean turning down business rather than colluding with the client. It means getting to the underlying issues and not just the surface or symptom level of the problem. Whatever the immediate or long-term purpose, our objective is to be successful. Client and consultant—both of us—want to come out of the consulting relationship winners, both of us feeling that we have contributed to "success" and "results." This implies that both the client and consultant have important roles to play and important responsibilities to carry out. So while there is a time and place for the other roles, a working relationship that is on-going and continuous can best be served using a collaborative approach.

Profile of Successful Consultants

In addition to the role we may take, there are certain abilities that help us succeed. Warner Burke (1987), in his book *Organization Development*, details ten abilities of successful consultants. His list includes the ability to (a) tolerate ambiguity; (b) influence; (c) confront difficult issues; (d) support and nurture others; (e) listen well and empathize; (f) recognize one's own feelings and intuitions quickly; (g) conceptualize; (h) discover and mobilize human energy, both within oneself and within the client organization; (i) teach or create learning opportunities; and (j) maintain a sense of humor. The list itself demonstrates that the interactional components of consulting are just as important as the technical ones.

The How

First Impressions

Creating a healthy client-consultant relationship demands that certain requirements be achieved. The relationship must first survive—be viable—before it can grow and flourish! In fact, whether it survives may be dependent on the first two minutes face-to-face with the client. The client may make up his or her mind on hiring you in that time frame. Though this chapter is not about entry into the client system or on how to market your services, there are some points to consider that enhance that first impression.

The first requirement is to *establish rapport and trust* with the client. One of the best ways this can be accomplished is by listening to the client. Especially with new prospective clients, our tendency is to concentrate on what we know and want, centered on ourselves, focused on the technical content and data rather than trying to understand what the client knows and wants and demonstrating to the client that we understand, at least at some level, what they are saying. We can do this by summarizing or paraphrasing the content and feelings the client shares with us. We also communicate this understanding via nonverbal behavior such as eye contact. Having properly prepared to speak with the client, which of course is a prerequisite to showing up, we need to leave our agenda and focus our attention and listening powers on the client. What is their view of the situation? What is it they want? What do they need? How do they experience their unique reality? It is not our job to judge or to sell our wares, but to connect with the client.

One of the skills that demonstrates connection to the client is the use of empathy. This is different than saying we agree they should not have gotten themselves into this fix in the first place! Empathy, defined by George and Cristiani (1990, p. 130), is "the ability to adopt the client's internal frame of reference so that the client's private world and meanings are accurately understood and clearly communicated back to her." Research has demonstrated that there are core conditions or dimensions associated with effective counseling. Empathic understanding is one of these. The others are genuineness or congruence, positive regard and respect, and concreteness or specificity of expression (George & Cristiani, 1990, pp. 126-133). Consultants would do well to use these skills to help form a solid basis for client trust.

Giving support to the client for their view, explaining that we can appreciate the seriousness of the situation and why meeting those milestones is so important to them, underscores that we will work to understand them and their point of view. We will work to determine what is important to them rather than having the pat answer to their every problem (the solution in search of a problem). We communicate that their problem is important. We may even communicate that it is solvable and workable and not hopeless. Fundamentally, by supporting the client's version of what is happening, we communicate that our agenda is their agenda, that the client—and the customer—is right. They have a right to their interpretation of their presenting problem. (After data gathering, we may or may not agree with their initial interpretation, but that is another matter.) The purpose at this early stage is to connect, to acknowledge the client's position—*not* to solve it.

A second requirement is to *establish credibility*. This begins at the surface level by appearance. Does the consultant look the part? Is he or she tastefully and appropriately dressed? What is appropriate? My common sense rule is to "fit in" the client's environment. If the firm is quite conservative, then conservative business attire is appropriate. If you are meeting the manufacturing manager on the line at the plant site, then business suits may not be necessary. Credibility can also be enhanced by association with people or firms the client recognizes or knows. If others the client respects know of a consultant or his/her firm, that can go a long way in assuring the client that the consultant is a credible resource. Endorsements or referrals also can mean a great deal. Satisfied customers are by far the best advertisement. Credibility also infers that the consultant has experience in a similar environment. For example, the consultant should explain to the client that this is not the first time he/she has worked in the banking or financial field or that he/she does have experience dealing with a union environment with a three-shift operation. It is very difficult to establish credibility, no matter how terrific one's expertise, if one is fresh out of graduate school and has little experience with which the client can identify.

Demonstrating competence is a third requirement. This is the consultant's technical expertise. Competence can be demonstrated partly by the kind of questions one asks and by stating how similar results have been achieved elsewhere: A consultant can show how, for example, he/she has been instrumental in helping the manufacturing facility achieve on-time performance. Focus on the achievements rather than all the technical steps that led to the achievement and how the results were better than .001 levels of significance. Having a portfolio of similar work may be one way to demonstrate competence without overwhelming the client with data and methodology. This can be samples of work that relate to the client's world and geared to their level of technical competence. One client may not care what computer operating environment a consultant used, others may care a great deal to make sure it is compatible with their own. However, many of us "techs" enjoy the technical work so much that we spend most of our time demonstrating it to a client in infinite detail, applauding the various bells and whistles we have created. We enjoy our work. We also tend to over explain, concentrating on the facts and data. The client may not understand or care. What they want to know is, are you capable and can you handle their needs appropriately, effectively and efficiently.

Take the second example at the head of this chapter, the one about the salesperson concerned about keeping a profitable key account. One way she checked my credibility was to see what happened on another account she knew I was working on. How satisfied were they with my work? How successful was the consulting engagement? When she found out that both the company and telecommunications client-account teams were able to come to a successful resolution of conflict, my credibility was established in her mind. During our first meetings, how I conducted myself, how I explained how I thought we might work together, and under what guidelines we would operate helped establish her perceptions of my competence. The crux, however, was establishing rapport and trust. She was a successful sales representative. She handled a key account for the company. The chief client was not happy—and her superiors thought things were business as usual. Should she raise this awful issue? What if she did? What if she did not? Could she trust me? She had a lot at stake to risk and did not need a consultant to make matters worse! Regardless of my technical expertise, how was I going to use it? Would I be an advocate? Would I support her raising a tough issue to her top management? Evidently, the answer was "yes." After much work by many people and some difficult feedback sessions, both the management of the company, and the key account and customer teams agreed to renegotiate their contract establishing a partnering arrangement between the two corporations, new fee structures, new positions and responsibilities, and an improved working relationship, and, by the way, increased profitability.

Contracting: Reaching an Agreement to Proceed

As in many things in life, the beginning is particularly important. If we start our consulting arrangement with clear expectations, not only about the outcome but also about how client and consultant(s) will operate, we are farther down the road to a successful experience. If, conversely, we are unclear about our expectations, needs, and desires, then we have paved a road that we would prefer in hindsight not to have traveled. When we adopt the pair-of-hands role regardless of its suitability to this situation, or push our most favored solution, or spend little or no time establishing rapport and trust, we are making that road that much more difficult for ourselves.

How to start down that road and navigate it effectively and test the client's commitment as we begin is what the first phase of consulting—contracting—is all about. The term *contracting* does not mean the legal contract (See Kuhnert & Gore, this volume), but rather how to reach agreement to proceed, whether it is formal or informal. It not only includes agreement on the work to be done, its scope, fee, timeline, and resource base, but more importantly, how the consultant and the client will operate together. Contracting in this broad sense goes beyond the letter of the agreement or legal contract to include such issues as, (a) how frequently the client and consultant communicate with each other, (b) how to share decision making during the life of the project, (c) how to ensure adequate monitoring and progress reports, (d) how to give and receive feedback on performance, (e) whether the collaborative role is the appropriate role, (f) whether the client is open to addressing root causes (beyond symptoms of the problem), and (g) whether the contracting itself can be renegotiated as situations warrant.

Some of the elements in this contracting phase that need to be addressed include communicating back to the client your understanding of his or her situation, negotiating the wants and needs of both client and consultant, testing the client's commitment to proceed, and in detailing the next action steps. It is not possible to go into further detail here about navigating the contracting meeting. For that I refer you to Peter Block's work, *Flawless Consulting* (1981). His discussion of contracting is one of the most usable and coherent ones that I have encountered.

To provide context, the other phases of consulting after contracting (reaching agreement to proceed) are data collection and analysis (getting a clear picture of what's happening), feedback and decision (sharing that picture in very clear terms and getting the client invested in acting on it), implementation (doing, implementing change), and evaluation (assessing value and impact) (Block, 1981).

As a result of the first contracting meeting, the consultant may determine that he/she needs more data or more time to put together a proposal. Another possibility is that through the discussion the consultant discovers that another client, perhaps the head of another business unit, also needs to be involved. In such cases, the next step may to be continue to contract at a later date or with other people. The contracting meeting itself may be short and to the point or drawn out and more complex requiring time and deliberation. In any case, contracting is *the* essential first phase.

Why is contracting, the reaching of agreement to proceed, so important? One of the key reasons is that the consultant's leverage is greatest at the start of a project. Think about starting a new job, even if someone has preceded you in the position, you have a unique and time-limited opportunity to mold the job, to make it conform to your requirements of a worthwhile and contributing occupation. Even if the goals are nonnegotiable, how you accomplish them, who you involve, how you go about it most often is not mandated. It is an opportunity to create your own environment and way of operating. So too in establishing a consulting contract. Both you and the client have an opportunity to negotiate a viable and open agreement, to ask for what you want and need in order to make the consulting engagement successful. The client is rare who does not want you to have what you need in order to accomplish his or her own objectives successfully! Yet we are often reluctant to ask for those really tough things we want in a client-consultant relationship, focusing instead on the tangible stuff. If you do establish a collaborative relationship, then you are partners in figuring out how to make it happen. There is shared responsibility and most importantly, shared commitment (see Larson & Brownell, this volume).

This assumes, of course, that you know your objectives, that you come in to the client informed and prepared. You have a game plan. But like any game plan you are flexible enough to change it depending on the wants and needs of the client.

Effective Negotiating

In an effective negotiation, you must understand the needs and wants of your counterpart. How clear are you about what the client wants? What is their perception of the problem? What are their expectations? Why now? What pressure are they under? What does "success" mean to them? What are they willing to offer? How do they like to work with consultants like you? Do they expect you to be the expert, a pair-of-hands, or a collaborative partner? Do they expect a miracle? What are their requirements, their timelines, their budgetary constraints, the political realities within which they work, their personal objectives and ambitions? The better informed you are, the better you will do in this negotiation process. After all, you want the consulting engagement to be successful, as does the client. It is imperative, therefore, to understand their frame of reference. How do they see it?

Psychologically, it is very important to communicate that we understand the client's frame of reference. Most of us prefer to work with people who are not only technically competent but who also have taken the time to hear and acknowledge us. We are a lot more likely to want to work toward mutually satisfactory (collaborative) solutions. We can do this by utilizing the skills discussed earlier: paraphrasing, summarizing, good attending behaviors such as positive eye contact, demonstrating empathy and giving support. Oftentimes, what we do instead of listening and all the above is to sell our side, deal with our requirements too early on, jump to our preferred solutions. Most often technically inclined professionals jump to the technical solutions and the facts and figures (where there is a higher comfort level) rather than deal with this soft stuff. Again, both kinds of stuff are important.

Once we have successfully demonstrated we understand the client's position, objectives, wants, and needs, it is time to offer our requirements in order to meet these objectives. Our requirements do not have to be in their final form. Our needs and the client's may change. One requirement we may have, then, is the ability to renegotiate what the consultants want and need in order to make the project successful. Recontracting and renegotiating is always acceptable. We will obviously need things like time, money, access to information, use of resources, and so forth. In addition, my recommendation is that we request nontangibles as well, such as feedback about how the project is going, access to our main client on a regular basis to plan next steps, the need for anonymity and/or confidentiality, returning phone calls, the right to disagree with the client. Each of us has to determine what is important and appropriate. If there are areas in which you and the client disagree, you will have to determine what is really critical for the success of the project and what would be nice to have. Ethical dilemmas could also arise. We will have to determine what we are willing to live with and what we can not do or cannot live with. Focus on areas of common agreement first, then on the disagreements. Argue your case in light of the client's needs, wants, and objectives. If we can demonstrate that what we want will help the client achieve what he or she wants, our case is much stronger. Think and communicate benefits to the client.

Moreover, your attitude in the negotiation process is also important. As Fisher and Ury (1983) of the Harvard Negotiation Project point out in *Getting to Yes*, the emphasis should be on mutual gain, a win/win result with issues decided upon by their merits rather than each side using bargaining chips to get their way. This approach is called *principled negotiation*. As a consultant you are entitled to ask for what is important to you to be successful. This includes both tangibles, like the use of administrative assistants, and intangibles, like respect and serious consideration for your ideas.

There is also a balance, in my mind, between demonstrating credibility and competence by discussing similar successful projects you have managed or potential methods of addressing the client's concerns versus listening and communicating to the client that you understand their unique situation. Focus should be on clearly stating client objectives more than enumerating potential methods. Understanding what the client is after is much more important than figuring out exactly what it is you are going to do about it. In fact, unless you are using the expert model (I—the consultant—know best), the client may even have some ideas (the collaborative model) on how to proceed!

There are some pitfalls to avoid. Be careful of technical jargon. We can lose some clients quickly. Also watch phrases like, "To be honest with you . . . " or "To tell you the truth . . . " Does this mean the consultant's been dishonest or untruthful up to now? Be wary of giving advice, overexplaining, overselling. If you look back at the discussion and it turns out to have been a monologue with you having the great majority of the air time, then you probably learned little about the client's reality.

In any consulting relationship, particularly growing and challenging ones, there is a continual balancing of needs: yours and the client's. You want the contract, the money, the opportunity to shine, the chance to enhance your reputation, the satisfaction of contributing to solid results, the security of steady employment, the opportunity of continuing and gainful follow-up work, and so forth. The client has wants and needs also. Some of these are task needs such as trimming expenses, meeting budget, increasing the use of technology, launching a new product successfully, as well as more personal needs and wants, such as looking good in front of his or her boss, superiors, and peers, being seen as a winner, removing doubt, rewarding friends, learning, being the one who brought in this consultant, making a difference or leaving a mark in the organization, being treated with respect and taken seriously by the consultant. These stated and unstated needs and wants of the client are integral to success. It is at this level as well as at the task level that consultants can use their consulting skills to enlist the client's knowledge, experience, and willpower to make that happen. Consulting at both levels increases the consultant's leverage and the client's ability to make the desired change happen.

A Perspective

The Client Organization

The consultant contracts implicitly with the whole organization. It is not just your immediate client who is involved. This implies that you will have to contract (reach agreement) with a multitude of clients in the client system.

For example, I once volunteered (right away I should have known better!) for an experimental project to coach first-line foremen to be better leaders. Although I had an agreement or contract with the corporate office for my special assignment, the foremen with whom I was to work and their general foremen had only a foggy notion of what I and the consulting team were doing there. After all, what did we know about the front forward fuselage assembly on a fighter aircraft? Not much. Not only that, we were here from corporate, to help. Right! It became quite apparent that we were in need of a number of contracts, not only with each foremen but with the whole chain of command. We therefore started at the top with the program manager of an entire aircraft operation, down to directors and superintendents, and back to the general foreman and his foremen. Specifying what both clients and consultants needed at every level and getting agreement about how to proceed and what were the deliverables was the key to what became a successful venture. So, before you set up your assessment center with in-box exercises and realistic managerial time constraints and pressures, make sure the organization at large and the leadership in specific is onboard enough to proceed. Asking yourself and your clients questions to determine the readiness of the organization to accept and support the intervention is paramount. After all, some systems are healthy and some are very sick. It is akin to an organ transplant. If you are not careful to check all the patient's vital signs, prepare the body properly, watch your timing, and so forth, despite your great technical skill, you may end up with a dead client, not to mention the aftereffects on the consultant!

Weisbord (1987) outlines some general rules that we all might well consider.

1. Is there a business case? Can the work be directly linked to how the business is run and how it contributes to the business objectives and strategies?
2. Is there opportunity? Is this the right time or are we in the middle of corporate downsizing or implementation of MRP-II (Manufacturing Resource Planning)?
3. Do we have the right people? Again, are we contracting our products and services with the real clients or are we dealing with the palace guard?
4. Is there energy? Do you feel the energy to overcome the inertia that invariably accompanies change? Are people willing to move on this now?
5. Is there leadership to drive the change or implementation? Are the key managers real sponsors? Are they committed? Are they willing to invest personal time and sweat to make it happen or are we dealing with lip service and posturing?

In the third example at the start of this chapter, a high tech division had embarked on the total quality management path. Over a year had gone by since its most recent incarnation using high-performance teams of employees to increase quality of all products and services. An assessment of progress was in order. A proposal, after appropriate input from a key senior executive, was put forward to the divisionwide steering committee in October. The idea, after much debate, was approved and sent to committee where it was changed, narrowed, refocused, and debated some more. After a number of starts and reapprovals, the actual division assessment was conducted in March with results reported a full half year later than the original proposal. Sometimes it takes this long or longer to do a proper job. It is also possible that some of the above general rules were missing! Certainly there was opportunity. Certainly the leaders of the business units were the right people to be talking with. However, was the linkage to running the business forcefully made? Was the energy to move forward strong enough in light of the day-to-day tight business picture which eventually led to lay offs? Was the leadership driving this assessment or was it preoccupied with more immediate and short-term survival issues? Though the example is real, we will leave these unanswered questions on the hypothetical plane for now. Besides, the past leadership might read this!

Personal Stress and Strain

Which brings us to facing some tough organization realities and the consultant's role. What do we do when we are in the unenviable position of having to confront some harsh realities within our own organization? How do we take responsibility to address the "real issues" when our client, the one who pays the bills, demands that we address the symptoms? What it takes is a lot of intestinal fortitude and acts of courage. Peter Block (1987) in his chapter "Facing Organization Realities" in *The Empowered Manager*, calls it "nonsuicidal courageous acts." As consultants, whether internal or external, we live and work in a political environment in which what is said means something else ("We need to contain costs" means "Restructure the business unit") and what is done is contrary to stated goals and objectives ("Quality is number one" versus "Get the product out on schedule no matter what"). No organization is free from these contradictions because every organization is full of people. People have a way of being less than totally consistent. Therefore, according to logic, organizations are not consistent either. Despite the left-brain logic about how functions are supposed to work, we find that the organization charts or the policies and procedures manuals have little to do with actual reality! That is the environment we work in whether we are internal or external consultants.

So what do we do? Know your values and be authentic to them. Who said it was going to be easy? As consultants we face dilemmas every day. The paying customer wants an evaluation of a mid-level manager who is causing trouble. You are expected to make the "right" recommendation. Or the client wants to know how knowledgeable we are about experimental design and the only thing you know is that you have designed experiments before, why not try again? Or its now obvious to you that the client's closed-mindedness is getting in the way of progress, but you do not want to offend him. Though there are big and little dilemmas, to be effective we have to be ourselves and live with ourselves. The more we compromise when our values tell us otherwise, the more we lose our integrity as consultants and the less value we will be to the client and to ourselves. The more we pretend to be somebody or something we are not, the more we invite disaster. It takes a willingness to risk, to change, to be vulnerable—just like we are asking our clients to do!

Being a consultant can be lonely business even if you work in a group. It takes long hours and hard work. Some days you need thirty hours in the one day you have available to get all the work done; other days you can sit and wait for the work to start. The job comes with stress and strain. If, on top of that, we try to do it all for the client, have all the answers and be the expert all the time, we take on the client's responsibilities and rob him or her of the gift of struggling with their own answers and working out their own solutions. We can burn ourselves out and the client will hardly know there was any heat.

Clients often get in their own way. Our job is to tell them. This means confronting the client with a description of their own behavior. For example, the client avoids moving ahead by explaining away the results of our study, or says that things have changed since you did this evaluation, or insists that yet another more comprehensive study be done just to be sure—these are times to confront the client with their behavior in a nonjudgmental way. We identify the resistance we are observing: you seem to be discounting what we learned; you are avoiding taking action by making alibis. Handling this resistance is inviting the client to handle their own behavior and to be accountable for it. It is easier to understand it than to do it.

The End: Partnerships and Choosing

There are a number of requirements such as establishing rapport and trust that is a requirement for a viable and healthy client-consultant relationship. When the relationship moves to the levels of growing and being challenging, the growth and challenge do not reside in the client alone. They reside in both the client and the consultant.

A partnership is not any easy thing to achieve. It means hard work and a personal investment of time and energy. It means knowing the strengths and weaknesses of your partner and of yourself so that together you both can use the best of the partnership to move forward. It means negotiating objectives and methodology. It means give and take. It means challenging each other to be whole while accomplishing business results. Solid partnerships are win/win where there is quid pro quo, needs of both client and consultant are met although not always equally. It means shared decision making, doing things on the fly, trusting. It requires on-going evaluation and critique. It means a balance between getting what you want and having empathy for the partner. It means making commitments and performing as you said you would and confronting each other and yourself when you do not. It means taking it all with a grain of salt, having fun, yet being serious. It means attaining a level of synergy that would be impossible by going it alone.

When we get down to it, it is our choice. We can create our own reality and challenge ourselves and our clients, or we can dutifully provide service and move on. Engaging is much more risky—and, by the way, fulfilling. It is also what we are teaching the client through modeling. We take responsibility as we expect them to. We act with them like we expect them to act with us. The real value we bring to the client is ourselves. And it is the gift we give to ourselves in the process.

References

Bellman, G. M. (1990). *The consultant's calling*. San Francisco, CA: Jossey-Bass.

Block, P. (1981). *Flawless consulting*. San Francisco, CA: Jossey-Bass.

Block, P. (1987). *The empowered manager*. San Francisco, CA: Jossey-Bass.

Burke, W. W. (1987). *Organization development*. Reading, MA: Addison-Wesley.

Fisher, R., & Ury, W. (1983). *Getting to yes*. New York, NY: Penguin.

George, R. L., & Cristiani, T. S. (1990). *Counseling theory and practice* (3rd ed.). Englewood Cliffs, NJ: Prentice-Hall.

Solomon, G. (1991, September 22). The consulting field keeps on growing. *National Business Employment Weekly*.

Weisbord, M. R. (1987). *Productive workplaces*. San Francisco, CA: Jossey-Bass.

5

Evaluation Skills Nobody Taught Me

GAIL V. BARRINGTON

Looking back over my event-filled career as an evaluator during the past 10 years, I wonder at how I could have been so unprepared for the trials and tribulations that this profession engenders. What skills could I have acquired to prepare myself? What suggestions could I pass on, based on my own experience, that would help smooth the way for future evaluators?

Program evaluation, as a discipline, has been addressed in numerous articles. There appears to be general agreement that university courses in program evaluation should include evaluation theory, research methodology, and evaluation process. However, Davis (1986) surveyed forty-three university-based evaluation courses, and found that only 40% addressed ethics, 23% standards, 14% professional resources, and 12% training.

Theorists such as Cronbach (1980) would suggest a doctorate in a social science as a minimum academic requirement. In addition, Cronbach's ideal educational program would include participation in interdisciplinary seminars, an apprenticeship, and an internship. From a practical standpoint, however, few would-be evaluators will have this luxury because of the cost in terms of both time and money. Many will move from other careers into evaluation as the need or opportunity arises. Many will also move out again, I believe, because the heat can become too great and they may not have the survival skills they need to cope.

Greiner and Metzger (1983) identify three critical skills that management consultants need. These include diagnostic skills, solution skills, and communication skills. The first two are problem-solving skills, which universities probably teach best. They involve the higher-level thinking skills of analysis, synthesis, and judgment, but all consultants need to ground these thought processes firmly in reality rather than theory. Communication skills may be taught in a number of ways and surely consultants can never know too much about human interaction. But evaluators, I would suggest, need three other skills in addition to those that Greiner and Metzger recommend for consultants. These include political skills, negotiation skills, and survival skills.

Political Skills

Though evaluation tends to be regarded as a research activity, I believe that it is just as much a political one. Having conducted the research is only half the battle: what remains is to present the information you have so painstakingly obtained and ensure that it is interpreted and applied correctly. This lies in the realm of small *p* politics rather than in the realm of science. Political skills cannot simply be acquired: rather they are practiced throughout one's career with increasing levels of proficiency. But there is never a point at which one can say, "Now I have enough," because one can never have enough skill. And therein lies the challenge.

Some of the political skills that I have learned include knowing the players, the policy environment, the political dimension, the power of communication, and the importance of timing. However, I am sure that there are others which I have just not encountered yet.

Knowing the Players

First of all, it is important to identify all the players in an evaluation enterprise. We are used to identifying stakeholder groups in evaluation, but perhaps a fresh perspective would be useful. In *The Politics of Expertise*, Benveniste (1972) suggests that policy researchers should revise their conventional view about relevant political actors. He refers to the client as the *Prince*, as in Machiavelli's Prince, who needs advice—but only when he wishes it. He is the politician, the management group, the city council, the school board. He contracts the services of the evaluator for a variety of reasons; some are formal and some are not.

The *Pundit* is the expert, the advisor, the sage. Her professional ideology is apolitical and her approach is interdisciplinary, conceptual, quantifiable, defensible. This is the evaluator and her own political views must be held firmly under wraps.

The *Lieutenants* surround the Prince and control the machinery of administration. They are the bureaucrats and are likely to be the evaluator's most frequent contact. They will either foster or impede the implementation of policy changes the evaluator may recommend and, therefore, their views must be valued from the beginning.

Actually, I have found that there is generally an intermediary level here of *Program Implementors*. These people are actually out in the field conducting the program. Without their critical input and support an evaluator's report will gather dust.

Finally, there are the *Beneficiaries*, those whose lives and purposes are affected by the programs themselves. Sometimes, Benveniste suggests, they are the *Victims*. He complains that too often communication with Beneficiaries is poor because the Pundits do not have the time, the desire, or the know-how to communicate effectively. As they are not paying the Pundit's bill, Beneficiaries can be overlooked as critical stakeholders.

The conventional role that the Pundit may enact is that of paying too much attention to the Prince, too little attention to the Lieutenants, and no attention at all to the Beneficiaries. An example of this approach in an educational setting would be personified by a program evaluator who never elicits the views of school children, who views teachers and administrators as drones, and who focuses only on the needs and wishes of the Department of Education and its steering committee.

I learned, at my peril, that teachers and principals, who are actually two very different types of implementors, will revolt if their information and control needs are not met. I have come to value the opinions of school children, for when they are taken in their own context, their perceptions are keen and valid. Department-based officials and steering committee members may have very little to do with these three groups and may be operating with limited information about what is currently happening in schools. More than once, I have found myself acting as an interpreter for the school-based population to the bureaucrats who have not taught for 20 years.

In a recent evaluation, I made the political mistake of adopting the Lieutenants' agenda too closely while neglecting the needs of the Prince who never attended any of our meetings. When the final report was produced, the Lieutenants commented, "This is excellent! Just what we need to tell us what to do next!" However, the Prince refused to attend the final meeting because, as he said, "This is the most horrible report I have ever read!" Guess who was paying the bill? Fortunately, thanks to the negotiation skills I had acquired over the years, I was able to prepare a second report for external release that satisfied the Prince's needs, and mine, as I was able to bill for it as well. That time I was lucky.

There are many political players to be aware of besides those identified by Benveniste. Others I frequently encounter are parents, trustees, union representatives, professional organizations, university professors, taxpayers, the general public, and the media. Not every group is critical to every study, but evaluators should analyze the political landscape and identify the critical players from the outset.

Knowing the Policy Environment

The evaluator needs to know about the policy environment in which the program exists. This environment includes the real context in which the program functions along with the program's past history, its philosophical evolution, and its former successes and failures. Another component of the environment is the conventional wisdom or folklore that may surround both the program and the organization. However misguided or inaccurate, these myths are a perceived reality that must be acknowledged as part of the collective memory. They are interesting to visit, albeit briefly, to determine the origins of certain beliefs people may hold about the program.

One school program I evaluated actually started because a trustee read an article about a similar program in an in-flight magazine. How many children benefited from that casual beginning! Another program at the university level that I evaluated evolved out of a conversation between a community college president and a university professor during a game of golf. In the long run, their commitment to golf was probably greater than their commitment to the program, which died an untimely death from lack of attention. Another government program I evaluated was initiated by a former employee of a historic fur trading company. There was more than a passing similarity between the program structure and a trap line!

Chelimsky (1987) argues that evaluators must be clear about their role in the policy environment. Rather than being an advocate, a reformer, or a partisan, the evaluator must be systematic, scholarly, independent, and a critical thinker. The purpose of an evaluation in a government setting, she argues, is to empower the decision maker by "bringing the best possible information to bear on a wide variety of policy questions" (p. 26). The research questions are not the evaluator's creation; rather they emerge in general terms from the political process and can later be refined by the evaluator for the purposes of the study. She views the translation of policy questions to evaluation questions as "one of the most sensitive and important political interactions in the entire process, [which is] fraught with risks" (p. 27).

If the evaluation cannot answer the policy question on the table, then it has failed, no matter how elegant its research design or how significant its findings. At the end of an evaluation when the chief executive officer says, "Yes, but is it a good program," this is not a simplistic question. Rather, it is the critical one and the evaluator must be able to state clearly, "Yes," or "No," and list the reasons for this conclusion.

Thus it is important to explore the policy environment in which the program exists. The context adds meaning to the program the way a setting enhances a jewel.

Knowing the Political Dimension

To be effective as a policy expert, Benveniste (1972, p. 80) believes that the Pundit needs some political savoir faire but suggests that there is no guaranteed way to acquire this skill. Exposure, observation, and experience may be the best teachers as this is an area in which theoretical knowledge falls short. Selecting a role model could be an effective way to develop this sixth sense. Watching how an experienced evaluator looks, dresses, and operates in a particular environment is an invaluable lesson.

A good way to gain experience, or to hone your skills, is to act as a subcontractor to another evaluator with more or different experience. That was how I obtained my first major evaluation contract. I began as a researcher in a support position to the principal consultant and observed his deeds and misdeeds closely. Then when he had to move away, the study was passed on to me to maintain and complete. Because the study was of five years' duration, I had ample time to cut my teeth as an evaluator before the final report was due. Many evaluation systems guiding my work today were developed during that "protected" period.

Knowing the players must be supplemented by becoming aware of how they interact. Sometimes the initiation of a program evaluation can become a political statement in its own right. If the evaluation is perceived as a challenge or a threat, the response of other players can have a major impact on study development or demise.

An evaluation should always be approached from the perspective that it may end up in the media. The spectre of front page exposure tends to add a degree of caution to my work. One study in which I was involved was terminated by the client as a result of a series of articles by a local editor on the topic I was exploring. Although my study was still on the drawing board, and hence not in the line of fire that time, the topic created so much political fallout that the client chose not to proceed. In another study, my client made front page news several times during the evaluation period and I once had to pass through television cameras in order to get into the building. In the final analysis, it was difficult to separate the study findings from the impact on the staff because of such a turbulent working environment. Whether directly or indirectly, then, the media exerts a significant force that should not be underestimated.

Knowing the Power of Communication

Throughout the evaluation process, communication with the appropriate players helps to keep them informed about how the study is progressing by providing them with accurate information. This keeps speculation and rumor to a minimum. I tend to produce monthly status reports that are one-page factual summaries of activities to date (e.g., number of phone calls made, number of contacts, number of completed interviews, and so on). In addition, emerging trends are highlighted. Generally, I have discovered that a policy of "no surprises" works best with clients.

Feedback loops are another important way to keep critical people involved. Having players respond to draft surveys, draft reports, and draft recommendations enhances ownership and accuracy of the findings. But this too can backfire. Players can interpret their involvement as doing your job for you! I would caution that the ground must be laid, particularly in qualitative studies, for legitimate player input or a paradigm conflict may ensue. It has been my experience that players with a scientific background may interpret your role as evaluator in terms of their own experimental or quasi-experimental research training. In their frame of reference, the evaluator as communicator, negotiator, or educator may be interpreted as the evaluator tampering with the data.

Chelimsky (1987) underlines the importance of spending time thinking about how best to present findings. She suggests that the important thing is to "answer the policy question as clearly and as simply as possible, to emphasize a few critical and striking numbers, and to do it all in such a way as to highlight these findings that give rise to policy action" (p. 32). Though the needs of the client will vary in terms of how technical the final report should be, a general rule is to provide summary data in the text and detailed tables in an appendix.

Although I rarely find time to prepare different reports for different audiences, I tend to structure reports in such a way that the needs of each audience can be met. For example, the "Executive Summary" provides a thumbnail sketch of the process and highlights critical findings and recommendations. It lends itself to an oral report, and is aimed at the Prince and his Lieutenants who will likely not have the time to read the actual report. The body of the report is aimed at the Implementors and is presented in a nontechnical style with brief easy-to-read tables and comments highlighted in context. The appendices are reserved for other Pundits. It is there that the validity of the methodology and procedures are reviewed. Generally, the Beneficiaries' information needs are not addressed in the report although a press release may be developed for the client to publish. Occasionally, upon request, I have produced a brief journalistic summary, but again to be distributed by the client.

Knowing the Importance of Timing

As part of that political sixth sense, timing can be all-important to successful implementation of study outcomes. In a legislative context, the evaluator must be aware of decision-making cycles to ensure that the final product dovetails with them. Sometimes, perfection must be sacrificed in order to achieve the goal of timeliness. In educational circles, decisions that will have an impact on next year's students have to be made by April of the previous year. Surveys that go out to teachers or students will have lower return rates in September (school start-up), December (Christmas holidays), January (examinations), March (Spring break), and June (burnout time). In a recent study we conducted involving disadvantaged senior citizens, we were instructed by our client not to survey or interview them in the two weeks subsequent to receipt of pension checks because of a belief that these seniors tended to indulge in alcohol while the money lasted. Sensitivity to timing issues can have a significant impact on evaluation success.

Thus, as we have seen, political skills are critical for the evaluator. Knowing the players, understanding the policy environment and the political dimension, and being sensitive to the power of communication and timing can maximize the success of evaluation research. Not surprisingly, they also support the survival of the evaluator.

Negotiation Skills

As an adjunct to political skills, negotiation skills need to be developed in fledgling evaluators. When I told a professor about my first evaluation contract, she said, "You'll never stop negotiating," and in a sense it has turned out to be true.

In fact, the "contract" part of negotiations has generally been easily accommodated by both me and my clients. It is after the contract is signed that negotiation begins in earnest: negotiation about the evaluation questions, the data base, the sample, the survey instrument, the file review, the literature review, the on-site visits, not to mention the final report, and the recommendations. Despite the preparation and acceptance of a clear work plan, I have found myself in severe conflict situations over methodology and interpretation of findings on several occasions. The issue can boil down to a conflict of paradigms with the plaintiff representing an entrenched quantitative, scientific perspective and the defendant representing the qualitative, naturalistic one. In the severity of each conflict situation, role of "parent" or "steering committee member" has peeled away to reveal basic core beliefs about the research process which could not be aligned with mine. All the political skills in the world would not have prepared me for this revelation. However, if I had possessed better negotiation skills or had known then that paradigm conflict is always out there waiting to raise its ugly head, I might have responded with more aplomb. As it was, I ended up on the defensive, sputtering about multiple realities and wondering if I should change careers.

Recently, I became aware of the Harvard Negotiation Project through a book entitled, *Getting to Yes: Negotiating Agreement Without Giving In*, by Fisher and Ury (1983). The book is based on studies and conferences conducted by a group that deals continually with all levels of conflict resolution, from domestic to international disputes. The methods used to negotiate with hijackers could probably have been effective for me as well. Fisher and Ury (1983) have four basic suggestions to use in order to get away from positional bargaining, which was the trap that I fell into. These include separating the people from the problem, focusing on interests not positions, inventing options for mutual gain, and insisting on the use of objective criteria.

Separate the People From the Problem

Fisher and Ury suggest that you should address the human side of the issue first by trying to deal sensitively with people as human beings and by separating your relationship with them from the substance of the issue. By putting yourself in their shoes, speaking their language, and presenting the issues in terms that are consistent with their values, much can be done to break down barriers and lessen hostilities.

When I deal with teachers, I always let them know that I have been a classroom teacher myself. Usually, a bond of shared experience is immediately forged that can withstand a fair amount of friction over specific areas of disagreement. When I talk to managers, I try to relate administrative or leadership experiences of my own and build a relationship from there. However, when I talk to nurses, I have to profess myself a medical klutz, which I am, while stressing at the same time my lengthy experience as an evaluator. Being a neophyte can be an advantage if you do not overplay it, as you can ask obvious questions with not-so-obvious answers. Usually, beneath the veneer of a new environment lie all the old familiar evaluation issues.

The point Fisher and Ury make is to look for commonalities upon which to build your relationship. A rerun of an argument I had over methodology with a particularly aggressive participant could have sounded like this:

Participant: You are doing this study all wrong! This is terrible! How can you possibly call this research?

Evaluator: That is an interesting perspective. I see you are interested in research.

Participant: Yes, I happen to be a senior researcher with the National Institute for Research in the Hard Sciences.

Evaluator: Well then, it's likely that you have a very scientific perspective. Perhaps you would be interested in looking at our data collection matrix that outlines our research questions and proposed methods of data collection. I'd be interested in your comments.

There is nothing like hindsight, of course, but another time I think I would try harder to understand what fuels the hostility.

Other suggestions they make to separate the people from the problem include making sure that they have a stake in the outcome, legitimizing their emotions but not getting drawn in yourself, and being an active listener. It is essential to forge a working relationship.

Focus on Interests, Not Positions

Fisher and Ury (1983) point out that no side has only a single interest. Each side actually has many interests, and some of them are shared. It is important to acknowledge their interests by restating them. They also suggest that you state the problem, preferably couched in a future scenario, before you provide a solution. Be concrete but flexible and have a variety of specific options up your sleeve. Be hard on the problem but soft on the people.

In a round of negotiations over a work plan, I was worried that my client had a positive bias and was only looking for positive outcomes. This made me nervous because I wondered how I could maintain a neutral third-party stance and come up with a final report that would be acceptable to both them and me. The dialogue went like this:

Evaluator: I see from the research questions you included in the Request for Proposals that you are hoping for some positive findings about the program.

Client: Yes, we are very enthusiastic about the program although it is still pretty new.

Evaluator: In a best case scenario, if the study results are really positive, what will you do with them?

Client: Well, we can use them in promotional materials, ask industry spokespeople to give testimonials at workshops, and use the information in our own motivational speeches.

Evaluator: That sounds really useful. But what about a worst case scenario? What if our findings are negative?

Client: Well, we really hadn't thought about that.

Evaluator: It is possible, though, that not all of the program sites will be equally successful. How can you use negative information so that it can be useful too?

Client: We could use it to improve our program or to plan new strategies. I guess it could be an opportunity, too.

Invent Options for Mutual Gains

Fisher and Ury (1983) suggest that the option pie can be expanded by inventing viable alternatives before trying to divide it up. Obstacles to this taking place include premature judgment, searching for a single answer, assuming that the pie is fixed in size, and believing that solving their problem is "their problem." Instead, their advice is to invent creative options, separate creation from judgment, broaden the number of options on the table, search for mutual gains, and invent ways to make their decisions easy.

Sometimes you can assist clients to solve their own problems. Acting as a facilitator at a staff retreat might be an effective way to solve a thorny issue. A particularly useful group process method is the *nominal group technique* as outlined by Moore (1987, p. 24). It allows for individual judgments to be pooled effectively in which situations of uncertainty or disagreement exist. Its structure helps to neutralize differences in status or verbal dominance among group members and is also useful for groups of strangers. I once diffused an explosive confrontation between some grass roots community groups and a not-for-profit organization through the use of this technique. Hostilities did not dissolve overnight but the process turned attention away from each other toward a focus on the structured generation of ideas which were then taken away for discussion in an ad-hoc committee.

Insist on Using Objective Criteria

Develop objective criteria and procedures for resolving conflicting interests. Then negotiate as follows:

1. Frame each issue as a joint search for objective criteria.
2. Be reasonable as to which standards are most appropriate and how they should be applied.
3. Never yield to pressure, only to principle.

This is where evaluators have to learn to say, "No." This is where ethics come into play, along with a clear understanding of the role of the evaluator, the research process, and good business practice. With all these guidelines clearly adopted as part of your personal philosophy, it is fairly easy to spot a situation in which principles apply and deviation is impossible. Usually it is enough to say so. For example, I will not change the actual research process. I will not entertain a conflict of interest. I will not change the data. I will not change my conclusions. I will not change my recommendations, although I am open to negotiation of a more useful wording. I will quit first. That is usually when a client realizes he has stepped over my invisible line and he usually backs off.

I think that Fisher and Ury's (1983) four suggestions have a lot of merit for evaluators. In a manner similar to developing debating skills, it seems appropriate for fledgling evaluators to practice these negotiating skills in a protected environment such as a classroom or seminar prior to taking them "on the road." Heightened skills in this area can, I believe, cut through a lot of potential hazards and heartache and allow the evaluator to focus on the job of evaluation.

Survival Skills

Finally, I think evaluators need some survival or life skills if they are to continue to function at a high level over long periods of time.

Keep Fit

Greiner and Metzger (1983) suggest that there is some bad news about consulting: it is "one of the most intense, frustrating, fatiguing and damnable professions one can choose" (p. 326). Their advice includes keeping fit, using relaxation techniques, traveling light, eating light, and taking vacations. Along with those stress reducers, I would seriously urge evaluators to polish up their sense of humor.

Strengthen Support Systems

A key survival technique is to strengthen support systems both at the office and at home. Appropriate training to keep the evaluation support staff current helps the evaluator to stay current as well. Sharing information, both evaluative and anecdotal, encourages the whole team to work cohesively and efficiently. In addition, family stability is critical. My family members certainly have their own needs, but by ensuring that their needs are met first, mine are met as well. By being very clear with them about my priorities, namely, that they are most important of all, I find there are few difficult decisions to be made and, in fact, they provide me with support without even being asked.

Stay Current

Another survival skill is keeping up to date by reading periodicals and attending professional seminars and conferences. Networks at the local level provide useful contacts and practical tips. Sometimes a shared terminology can be very comforting, for evaluators work in isolation and they tend to embrace other evaluators when they can find them—which is why we are such a friendly group. There are likely more resources available in the community than you realize. For example, I became a Certified Management Consultant because of the basic similarity of the work and because their organization offered a code of ethics to clients.

Another way to keep current is to look for speaking engagements, to offer workshops and seminars, or to teach program evaluation at your local university. Each of these activities requires that you catch up on your reading and formulate current practice into conceptual frameworks. Finally, one can stay up to date by occasionally working with colleagues on a project in a subcontract arrangement. A bird's-eye view of how another evaluator functions can call some of your own practices into question. The reexamination can be healthy.

Foster Self-Reflection

An area that tends to be pushed aside with the demands made on an evaluator's time is that of reflection and introspection. A developing knowledge of self pays high dividends. This is an area that can certainly be fostered in the classroom. Once the concept is entrenched, it maintains a life of its own—a sort of substratum of personal narrative. I recently taught a graduate seminar in qualitative research methods and gave each student a notebook on the first day of class in order to keep a journal. Knowing how students' minds work, I encouraged them in this process by suggesting that part of their final grade would be awarded for the summary of their mental journey in a methodological appendix (as suggested by Lareau, 1987) to be attached to their final paper. We also took a look at personal learning styles before getting into the content of the course. Feedback from the students was positive and the research proposals they produced were competent.

Reflection is also fostered by reading widely for recreation. Characters like Madame Bovary, the Duchess Sanseverina, Elizabeth Bennet, Copperfield, Rumpole, and Roskolnikov, whether for their wisdom or folly, remain with me as both friends and classic examples of human behavior. A number of business schools have found that the great works of literature enrich, motivate, and provide lessons about leadership and human nature that cannot be surpassed.

Get Involved in the Community

Evaluators complain that they do not have enough time for their personal life, let alone time to be a volunteer. I would suggest, however, that community involvement, such as being on a volunteer board, pays off in a number of ways. First of all it can allow you to work with the implementors and recipients of social programs, to meet them as equals in a nonevaluation context. The perspective you gain can be invaluable to your work. Second, you can make connections in the community with high profile individuals in other walks of life and you can learn from their skills, not to mention gaining their friendship. Community involvement can give you higher visibility that in the long run can lead to more contracts and greater credibility. Finally, the volunteer work you do can add to your own sense of accomplishment, something which evaluation work seldom does because we rarely have the opportunity of seeing our recommendations enacted.

Keep an Escape Hatch Open

I was very interested to hear the confession of one of the senior executives of a group of trust and investment companies that failed spectacularly a number of years ago in Alberta. He said that they had never planned for failure, only for success. To me it seems shortsighted to only view the up side of a situation. Evaluation is a taxing activity. As Cronbach (1980) points out, the market for evaluators has been capricious and will probably remain so. With its logistical and political requirements being what they are, many people may not consider it as a lifelong career. Greiner and Metzger (1983) see this as part of the good news about consulting. Many people regard it as a stepping stone from one career to another. They suggest that as many as 60% of consultants remain in the field for 3 to 6 years and then move on to a choice job at the director level. About 30% stay for about 10 years and then move into private industry at the vice-president level. The remaining 10% are either university faculty or senior partners who are making too much money to think of leaving. I do not have equivalent figures for evaluators but believe that at least the proportions may be similar.

The rest of the good news is that both the tremendous challenge of independence and the richness of the learning involved keep one coming back for more. Rossi (1987) suggests that the excitement involved in the research itself, as well as your potential long-term impacts on the program are intrinsic rewards. My view is that few occupations provide the same degree of satisfaction; however, would-be evaluators should be warned, inoculated, inured to the hazards awaiting them in the field. Evaluator training needs a good shot of reality therapy.

References

Benveniste, G. (1972). *The politics of expertise*. Berkeley, CA: Glendessary Press.

Chelimsky, E. (1987). The politics of program evaluation. *Society, 25*(1), 24-32.

Cronbach, L. J., & Associates. (1980). *Toward reform of program evaluation*. San Francisco: Jossey-Bass.

Davis, B. G. (1986). Teaching of evaluation across the disciplines. *New Directions for Program Evaluation* (No. 29). San Francisco: Jossey-Bass.

Fisher, R., & Ury, W. (1983). *Getting to yes: Negotiating agreement without giving in.* New York: Penguin.

Greiner, L., & Metzger, R. (1983). *Consulting to management.* Englewood Cliffs, NJ: Prentice-Hall.

Lareau, A. (1987). Teaching qualitative methods: The role of classroom activities. *Education and Urban Society, 20*(1), 86-120.

Moore, C. M. (1987). *Group techniques for idea building.* Newbury Park, CA: Sage.

Rossi, P. (1987). No good applied social research goes unpunished. *Society, 25*(1), 74-79.

6

The Growing Importance of Multiculturalism for Independent Consulting

CARL L. JENNINGS

The ability of consultants to be effective in present-day American organizations is inseparable from their knowledge of and sensitivity to the changing demographic composition of the workplace. According to research conducted by the Hudson Institute (1987), there will be a dramatic increase in the numbers of minorities, women, and immigrants entering the work force between now and the year 2000. This demographic change has major implications for consultants with regard to the opportunities and challenges that a multicultural work force presents. Given this emerging scenario, previously existing attitudes among America's managerial elite, levels of comfort with interpersonal relationships, intergroup cooperation, and organizational effectiveness all have to be viewed differently. A new perspective is essential, and it will provide challenges and opportunities for organization development (OD) consultants and other applied researchers dealing with organizations.

This chapter provides a brief sketch of the demographic and cultural changes in American organizations, and the implications and challenges these changes pose for organizational leadership. The contributions made by OD as a profession to understanding multiculturalism will also be explored. In addition, specific consulting skills will be examined. In closing, I will put forth conclusions and recommendations for consultants to consider.

The Changing Demographics of the Work Force

"Business as usual" is rapidly becoming a thing of the past. Over the next nine years, white males will represent only 15% of the net increase in the labor market; white females, 42%; native and nonwhite men, 7%; native nonwhite women, 13%; immigrant men, 13%; and immigrant women, 13%. These data further indicate that 85% of the net increase of entrants into the work force will be women, people of color, and immigrants (Hudson Institute, 1987).[1] These data indicate that, for the first time, the traditional white male managerial elite will have to begin developing the competence in dealing with larger numbers of work force entrants who are female and/or of another culture.

The implications of these changes for organizational management and leadership are broad. The differences in values held by women and nonwhite ethnic groups present a unique set of challenges. For example, traditional members of American organizations place a great deal of concern and emphasis on the primacy of task (agentic), whereas women and members of other various racial and ethnic cultural groups value an empathic and communal approach. Given this scenario, leadership may need to create alternative organizational climates and environments. Thus, management should bring together and support *all* human resources organized around tasks that must be accomplished to ensure organizational growth and survival.

The current changes represent a major challenge to the preexisting preferred attitudes and other psychosocial biases that have combined to create a climate wherein women and people of color still risk being excluded from areas in which they could make much-needed contributions (Jennings & Wells, 1989). For example, there is a belief among some white male managers that women and people of color are not competent to serve in leadership roles. Perceptions and distortions of this kind are due in part to the impact of history operating as a process of socialization that influences how one views groups different from his/her own. A further description of these dysfunctional attitudes and barriers follows.

Psychological and Structural Barriers to Success

Jennings and Wells (1989) maintain that a systemic ethos underlies American organizations creating status anxiety among white males when women and people of color move beyond "threshold positions." Threshold positions are defined by Jennings and Wells (1989) as the highest, acceptable positions that women and minorities are permitted to hold in organizations. Depending on their individual tendencies, middle managers and "gate keepers" can be motivated to demarcate threshold boundaries for ethnocentric, sexist, or racist reasons. When members of these groups gain access to higher organizational positions and resources, it evokes a sense of encroachment on white entitlement (Jennings & Wells, 1989). These forces combine to create organization-wide barriers experienced by women and people of color on a day-to-day basis. These barriers impose limited access to mentorship opportunities, or create power imbalances due to disproportionate white male involvement as mentors. They also result in limited access for most nonwhites to powerful informal networks, and lack of access by women and people of color to key policymaking positions. The comparatively disproportionate number of white male executives and senior managers expected to provide mentoring experiences in American organizations accounts for the tensions and resistance experienced by women and people of color trying to find positive mentoring experiences (Thomas, 1989, p. 90). These are only the outward manifestations of any one or combination of traditional managerial preferred attitudes, however. The deeper commonality they all share is that they facilitate the creation of barriers to advancement for underrepresented groups.

For some, permeating these barriers can engender feelings of another substantial barrier to inclusion and success—*tokenism*. Women and people of color who function as tokens in organizations experience loneliness and unwarranted pressure to perform (C. S Jennings, personal communications, October 12, 1991; Kanter, 1977). Often they do not know how to judge themselves when other people's standards have a different cultural context. For example, the tendency of blacks to be more affective, speak louder, and display a different time orientation in mixed social contexts can often result in miscommunications among blacks and whites. Socializing can be difficult because they feel they can never let their guard down. It is as if blacks are always working. Sometimes they are embarrassed by being held up as a symbol or spokesperson for their group, while at other times, they are confused because they do not know whether people really value their knowledge and skills or believe that their presence merely fulfills an EEO requirement.

Another attitudinal barrier has to do with a *devaluation of diversity* by managers and workers. In situations in which diversity is advocated for legal reasons, some women and people of color may resent diversity efforts as much as many whites. Many competent and highly capable blacks, other people of color, and women do not like the stigma attached to hiring and promotion decisions for the purpose of complying with affirmative action guidelines. Although many such highly competent people would never be hired were it not for affirmative action policies, they resent them nonetheless. Some whites tend to dislike multiculturalism because they feel that competence and standards are sacrificed, and that perhaps their entitlement is violated. Competent leadership is needed to help organizations manage these multicultural issues.

Multiculturalism: The Leadership Challenge

Multicultural realities in the 1990s are being shaped by demographic shifts and an unanticipated economic downturn within America, as well as global competition from without. Faced with growing competition from Japan, West Germany, and other Asian and European countries, America is being forced to reexamine its attitudes and values about working and doing business with culturally different people. These developments highlight the need to view multiculturalism as a necessary and inseparable dimension of overall American organizational improvement efforts. Dertouzos, Lester, and Solow (1990), in their book, *Made in America*, acknowledge that the influx of people of color and immigrants into the work force over the next eight years will create a dynamic tension between worker ability and the demand for greater and more complex skills. These circumstances clearly pose a formidable challenge for leaders and managers. They recast multiculturalism as an area of concern inextricably tied to issues of quality, productivity, and profit. Faced with these circumstances, it is senseless and counterproductive to persist with the old rationales for excluding women and people of color from the upper levels of American organizational life.

One of the principal advantages of multiculturalism is the diversity in perspective and approaches to problem solving that it provides. A possible disadvantage for women or people of color in today's organizational and business environments is the difficulty experienced in, if not total exclusion from, policymaking positions. Generally, women and people of color find it easier to obtain employment that involves the implementation of policy rather than its formulation (E. J. Nichols, personal communications, May 3, 1989). If this practice continues, the current trends indicated by the Workforce 2000 data suggest that a massive breakdown in American businesses and organizations is imminent. The shrinkage in the number of white males entering the work force, combined with the need to better manage a multicultural organization, makes the practice of excluding women and minorities from policymaking positions hard to sustain.

In view of these dramatic transformations impacting American organizations, leadership has a tremendous responsibility. In this new context, leaders must be passionate and inspirational about *all* people in their organizations and about their mission, vision, and goals. Through this passion and inspiration, they ignite a "can do" spirit within organization members. This spirit is necessary for a proactive response to change that is necessary for furthering growth and development.

One of the biggest challenges confronting today's leaders is their ability to continually be architects of experience in an environment so turbulent that it has been described as "permanent white water" (Vaill, 1989, p. 2). In addition to being responsible for determining organizational direction through articulating an inspired vision, organizational leaders are responsible for managing all resources and determining how they interrelate for high-quality product and/or service provision. Determining the necessary interrelationship of all resources will require an understanding of the full impact of changing demographics on leaders and their organizations. This means helping organization members understand and accept the change from what the organization *was* to what it is *becoming*. The impact of change on old and new organization members makes leadership responsible for helping all organization members understand how their relating to one another influences how they work together. During this phase, it is important for leadership to help members of all groups manage the tendency to revert to the behaviors they know best when under stress. Typically, these behaviors are at best offensive and at worst counterproductive. Understanding the likelihood of these tendencies in a multicultural setting is very important because of the higher potential for intergroup conflict and misunderstanding.

In today's organizational environment, leadership and management need to model acceptance and commitment to diversity. It is important that all members of the organization feel that they have the fundamental respect of their superiors, co-workers and subordinates. It is important that all levels of management embrace multicultural diversity and demonstrate this commitment if they truly desire its becoming a value to which the total organization is committed.

The accomplishment of desired organizational outcomes requires leaders' willingness to commit to the following:

- Being eager and enthusiastic about getting state-of-the-art information and technologies to deal with the various issues and needs that can emerge in a multicultural organization. In a rapidly developing global economy in which *information* is becoming the dominant source of wealth creation, such attitudes and behaviors will be critical for organizational survival (Toffler, 1990, p. 9). In view of the fact that accurate information is critical as the basis of good decisions, it is essential that management always have access to the highest quality information to help in the decision-making process. With regard to multiculturalism, it is becoming increasingly important for leaders and managers to stay informed about the necessary concepts and practical skills essential for managing multicultural organizations. Organizations need to cultivate a climate and culture wherein members of *all groups can make their unique contributions to the realization of the organizational mission.*

- Viewing the multicultural organization out of necessity, as an entity that must value learning in order to support desired levels of productivity, development and health (Vaill, 1989, p. 25). This requires engaging in ongoing self-examination about what senior management is doing to better serve and support the creation of a multicultural organization through fulfilling their responsibilities as managers. This involves encouraging unconverted management and staff to fully accept relational, communicative and organizational competence as essential for better multicultural relations and organizational success and development.

- Leadership needs to interact at all levels of the organization, encouraging thinking and discussion about mission, vision, goals, and objectives and how everyone can better support the creation of a multicultural organization by carrying out their respective portion of each strategic element. All levels of management should always attempt to help organization members understand how their respective efforts contribute to total organizational functioning.

- Modeling diversity by working toward forging a common vision of the organization that incorporates an inclusive multicultural perspective and evokes committed action from all organization members. To accomplish this, leadership must shape organizational values about multiculturalism through upholding those behaviors identified as important through day-to-day interactions with *all* organization members.

- Modeling the commitment to open, clear communication and feedback at the interpersonal, intergroup, and organizational levels is very important.

Through this commitment, the organization can continually monitor multicultural relations and other processes needed to support the creation of products and services. It is especially important that organization members learn how to competently give and receive corrective feedback. This allows the organization to identify and correct those processes that must be improved for top performance.

- Clearly communicating all policies and procedures to people in a direct and genuine way with representation from all cultural groups working at every level of the organization. To communicate and articulate persuasively in a multicultural setting necessitates leadership's willingness to want to understand the communicative preferences and values of those people who are different from themselves. The extent to which they are capable of doing this will determine their level of effectiveness in successfully articulating a common frame of reference.

- Facilitating the establishment of organizational or departmentwide workshops in which output gaps exist. This is suggested for three important reasons. The first is to revisit the organization's mission, vision, and goals so that organizational members clarify their understanding about the importance of their responsibilities in relation to multiculturalism and the desired levels of productivity. Furthermore, the experiential portion of these workshops will provide management with invaluable information as to where the gaps are, between what staff understands and does, and what must be accomplished to achieve designated goals. Finally, this data can provide the basis for staff-development programs and supervision.

It is critical that organizational leadership focuses on the training and development needs for new work-force entrants and all management. It is more important to work on these issues than to get caught up in the sensationalism of misinterpreted numbers about groups of people entering the work force. Henceforth, the ability to manage a multicultural organization will determine the extent to which American-based organizations can improve quality, productivity, and profits in today's global environment.

The implications of these developments for independent consultants are considerable. In addition to knowing one's area of expertise, it will be necessary for consultants to understand how these issues impact the experiences and priorities of the organizations with which they work. More specifically, consultants are expected to help their clients understand the impact of change on the various departments within the total organization and how that change can be managed. Toward this end, OD consultants can contribute greatly.

OD and the Multicultural Organization

Organization development, an approach to organizational consulting that grew out of the social and applied behavioral sciences, continues to be a major force among current consulting approaches (Sikes, Drexler, & Gant, 1989). The increased appreciation for OD has to do with its organizationwide perspective and its focus on human behavior as a key factor in determining managerial and organizational effectiveness. The core group-improvement strategies from which OD emerged had, as a basic concern, a greater appreciation for racial and religious differences as reflected among the diverse groups in American communities (Morrow, 1977).

This focus on diverse human behavior highlights the most critical boundary that managers and leaders must be able to effectively manage to avoid irreversible chaos. Of all the areas presently competing for the attention of managers and leaders, interpersonal, group, and organizational relations, within and between different racial, gender, and age groups, are among the most pressing.

Facilitating understanding and exploring attitudes about these differences have always been associated with OD in some way since its inception. Kurt Lewin, one of the major contributors to the development of core OD technology, was involved in the use of these methods to combat racial and religious intolerance in Connecticut in 1946 (Morrow, 1977). These interests and activities culminated in the development of theoretical and practical strategies and methods that provided the basis for the further development of approaches for addressing issues of diversity. The work and research of Kurt Lewin, Ken Benne, Ron Lippitt, and Leland Bradford resulted in the founding of the National Training Laboratory (NTL) Institute for Applied Behavioral Science. Over the past forty years, NTL has committed much of its time and resources to broadening our understanding of issues of diversity so that all people can work and live together with greater appreciation and understanding.

OD consulting is distinguished from other forms of consultation by the emphasis it places on the importance of how best to work with and support organization members. OD consulting accomplishes this by focusing on the necessary interdependence of all people and departments essential to high performing organizations. Table 6.1 further differentiates OD consulting from human resource development and program evaluation consulting, which are alternative consulting pro-

Table 6.1 Comparison of Organizational Consulting Approaches

	Organizational Development	*Human Resource Development*	*Program Evaluation*
Focus	Typically system wide, divisional or departmental (smaller projects are worked on in some instances, e.g., one-on-one consultation, interpersonal problem solving)	Management and development of an organization's human resources	Quantitative and qualitative assessment of organizational processes in terms of their actual versus intended outcomes, helps determine whether or not an organization is achieving its goals
Methodology	Involves use of participant observations, surveys and interviews, process consultation, team building, strategic planning, leadership development, interpersonal communications and relations, sociotechnical systems, diagnosis and analysis and multicultural diversity	Executive development skills training, employee relations, compensation, strategic and human resources planning	Internal consulting, staff reductions and relocations, and implementation of organizational policies and procedures
Intended Outcomes	Increase problem solving and (org.) self renewal capacity and effectiveness Enhances individual and group performance by monitoring organizational health, productivity and the quality of work life	Efficient and effective management of planning and utilization of *all* human resources	Identification of performance gaps as contrasted with organization mission and goals Provides feedback on necessary corrective measures

fessions that may also confront multicultural issues. Other types of organizational consultants focus on more specific issues such as office systems technologies and management skills training as a primary means of organizational improvement. Although these are necessary, consultants working in such areas generally lack expertise in dealing with attitudes, behaviors and the range of human conflict at varying systemic levels in today's organizations.

OD consulting is an organizationwide planned approach that has the commitment of top management. Many of its activities involve working with individuals and groups to help the organization develop the capacity for self-correction. This is accomplished through developing new methods of problem solving, improving interpersonal and intergroup relations, and changing organizational norms in order to promote a healthier and more productive climate.

One of the primary activities of an OD effort is *process consultation*, which takes place throughout all stages of the OD intervention. A basic assumption of this activity is that it is impossible for either the consultant or management alone to properly diagnose organizational issues. Given this reality, the manager and consultant "must share in the process of diagnosing what may be wrong" (Schein, 1987, p. 30). The client "must be actively involved in the process of generating a remedy because only the client ultimately knows what is possible and what will work in his culture and situation" (Schein, 1987, p. 30). Process consultation can be a useful tool for understanding the fundamental dynamics of multicultural relations. Process consultation aids in understanding multicultural relations through the emphasis placed on interpersonal communications and relations. The initial focus on the importance of open, concealed, blind and unknown aspects of interpersonal communications, as indicated by Luft (1970), led to the need to also consider the importance of culture, gender, and age. Given the importance of subtlety in interpersonal communications and its relationship to the quality of human interaction, racial, cultural, gender, and age differences also became obvious factors that influence productive working relationships that warranted special attention. Another distinction of OD is the belief that organizational change can be facilitated and haphazard occurrences can be avoided. Prior to the emergence of OD, organizational responses to change were thought to be haphazard out of necessity.

Viewing organizations as a multilevel, dynamic, interactive process has conceptual and procedural advantages. OD consultants are aware of the multilevel needs and processes that operate in all organizations, from the intrapersonal through the organization/environment interface. A consultative approach should be useful in attempting to understand

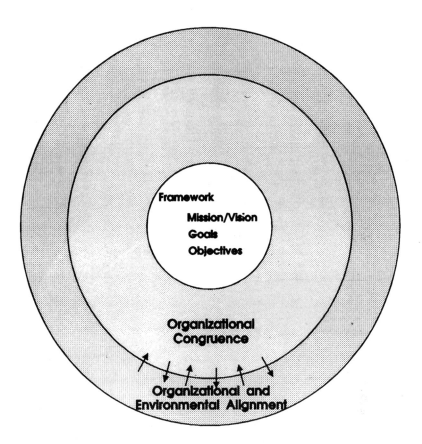

Figure 6.1. The Jennings and Jennings Approach to OD Consulting

the inner- and inter-workings of an organization. The Jennings and Jennings approach is a global model useful for responding to the full range of organizational issues. In instances in which the organizational issues are multicultural, the model would be used as indicated (see Figure 6.1). The approach involves exploring three broad domains as an interdependent system. This helps to determine the source of organizational dysfunction from the intrapersonal through the organization/environment levels.

As shown in Figure 6.1, the model begins with an examination of the organization's framework, which consists of mission, vision, goals, and objectives. At this level, an analysis of an organization's framework can indicate the basis for multicultural issues. For example, if there were no statements of value and fairness relative to multiculturalism in the organization's mission or goals, the omission could be an indication of multicultural problems.

Next, the nature of intrapersonal, interpersonal, group, intergroup (e.g., interdepartmental) relations necessary for organizational congruence are examined. Consultants typically gain entry into an organization at the point of stress or conflict identified by senior organization members. For purposes of illustrating the Jennings and Jennings model, I will proceed sequentially. Having examined the organization's framework, I would continue with a further analysis of intrapersonal, interpersonal, group, and intergroup/departmental relations. Should my analysis indicate that the organizational issues are multicultural, I would utilize an intervention appropriate to that level. For example, if the issue was at the *intergroup level*, I would use Nichols' PACD (Philosophical Aspects of Cultural Difference; E. J. Nichols, personal communications, May 3, 1989). One of the ways this method illustrates intergroup conflict between whites and people of color is to highlight the culturally based value differences that exist between groups and how they conflict in organizational settings. To demonstrate white attitudes about affirmative action, for example, Nichols uses magic markers as symbols of the organizational resources for which women and people of color and white men compete. By distributing a seemingly disproportionate number of the markers to people of color and women, he demonstrates how some whites experience this phenomenon as reversed discrimination (E. J. Nichols, personal communications, December 4, 1991). Finally, the degree of alignment between the organization and those important forces in the environment, upon which it depends for survival, are examined. These could include government agencies and regulators, other businesses, community groups, environmental organizations, and the full range of educational institutions.

No matter what type of diagnostic activity or intervention is used to understand and to facilitate change in organizations, a theoretical framework is necessary to provide context to the issues that emerge. The Wells and Jennings (1989) analysis is a framework that can be used to explain the dynamics operative at the *organizational level*. This paradigm provides insight into multicultural organizational behavior through combining research findings in comparative history and political science, advances in psychoanalytic object-relations theory, studies on the operation of unconscious processes in social systems, work in theories of group relations and organizational diagnosis and change, and selected research on black managers (Jennings & Wells, 1989; Wells & Jennings, 1983). These theories and disciplines are integrated to create a diagnostic perspective that explains the barriers women and people of color experience when they attempt to move up in American organizations (Jennings & Wells, 1989; Wells & Jennings, 1983). A specific diagnostic tool that can be used within the Wells-Jennings analytical framework is the *cultural audit*, which involves observations, interviews and surveys (L. Wells, personal communication, November 10, 1991).

At the *interorganizational level, stakeholder analysis* could be used to manage the interorganizational interface. Stakeholder analysis focuses on understanding the environmental influences that impact the stakeholder's organization (Alkhafaji, 1989). In addition to the focal corporation (or organization) it takes into consideration employees, suppliers, investors, lenders, debtors, consumers, and government. Strengths, weaknesses, opportunities and threats (or SWOT as the method is called) are thoroughly investigated. The intended outcome is that the interests of the various stakeholders and those of society as a whole are served through this approach (Alkhafaji, 1989).

Although stakeholder analysis does not speak explicitly to multi-culturalism, its relevance is suggested by the emphasis placed on the importance of managing the various interest groups that make up an organization's constellation of relationships. The way organizations manage multicultural diversity has major implications for how such issues are managed among stakeholders in the external environment.

Strategic management is another approach that could be used for managing the interorganizational interface within or without the parameters of the Jennings and Jennings consultative approach. Strategic management is concerned with the formulation and implementation of the necessary goals, objectives, policies, and plans for achieving desired organizational outcomes (Hammermesh, 1990). Through the incorporation of the values of key implementers and one or a combination of the following analytical methods—linear planning (top down and/or bottom up), portfolio analysis, industry and competitive analysis, or scenario planning—a strategy is formulated and implemented. The desired outcome is the pursuit of a cogent, reflexive, and viable strategy based on a comprehensive analysis of interorganizational forces and relations that will lead to success. Again, while this approach does not focus on multicultural diversity specifically, there are aspects that lend themselves to multiculturalism. For example, the values of the key implementers are critical for establishing an organizational culture and climate that upholds the importance of multiculturalism both within and among today's organizations. Furthermore, it would be in the interest of leadership to ensure that all analyses and strategy development were relatively free of culturally based distortions and biases. Accomplishing this would involve the use of an appropriate intervention strategy intended for use in understanding multicultural relations.

The major challenge to OD consultants involves their ability to help organizational leaders effectively manage (a) process issues—*how* things happen through people and procedures, and (b) content issues—*what* must be done that is specialized or of a technical nature. The following includes examples of interventions used to support organization leaders and their change efforts at and between the various organizational levels. The appropriateness and dimensions of these interventions for organizational or multicultural issues is indicated by their distinctive function illustrated in Table 6.2. The major difference between the two classifications of intervention is that one deals specifically with multicultural diversity, and the other describes interventions for general organizational concerns. The commonality between the two classifications of intervention strategy is the importance of understanding interpersonal, group, and system-level processes, that are essential for managing multicultural as well as other organizational issues.

Given OD consultants' expertise in managing large-scale change, with their help, organizational leaders can better influence and respond to a rapidly changing and turbulent environment. Disjunctive interdepartmental and intergroup relations heighten levels of organizational stress. These dislocations can lead to declining productivity and organizational instability. By helping organization leaders to see the current intergroup and multicultural challenges as an opportunity and not a danger, OD consultants can make needed contributions. To be effective in this way, new and practicing OD consultants must be committed to learning.

This commitment to learning must exist at two levels: one is a lifelong pursuit of self-development and knowledge, the other involves a parallel commitment to keeping up with the theoretical and conceptual

Table 6.2 Comparison of Organizational and Multicultural Strategies

Organizational Levels	Organizational Intervention Strategies	Multicultural Intervention Strategies
Intra Personal	Growth groups, Myers Briggs Type Indicator, Gestalt Therapy	Cultural awareness workshops, Race Relations Competence Workshop
Inter Personal	T-groups, sensitivity training, Leadership Effectiveness Training	Cultural awareness workshops, Race Relations Competence Workshop
Group Level	SYMLOG (Systematic *Multiple Level Observation of Groups), Nichols' PACD, Tavistock Labs, Oshry Power Labs, Star Power	Wells' CARS (class, age, race, sex) labs, Counseling from a Cultural Perspective workshop
Inter Group	SYMLOG, PACD, C-Group	PACD, CARS, Wells-Jennings Analysis, Race Relations Competence Workshop
Organizational	Gestalt, Total Quality Management, Organizational Analysis and Diagnosis	Wells-Jennings Analysis, Cultural Audit
Inter Organizational	Stakeholder Analysis, Strategic Management	

frameworks and behavioral technologies necessary for working in both traditional and the new multicultural environment.

In the new multicultural environment, successful leaders will be those individuals who discover how to stimulate the desire and capability to learn at all organizational levels (Schein, 1985; Senge, 1990). From now through 2000 and beyond, multiculturalism will pose a tremendous challenge to American organizations. What follows are suggested knowledge and skills essential for understanding and managing a multicultural work force.

Multicultural Literacy

To manage the multicultural work force, leaders and organizational members must have a better understanding of cultural differences. One of the differences between whites and people of color, suggested by Nichols (personal communication, December 4, 1991) is time orientation. Anglo-Americans conceptualize time as a discrete, tangible construct. Time is linear and sequential. Thus, for example, whites prefer to complete specific tasks within a designated time frame during the course of the work day. A variety of different ethnic and cultural groups, including African Americans, experience time in a nonsequential, cyclical or infinite way. An African-American individual (or other person of color), then, might indicate a preference for working on the tasks nonsequentially and across time periods, but completing all of them by the end of the project or work period. If the supervisor in this instance was an individual with a strong Anglo-American time orientation, this preference could become a major organizational issue. Another issue here could be the supervisor's desire to impose his/her preferred system of logic or method of problem solving which might be counterintuitive to the culturally different subordinate.

Another culturally based difference between whites and people of color is space orientation. For example, blacks tend to interact at much closer proximity to people than do whites. Other nonwhites also display this tendency (e.g., Hispanics, Arabs, and Native Americans). It is important to note that some whites from the Mediterranean region also exhibit these behaviors (Hall, 1959). These observations illustrate culturally based behavioral patterns among a significant number of people in each group. The statements do not apply to all members of these groups and they are not intended to be stereotypical.

In addition to awareness of these types of cultural differences, having an awareness of how systems theory operates at the intrapersonal through the organizational/environmental levels is very useful for OD specialists. It is also necessary to have some knowledge of the behavioral and social sciences. More specifically, it is important to develop skills in the following areas: self-insight and awareness, multicultural communications and relations, race relations, women's issues, age issues, issues of the physically challenged, conflict management skills, group relations and process skills, sensitivity to time and space across cultures, organization analysis and diagnosis from a multicultural perspective and an understanding of the philosophical basis of cultural difference. Individuals interested in multiculturalism need to seriously consider these areas. It is common for individuals to have a graduate degree or at least a bachelor's degree in the behavioral or social sciences. However, it is also important to get as much practical experience as you possibly can. This is the only way to appreciate the efficacy of theory combined with practical skill for managing complex, large-scale multicultural and other organizational issues.

Finally, I would encourage students, practitioners and interested applied research academicians to seek opportunities to learn more about the application of OD to multicultural organizations. If you are at a college or university, you can start by taking a human interaction lab or a communications lab. I suggest these to begin with because they will provide a basic understanding of applied behavioral science concepts and skills. It is important to know and experience these concepts and methods because they are the basic building blocks of OD.

Once you have had these experiences, you may pursue your personal and professional development further by participating in a group relations conference or conflict management lab. While you are learning, it is also important to gain practical experience so you can learn how to apply your knowledge to real world organizational problems and issues. If you are not in a professional setting in which there is someone to mentor you or provide direction, you can gain experience through human resource and OD programs or courses that have working in a client system as part of their requirement.

There are organizations that provide opportunities for these specialized learning opportunities. The NTL Institute for Applied Behavioral Science is one of the premier organizations in the world that educates people about interpersonal and systemic dynamics. Other organizations that provide useful learning experiences are the A. K. Rice Institute and its nationwide affiliates, University Associates, the Center for Creative Leadership, and the American Society for Training and Development. Through individual pursuit of such efforts, organizations will have better qualified people equipped to serve and negotiate an unpredictable multicultural environment with greater clarity, certainty, and much needed direction.

Concluding Comments

Organization development consultants are particularly well suited to address issues of multiculturalism because their philosophical and methodological framework is grounded in a systemic interdependent process that requires multiple levels of analysis for understanding organizational behavior. Given the diversity represented by new workforce entrants, OD's emphasis on human interactive processes can provide direction for understanding the various problem-solving styles these new entrants bring to the workplace. For future organizational success, management will need a practical understanding of these differences to continue the development and refinement of product and service outcomes. OD and applied research consultants have a disposition to foster organizational growth within a human-relations context as well as a variety of tools and techniques that leaders and managers will find indispensable in their efforts to manage the multicultural evolution. Students, practitioners, and applied research academicians have an invaluable opportunity, as well as perhaps an obligation, to pursue multicultural knowledge and experience.

Note

1. It is important to remember that these numbers only represent a net increase, that is, the composition of the increase in the labor market, minus that portion that will leave for retirement or other reasons.

References

Alkhafaji, A. (1989). *Stakeholders approach to corporate governance: Managing in a dynamic environment.* New York: Basic Books.

Collins, E. G. C., & Devanna, M. A. (1990). *The portable MBA.* New York: John Wiley.

Dertouzos, M. L., Lester, R. K., & Solow, R. M. (Eds.). (1990). *Made in America: Regaining the productive edge.* New York: Harper Perennial.

Hall, E. (1959). *The silent language.* New York: Doubleday.

Hammermesh, R. G. (1990). Strategic management. In E. G. C. Collins & M. A. Devanna (Eds.), *The portable MBA.* New York: John Wiley.

Hudson Institute, Inc. (1987). *Workforce 2000: Work and workers for the 21st century.* Indianapolis, IN: Author.

Jennings, C. L., & Wells, L., Jr. (1989). The Wells-Jennings analysis: A new diagnostic window on race relations in American organizations. In W. Sikes, A. B. Drexler, & J. Gant, (Eds.), *The emerging practice of organization development*. Alexandria, VA: NTL Institute and San Diego, CA: University Associates.

Kanter, R. M. (1977). *Men and women of the corporation*. New York: Basic Books.

Luft, J. (1970). *Group process*. Palo Alto, CA: Mayfield Publishing.

Morrow, A. J. (1977). *The practical theorist: The life and work of Kurt Lewin*. New York: Teachers College Press.

Schein, E. H. (1985). *Organizational culture and leadership*. San Francisco,: Jossey-Bass.

Schein, E. H. (1987). *Process consultation: Lessons for managers and consultants*. Reading, MA: Addison-Wesley.

Senge, P. (1990). *The fifth discipline: The art and practice of the learning organization*. New York: Doubleday/Currency.

Sikes, W., Drexler, A. B., & Gant, J. (Eds.). (1989). *The emerging practice of organization development*. Alexandria, VA: NTL Institute.

Thomas, D. H. (1989). Mentoring and irrationality: The role of racial taboos. *Human Resource Management, 28*, 279-290.

Toffler, A. (1990). *Power shift: Knowledge, wealth and violence at the edge of the 21st century*. New York: Bantam Books.

Vaill, P. B. (1989). *Managing as a performing art*. San Francisco: Jossey-Bass.

Wells, L., Jr., & Jennings, C. L. (1983). Black career advancement and white reactions: Remnants of "Herrenvolk democracy" and the scandalous paradox. In D. Vails-Weber & W. J. Potts (Eds.), *1983 Sunrise Seminars*. Arlington, VA: NTL Institute.

PART III

Making It Better:
Tools, Techniques, and Advice for Improving Applied Psychological Consulting

7

Ethical and Professional Guidelines for Construction and Use of Contracts

KARL W. KUHNERT
BARBARA A. GORE

A critical demand of every consultant is to communicate effectively with the client. This is never more true than when the consultant and the client negotiate the terms of work the consultant is to perform. Clearly articulating objectives and expectations in a legal document such as a contract is one of the most difficult challenges a consultant faces. Poor communications between parties can prove devastating to the reputation of the consultant and the consulting firm, as well as to the client organization and to the reputation of the profession.

This chapter is designed to show how a well-constructed legal document between a consultant and a client can (a) increase the likelihood of the consultant maintaining professional and ethical standards, (b) educate the client about the ethical and professional standards of psychologists, (c) provide a forum for establishing rapport and trust between the consultant and client through open discussion of the expectations and responsibilities of each party, and (d) protect the consultant against charges of negligence or other legal misconduct.

Knowledge about the elements and components of a contract is crucial, but knowing how contracts can facilitate the establishment of

AUTHORS' NOTE: We gratefully acknowledge Annette Stanton, Ronald G. Downey, and Aita R. French for their critical comments on earlier drafts of the manuscript.

ethical and professional standards of practice is the most important focus for consultants. In a recent survey, psychologists providing services to police departments indicated that 55% had encountered an ethical dilemma (Zelig, 1988). The most common conflicts were related to issues of confidentiality, dual-role relationships, and balancing the ethical standards of the psychologist with the needs of the agency. These ethical conflicts are representative of those most likely to be encountered by organizational consultants as well. How do consultants protect themselves and fulfill the needs and expectations of the organization and the individual employees simultaneously?

The "Ethical Principles of Psychologists" (APA, 1990) describe ideals that guide the practice of psychology. Most often, these principles are thought of in reference to clinical practice rather than the organizational setting. However, they are quite applicable to industrial organizational (I/O) psychology and to many areas of applied psychological research generally. Most often, in the practice of clinical psychology, there is a focus on the individual client or the immediate family unit. Even though the issues in clinical settings are more personal and private, the I/O psychologist often has the welfare of hundreds, even thousands, of individuals to consider. In addition to this heavy burden, I/O psychologists must also consider and protect the interests of the organization. Because of the double client-practitioner relationship created by the responsibility to the organization and the employee, I/O psychologists face many complex issues when conducting projects or research in organizations.

The Need for a Good Contract

Contracts are usually thought of as evil things to be avoided at all costs because they contain too much legal jargon and are often unclear. As Schwitzgebel and Schwitzgebel (1980) admit, the average legally naive person "will probably experience confusion, boredom, anxiety, or anger when reading the law," and contracts are no exception (p. 2). In fact, this is probably one of the most comprehensive areas of study in most law schools. However, a contract is the best way to capture or operationalize an agreement between two parties and to ensure that both act accordingly. Although it is important to understand contracts in general, it is also critical for consultants to focus on how contracts can help address their professional, legal, and ethical interests.

The Definition of a Contract and Its Elements

The American Law Institute (Morawetz, 1925) defines a contract as a promise, or set of promises, for which the law gives a remedy if it is breached, or the performance of which the law recognizes as a duty. In other words, a contract is a statement about how each party to the contract should perform. An enforceable contract must be clear as to the rights and duties of each party so that in the event of a problem, an arbitrator or judge can determine what each party must do. The duties should be spelled out in plain language rather than legal jargon so that no misunderstandings arise and legal fees for *interpretive services* are avoided. Because contracts are typically drawn up by the party providing the services and ambiguities are interpreted against the preparer of the contract, consultants drafting their own contracts must make certain that the language is clear.

There are four basic elements to a contract (Privette, 1985). First, there must be an offer and acceptance. One party proposes a deal and the other accepts. The courts call this a "meeting of the minds" because there must be understanding by both parties before the offer is truly "accepted." This has direct implications for the concept of informed consent as it relates to the client making a decision about accepting the proposed services. Has there been a meeting of the minds when important information is glossed over, the potential risks are minimized, or the repercussions are not fully explained?

The second aspect is consideration, which is the exchange of promises that binds the agreement. The consultant receives payment, and the organization receives the consultant's services. Unless both parties are getting something from the agreement, it is not binding.

The third element of a contract is that both parties are capable of entering into it. The parties cannot be minors or mentally incompetent. Incompetence can include a disability caused by drug use or physiological problems. Although these particular examples may seem inappropriate for organizational consulting, the concept is very applicable. A person or organization could be considered "disabled" by a lack of pertinent information about the methods, risks, or any other factor that could affect the ability to make an informed decision. To establish the requirements for informed consent, the consultant must accurately present all important information about the project.

Finally the purpose of the contract must be legal. If not, the contract is null and void.

The Components of a Valid Contract

According to Privette (1985), a valid contract must contain four essential parts: (a) the identification of both parties, (b) the description of the terms, (c) the description of the consideration for both parties, and (d) the execution of the contract by signing. Although all elements are important, the terms section of the contract is usually the most critical, and longest, because it describes the rights that each party has and what duties each must fulfill in the performance of the contract.

After two parties enter into a contract, one party or the other may discover an error or omission. Instead of voiding the contract and starting over, the parties can enter into an agreement to add material to or remove material from the contract. This is done by stipulation, a written explanation of how the original contract is being changed. The stipulation is then made part of the contract and is "executed" in the same manner as the original contract.

When negotiating a contract it is important that the consultant does not agree to anything in writing, for any reason, prior to signing the final contract. This includes all material that may be incorporated into the contract at a later time. An informal written agreement may have all the necessary elements of a contract, and a consultant would be bound by it. This is especially important in that in some states a written agreement may not need the element of consideration to be binding. For example, a contract could still be valid even if an agreement for payment of fees is not included.

The need for consultation with a lawyer cannot be emphasized enough. Ideally this consultation should take place during the negotiation phase, *before* any agreements have been signed, to determine if there is a binding contract that will protect the interests of the consultant. The consultant is expending time and money toward the completion of the project: the loss may be substantial if a company refuses to pay or a court rules that the consultant is not entitled to collect the balance of the fees for services. By comparison, the legal fee for a contact review would be small. This loss is in addition to the legal fees incurred in litigation of the dispute. Consulting a lawyer is also important because most organizations will have a lawyer review the contract with their interests in mind before they sign.

Role of Contracts in Establishing Ethical and Professional Standards

What happens when the client makes a request to the consultant that is unethical or contrary to standards of professional practice? Every practicing psychologist must face the difficult task of balancing the interests of the client with the ethical and professional standards of the profession. The nature of the conflict is specific to each situation and should be resolved in light of the situational demands and the quality of the relationship between the psychologist and the organization. How does a consulting psychologist prevent the organization from making requests that are unethical or unprofessional for psychological practice? Drafting and negotiating a contract for consulting services is a good way to educate the organization about the ethical and professional standards of psychologists, before the organization makes requests that may be psychologically unethical. Negotiation is also an excellent forum for establishing rapport and trust between the two parties through open discussion of the expectations and responsibilities of each party.

It is especially important that the goals of the project are stated explicitly. Management in organizations often has unrealistic expectations about what can be accomplished in a project and what they should expect in terms of real changes in the organization. Misunderstandings can prove devastating to the reputation of a particular psychologist, the field of psychology as a whole, and the health of the organization. It would be unfortunate if the project were halted due to misunderstandings or if the project outcomes were unacceptable or disappointing to management. Such problems are avoided by better communication during the negotiation of the contract, and subsequently the organization, the psychologist, and most importantly the individual employee will avoid embarrassment and/or harm.

It is also important that negotiations and the final contract address other ethical issues. These topics include how the data are collected and by whom. If confidentiality is necessary for candid and honest information by employees, the data should be collected only by the consultant and his/her assistants. In the specific case of survey data, the consultant is wise to have subjects mail or deliver the survey data directly to the consultant's office with no contact with the data by anyone in the organization. If individual or group interviews are conducted, no one from the organization besides the interviewees should be present or given information concerning the outcome of the interview.

Other important decisions concern who has access to the data, what form the data are in, and for what purposes they may be used. If the data are made available to the organization and the data collection is anonymous, it is important that no individuals be identified. This is usually accomplished by aggregating the data across departments, or in other ways that are meaningful, before they are made available to the organization. Evaluation of the consulting project is another area of relevance to the contract negotiation. The psychologist and client organization should determine by what standards the project outcome is evaluated and by whom this is done. This evaluation process should be explicit in the contract, and is obviously based on the results of prior planning and communication between the two parties concerning important topics such as goals, methods, and expectations. It is also wise to develop a plan for the evaluation and review of the consultant-client relationship during the project.

Role of Contracts in Preventing Charges of Negligence

Malpractice, a subcategory of negligence, is "conduct which falls below the standard established by law for the protection of others against unreasonably great harm" (Schwitzgebel & Schwitzgebel, 1980, p. 250). In order to prove negligence, the plaintiff must show (a) a duty on the part of the professional, (b) that there was a breach of that duty, (c) an actual loss or injury, and finally (d) a causal link between the professional's negligence and the injury. The important factor in most malpractice cases is the standard of care to which the professional is held.

The standards that are recognized by the law are different for professionals and laypersons. The standards of conduct for professionals are set by custom, statute, or professional rules and are implicit in the contract. Even if these standards are not stated explicitly in the contract, the professional is held to these standards. Professionals cannot remove responsibility of negligence by a statement to this effect in the contract. It is constitutionally invalid for psychologists to exempt themselves from claims of negligence. This is legally unacceptable and would void the contract (Schwitzgebel & Schwitzgebel, 1980). It is also wise to be careful when claiming to be a specialist in a particular area. "Specialists" are held to higher standards than the usual practitioner, and all that is needed to certify a consultant as a specialist is his/her own claim of specialty knowledge (Schwitzgebel & Schwitzgebel, 1980).

It is interesting to note that most courts rely on expert testimony rather than any available written standards of practice (Schwitzgebel & Schwitzgebel, 1980). In some cases the defendant has even been accepted as an expert witness in his/her own case. Even though this practice is rare, it highlights the point that the "standards of care" recognized by the courts may not be those endorsed by the American Psychological Association. In fact, many members of the legal profession may not even be aware of the standards for psychological care. It is important to note, however, that in most cases the standards for practice established by the American Psychological Association would be more stringent than the courts.

"Ethical Principles of Psychologists" (APA, 1990), *Standards for Educational and Psychological Tests* (APA, 1985), *Principles for the Validation and Use of Personnel Selection Procedures* (APA/SIOP, 1987), and the *Uniform Guidelines on Employee Selection Procedures* (EEOC, 1978) are a few of the documents that address the standards of care to which I/O psychologists are ultimately held. This is obviously a massive amount of information, and all of it is considered important. However, there are a few issues that are particularly pertinent to practice in organizational settings and should be addressed in any contract for consulting services.

Confidentiality

Confidentiality and the appropriate use of data are probably the most important issues to be discussed and included in a contract with an organization. The *Casebook on Ethics and Standards for the Practice of Psychology in Organizations* (Lowman, 1985) recommends clarifying with the organization all potential uses of data with all concerned parties including participants, supervisors, and personnel officials during negotiation. The *Casebook* (Lowman, 1985) also suggests that psychologists establish clear ground rules about how the results are communicated, to whom, and how the data are maintained. Psychologists "should be aware that data regarded as confidential may be sought by interested parties and take steps to protect the data" (Lowman, 1985, p. 45).

In this regard, all psychologists should be familiar with the laws governing confidentiality in the state in which they practice. A plaintiff can require that a psychologist testify even though participants were told the information would be kept confidential and the contract stated explicitly that the information would not be released. In 27 states in which psychologists have privileged communication by statute, they can successfully avoid testifying in court. However, the courts may be able to subpoena their records and, ultimately, psychologists may not succeed in protecting confidential information (Schwitzgebel & Schwitzgebel, 1980). The best protection for the consultant is to come to terms with the client on how the data are to be used, and include a statement to that effect in the contract for services. This will give the consultant more leverage to protect the information from inappropriate dissemination and/or use. Legalities aside, it is always important to remember that discretion goes a long way toward helping build trust among people (Golembiewski, 1990).

Research With Human Participants

Even though most consulting projects are not considered "research," psychologists must make every effort to protect the interests of the employees and other personnel who participate in the project. This is especially important when using assessment techniques and psychological tests. As discussed above, psychologists must protect the confidentiality of the information if it was promised as well as ensure that any information that is released is not misused.

There are several issues that are not explicitly covered in the "Ethical Principles" that could result in litigation. Psychologists must be aware of these issues and consider them in designing and conducting organizational projects. The main issues are invasion of privacy and misrepresentation. An invasion of privacy is usually defined as that which is "highly offensive to the reasonable man (sic)" (Schwitzgebel & Schwitzgebel, 1980). Many psychological test items could be considered invasions of privacy. Many people fail to see the need to reveal certain information and, as we know, some questions have very little face validity. In order to dispel the suspicion and uneasiness of the test takers, it is suggested that the purpose and rationale of the data collection be explained to them as clearly as possible. It is also good practice to include reliability and validity information in the work proposal and to state in the contract that the *Uniform Guidelines*, "The Ethical Principles of Psychologists" (APA, 1990), *Standards for Educational and Psychological Tests* (APA, 1985), and *Principles for the Validation and Use of Personnel Selection Procedures* (APA/SIOP, 1987) will be used to guide the project. This provides support for the psychologist by explicitly stating that the work must be performed in accordance with ethical and professional guidelines, in addition to providing protection for the participants from unfair discrimination and misuse of personal information.

Misrepresentation or deceit is another area of concern for the protection of participants. When fraudulent assurances of little or no risk are given or there is a failure to disclose risks that can be reasonably foreseen, the psychologist has misrepresented the study to the participants. Potential risks must be described as accurately as possible to allow the participant to make an informed decision about his/her involvement in the project. When a psychologist asks a person to participate, the decision to participate must be voluntary and with complete understanding of the risks involved. Without this understanding, the participant has not been completely informed, and it might be successfully argued that the research contract has been breached or is not even valid. It is the responsibility of the psychologist to inform the organization of these requirements and to gain management's cooperation to fully inform the participants of all information that would affect their decision to participate.

There is also a clear obligation to give meaningful feedback to any employees who are examined or assessed unless explicit exceptions are discussed and agreed upon before the project begins (Lowman, 1985). In any event, this condition must be made clear to the individual participant. It is advisable to inform participants who will have access to the data and how the data will be used. This protects the rights of the employee and helps ensure that the organization does not misuse the information. Telling the employees how the information is protected from misuse will also help to convey a concern for their welfare and possibly increase their trust in the organization and the psychologist. When working in an organizational setting, psychologists must assess the effects of a project or intervention on relevant groups and individuals before accepting and beginning the project. If this is not possible, a continual assessment of the use of information is essential to guarantee that information is used properly (Lowman, 1985).

Summary

Contracts are tools that are used to capture an agreement between a consultant and a client. The goal of the authors was to give the reader a basic understanding of contracts and to present ways that contracts can be utilized to accomplish the many goals of psychologists as consultants. Although they seem to have a power and existence unto themselves, contracts are only reflections of an understanding or formal dialogue that has been established between the consultant and the client. In this view, contracts are actually statements of the minimum standards that will govern the practice of the consultant. As industrial/organizational psychologists, it is our goal and responsibility to go beyond these minimum standards. However, the importance of these minimum standards should not be diminished. Only by adequately defining the starting point can we come to realize the factors and processes that will be crucial to the success of our efforts to go beyond them.

A Sample Contract

A discussion of a hypothetical contract will provide a concrete example of how the issues discussed above as well as others can be incorporated into an agreement. A few general suggestions include: (a) use plain language to ensure complete understanding, (b) consult a lawyer when negotiating and especially before signing a contract, (c) highlight or somehow draw attention to important parts of the contract by underlining or printing those sections in bold letters, and (d) because there is no guarantee of renegotiation or clarification, do not sign any contract that is not *totally* acceptable.

Appendix 7. A

CONSULTING PSYCHOLOGISTS
521 RESEARCH PARKWAY
ATLANTA, GA 30032

Ms. Pat Smith
Personnel Director
Widgets International, Inc.
Des Moines, Iowa 67789

Dear Ms. Smith:

Attached are materials relating to the development of a selection system for the Marketing Division of Widgets International. Additionally, these materials propose conducting six individual job content validation studies for the jobs in the Marketing Division.

THIS SUMMARIZES WHAT WILL BE DONE AND ALERTS MS. SMITH TO WHAT WILL BE DISCUSSED.

The accompanying flow chart reflects the different steps that must be executed to complete the work described in the first paragraph of this letter. This also summarizes the content validation methodology we propose to use.

PROVIDE FLOW CHARTS AND GRAPHS THAT CAN BE READ EASILY. IF THE INFORMATION IS NOT "USER FRIENDLY," THE COMPANY MAY MISS INFORMATION THAT IS IMPORTANT.

A second attachment reflects a cost of $38,000 to Widgets International for receiving these services partitioned into consultation fees and expenses. The timeline for the completion of key phases of the project and final deadline are also given. The contract guiding the delivery of these services is labeled Attachment A.

IT IS IMPORTANT FOR CONSULTANTS TO PROVIDE A TIMELINE FOR THE PROJECT. IF THE CONSULTANT EXPERIENCES ANY PROBLEMS DUE TO THE ORGANIZATION NOT FURNISHING INFORMATION OR NEEDED DATA, IT IS IMPORTANT TO INFORM THE ORGANIZATION THAT THERE MAY BE A DELAY IN MEETING THE DEADLINE DUE TO NO FAULT OF THE CONSULTANT. IN RETURN THE CONSULTANT SHOULD INFORM THE ORGANIZATION IF ANY DELAYS ARE

EXPECTED DUE TO PROBLEMS THAT ARE EXPERIENCED BY THE
CONSULTANT. THIS KIND OF COMMUNICATION SHOULD CONTINUE
THROUGHOUT THE PROJECT, NOT JUST IN TIMES OF DELAY OR
TROUBLE, IN ORDER TO ESTABLISH RAPPORT AND FACILITATE
UNDERSTANDING.

In closing, I believe that the attachments transmitted by this letter are
consistent with the earlier discussions which involved various Widgets International officials. We enjoyed working very closely with the officials and we
value the input from the employees.

STATEMENTS LIKE THIS LET THE COMPANY KNOW THAT THE
CONSULTANT HAS MET WITH THEM AND IS MAKING A REAL EF-
FORT TO ADDRESS THEIR NEEDS.

If you have any questions, feel free to contact me at (100) 123-4567.

Sincerely,

R. T. Gordon
Senior Psychologist

THE CONSULTANT MAY REFER TO HIM/HERSELF AS A PSYCHOLO-
GIST IF HE/SHE IS LICENSED. IF THE CONSULTANT IS NOT LICENSED,
A TERM THAT IS APPROPRIATE AND NOT MISLEADING SHOULD
BE USED.

ATTACHMENT A
AGREEMENT FOR SERVICES

This contract will set forth on May 29, 1990 the mutual understanding with respect to the consulting services (the "Project") to be performed by Consulting
Psychologists (the "Consultant") for Widgets International (the "Company").

THIS STATEMENT SPECIFIES THE DATE THE CONTRACT BECOMES
BINDING AND IDENTIFIES THE PARTIES TO THE AGREEMENT.

Services to be provided:
It is mutually agreed that such service will be undertaken and conducted according to the conditions described in the attached: (1) letter of transmittal,

(2) Work Flow and methodology chart, and (3) budget, all dated May 29, 1990, which are incorporated into the contract by reference.

THIS SECTION INCLUDES THE WORK PROPOSAL AND THE BUDGET IN THE CONTRACT BY REFERENCE AND SIGNIFIES THAT BOTH PARTIES AGREE TO THESE DOCUMENTS.

Term of the contract:
This agreement covers the period from May 29, 1990 to December 31, 1990. The final project report will be presented on or before December 31, 1990, provided, however, that a delay in signing the agreement beyond May 29, 1990, may cause the due date for completion to be forwarded to a later date that the two parties shall mutually agree upon.

THIS CLAUSE SAYS WHEN THE CONTRACT WILL BEGIN AND END. IT ALSO ALLOWS FOR A DELAY OF THE START OF THE PROJECT IF THE DATE OF ACCEPTANCE BY THE COMPANY IS ANY LATER THAN THAT STATED. WITHOUT THIS, THE CONSULTANT COULD BE OFFERING THE COMPANY A CHANCE TO RENEGOTIATE THE EN-TIRE CONTRACT IF THERE WERE A DELAY.

Payment:
In consideration of the services performed, the Company will pay the Con-sultant a total amount of $38,000, half ($19,000) of which will be payable on September 15, 1990, the midpoint of the project, and half ($19,000) of which will be payable at the completion of the Project and the Company's receipt of the Final Report as described below. The money shall be expended for com-pletion of the Project in a manner to be determined by the Consultant for sala-ries, wages, supplies, indirect costs, and other expenditures outlined in the at-tached budget. The Consultant and the Company mutually agree that funds may be transferred from one identified cost category to another at the Consultant's discretion.

THIS SECTION COVERS THE CONSIDERATION GIVEN TO BOTH PAR-TIES. THE CONSULTANT GETS MONEY AND THE COMPANY GETS SERVICES. ALSO, IT IS IMPORTANT TO STATE THAT THE CONSUL-TANT HAS CONTROL OVER THE TRANSFER OF FUNDS FROM ONE BUDGET AREA TO ANOTHER. IF THERE IS A CONFLICT, WITHOUT THIS PROVISION, THE COMPANY COULD SAY THAT THE CONSUL-TANT ACTED INAPPROPRIATELY BY TRANSFERRING FUNDS FROM ONE CATEGORY TO ANOTHER.

IT IS ALSO IMPORTANT TO NOTE THAT IN THIS CONTRACT FINAL
PAYMENT IS DUE UPON RECEIPT OF THE FINAL REPORT AND NOT
UPON THE COMPANY'S ACCEPTANCE OF IT. IF THE COMPANY
NEVER FORMALLY "ACCEPTED" THE REPORT, THEY COULD USE
THIS AS AN ARGUMENT AGAINST PAYING THE FINAL FEE. THE
POSSIBILITY OF THIS MAY BE SMALL, BUT IT HAS HAPPENED. THE
PSYCHOLOGIST MUST JUDGE EACH SITUATION TO DETERMINE IF
THIS IS NECESSARY.

Confidentiality:
In order to perform the obligations described in this agreement, the Company
agrees to disclose certain information concerning the Company, its organization, policies, and procedures. The Consultant considers all such information
about the Company and its affiliates, and the recommendations, reports or
other work produced during the performance of the services of this agreement, to be confidential information. Only authorized representatives of the
Company will be given access to this information unless explicit permission
is obtained in advance from appropriate Company representatives. *Any data
collected in the performance of these services that is promised to the individual employee to be confidential will be held in such confidence by the Consultant and not released in any individually identifiable form to the Company unless required by law. Data collected for these purposes may not be used for
other purposes unless employees are informed in detail of such purposes and
consent is obtained from each employee.* Any interns, assistants, and employees of the Consultant that assist in the performance of the Project will execute
an agreement containing confidentiality obligations identical to those contained in this Agreement with respect to the Confidential Information received by them.

THIS CLAUSE IS INCLUDED TO INFORM THE COMPANY ABOUT THE
NATURE AND USE OF CONFIDENTIAL INFORMATION. IT IS ALSO
A PROMISE THAT THE CONSULTANT WILL KEEP INFORMATION
ABOUT THE COMPANY CONFIDENTIAL. IT IS IMPORTANT THAT AS-
SISTANTS TO THE CONSULTANT SIGN A PLEDGE OF CONFIDENTI-
ALITY AS WELL. THIS CLAUSE DOES NOT COVER THE RELEASE OF
INFORMATION TO THE INDIVIDUAL EMPLOYEE. ANY PROVISIONS
FOR FEEDBACK TO THE EMPLOYEE COULD BE PLACED HERE OR
IN THE WORK PROPOSAL AND INCLUDED BY REFERENCE.

Professional Standards:
*As licensed psychologists, the Consultants are bound by the Ethical Principles
for Practice set forth by the American Psychological Association (APA) and
the Equal Employment Opportunity Commission (EEOC) Guidelines. These*

guidelines will be adhered to in every aspect of the Project. Any requests or requirements made of the Consultants or their representatives by the Company in the performance of this Project that violates the APA or EEOC Guidelines will be just cause for termination of this Agreement. The Consultant will then be exempt from any and all liability arising out of the performance of the Agreement. The Company will then assume any and all liability arising out of the performance of the Project including but not limited to counsel fees incurred in connection with the defense of any action brought against either party whether the liable action is won or lost by either party to this Agreement.

BY INCLUDING THIS CLAUSE, THE CONSULTANT IS DEFINING THE STANDARDS OF PRACTICE THAT WILL BE CONSIDERED APPROPRIATE. THIS COULD BE A HELP IF DURING LITIGATION THE PLAINTIFF TRIES TO BRING IN AN EXPERT WITNESS TO ESTABLISH STANDARDS OF PRACTICE THAT ARE NOT CONSISTENT WITH THOSE REFERENCED IN THE CONTRACT. THE CONSULTANT COULD ARGUE THAT BOTH PARTIES AGREED TO THESE STANDARDS AND THEREFORE THEY SHOULD BE THE STANDARDS CONSIDERED IN ANY LITIGATION. THIS CLAUSE ALSO RELIEVES THE CONSULTANT FROM THE CONTRACT IF THE STANDARDS ARE NOT FOLLOWED AND FROM FUTURE LIABILITY ARISING OUT OF PORTIONS OF THE PROJECT THAT WERE COMPLETED BEFORE THE CONTRACT WAS BREACHED.

Arbitration Agreement:
Any controversy or claim arising out of or relating to this Agreement, or the breach thereof, shall be settled by arbitration in accordance with the Rules of the American Arbitration Association, and judgment upon the award rendered by the arbitrator(s) may be entered in any court having jurisdiction thereof.

THIS SECTION IS RECOMMENDED BY THE AMERICAN ARBITRATION ASSOCIATION. SETTLING DISPUTES BY ARBITRATION IS USUALLY LESS COSTLY AND LESS TIME CONSUMING THAN COURT LITIGATION. THE INCLUSION OF THIS CLAUSE SHOULD BE BASED ON AN ANALYSIS OF THE SPECIFIC SITUATION. IT COULD BE ADVANTAGEOUS TO DELETE IT IN SOME SITUATIONS.

Final Report:
The company will be provided with a final report (the "Final Report") that includes an accurate and complete report of the method, all results, conclusions, and recommendations. This report will be prepared according to the EEOC Guidelines for validation reports.

THIS SIMPLY STATES THAT THE COMPANY WILL RECEIVE A FINAL
REPORT AND TELLS WHAT THAT REPORT WILL INCLUDE. PROB-
LEMS WITH REPORTING THE RESULTS ACCURATELY OR PRES-
SURE FROM THE ORGANIZATION TO SLANT THE RESULTS IS
SOLVED BY STATING THAT THE REPORT WILL BE ACCURATE AND
COMPLETE. THE REPORT WILL ALSO SATISFY THE EEOC GUIDE-
LINES.

Delay of Project:
The company shall hold the Consultant blameless in the event of one or more
emergencies which significantly disrupt the Project, including but not limited
to, the death, injury, illness or other non-availability of key personnel; natural
disasters; accidental erasure, alteration, or destruction of data, records or other
key project materials; delays in carriers; governmental acts and regulations;
or other related events. The Consultants shall exercise reasonable care in the
performance of their duties to the Company.

THIS SECTION EXEMPTS THE CONSULTANT FROM THE CONSE-
QUENCES OF EVENTS BEYOND HIS/HER CONTROL. IT IS ALSO A
PROMISE THAT THE CONSULTANT WILL USE CARE IN PERFORM-
ING HIS/HER DUTIES.

Ownership of work; Publication:
Ownership of the Final Report or other works produced by the Consultant for
the Company under this Agreement shall be the property of the Consultant.
Should the parties to this agreement decide that it would be advantageous to
publish the Final Report or a summary or any portion of the Final Report, the
determination of this may be made jointly by both parties, provided that the
Consultant may publish the results as a case study with no identification of
the Company if no other agreement is reached.

THIS CLAUSE MAY NOT MAKE IT PAST THE FIRST PHASE OF NEGO-
TIATION, HOWEVER, IT WOULD NOT HURT TO INCLUDE IT IN ORDER
TO SEE HOW THE COMPANY RESPONDS. THEIR RESPONSE COULD
ALERT THE CONSULTANT TO POTENTIAL PROBLEMS IN THE RELA-
TIONSHIP. AS IT STANDS, THE CLAUSE PROVIDES THE CONSULTANT
WITH OWNERSHIP AND ALLOWS THE CONSULTANT TO PUBLISH
THE RESULTS AS AN UNIDENTIFIED CASE STUDY WITHOUT FIRST
ASKING THE COMPANY FOR PERMISSION OR NOTIFICATION.

NOTE: OWNERSHIP AND PUBLICATION MAY ALSO BE ADDRESSED
SEPARATELY IF NEEDED.

Termination:

This Agreement may be terminated by either party at any time upon ten (10) days' written notice. In the event of termination, the Consultant will be compensated for actual costs and cost commitments incurred up to the date of termination. The Company agrees to make these reimbursements to the Consultant within twenty (20) days of billing.

THIS CLAUSE ALLOWS THE TERMINATION OF THE CONTRACT WITH THE AGREEMENT THAT THE CONSULTANT WILL BE REIMBURSED FOR EXPENSES.

THIS SEEMS TO BE STANDARD PRACTICE SO THE CONSULTANT SHOULD NOT BE HESITANT TO PUSH FOR THIS.

Notices:

All notices required or permitted to be given under this Agreement shall be in writing and delivered personally or by sending such notice by registered or certified mail, postage prepaid, addressed

  if to the Consultant: Consulting Psychologists
           521 Research Parkway
           Atlanta, GA 30032

  if to the Company: Ms. Pat Smith
           Personnel Director
           Widgets International, Inc.
           Des Moines, Iowa 67789

Independent Contractors:

Each of the parties is an independent contractor and nothing contained in this Agreement shall be deemed to constitute the relationship of partners, joint venturers, nor of principal and agent between the parties. Neither party may hold itself out third persons as purporting to act on behalf of, or serving as the agent of, the other party.

Severability:

If any term, condition or provision of this Agreement shall be found, by a court of competent jurisdiction, to be invalid or unenforceable, or to violate any Federal or State law, then the term, condition or provision so found shall be deemed severed from this Agreement, but all other terms, conditions, and provisions shall remain in full force and effect.

THIS CLAUSE ALLOWS FOR THE EXCLUSION OF ONE CLAUSE OR SECTION WITHOUT THE ENTIRE CONTRACT BEING DECLARED VOID.

Governing Law:
The validity, interpretation and performance of this Agreement shall be governed in accordance with the laws of the State of Georgia. This document constitutes the full understanding of the parties, and is a complete and exclusive statement of the terms of their agreement. This document supersedes all previous agreements, either oral or written, between the parties. No terms, conditions, understanding, or agreement designed to modify the terms of this agreement shall be binding unless they are made in writing and signed by each of the parties.

THIS CLAUSE IS ESPECIALLY IMPORTANT IF THE CONSULTANT PRACTICES OUTSIDE HIS/HER STATE OF RESIDENCE. EVEN THOUGH THIS IS GOOD PROTECTION, CONSULTANTS SHOULD BE FAMILIAR WITH THE LAWS OF STATES IN WHICH THEY PRACTICE OR CONSULT A LAWYER FOR INFORMATION THAT MAY AFFECT THIS CONTRACT. IT IS ALSO IMPORTANT BECAUSE IT OVERRIDES ALL PREVIOUS ORAL AND WRITTEN AGREEMENTS. IF ANYTHING IN THE CONTRACT CONTRADICTS WHAT WAS DISCUSSED, THE CONSULTANT SHOULD NOT LET IT GO UNMENTIONED.

The Agreement is approved and accepted by both parties and is executed by the signatures of authorized representatives of both parties. Both parties have read the above contract and have indicated that they understand it.

R. T. Gordon	Pat Smith
Senior Psychologist	Personnel Director
Consulting Psychologists	Widgets International

WITH THE SIGNING OF THE CONTRACT, IT HAS BEEN EXECUTED AND IS LEGALLY BINDING. IT IS IMPORTANT THAT BOTH PARTIES STATE THAT THEY UNDERSTAND THE CONTRACT SO THAT THE COMPANY CAN NOT CLAIM THAT THEY WERE CONFUSED ON AN ISSUE OR PROVISION. THIS WOULD ALSO BE IMPORTANT IN PROVING INFORMED CONSENT.

NOTE: IF THE COMPANY WILL NOT LET THE CONSULTANT RETAIN OWNERSHIP OF THE DATA AND THE REPORT, HE/SHE SHOULD MAKE EXPLICIT PROVISIONS FOR THE APPROPRIATE USE, DISSEMINATION, AND CONTROL OF THE DOCUMENTS. THIS COULD BE ACHIEVED BY HAVING THE COMPANY AGREE TO SIGN A POSTWORK CONTRACT BEFORE THE INFORMATION WILL BE RELEASED. THE CONTRACT COULD OUTLINE THE USE OF THE INFORMATION AND STIPULATE HOW THE CONFIDENTIALITY WILL BE MAINTAINED. IT WOULD ALSO BE WISE TO PUT A COVER LETTER ON THE ACTUAL DOCUMENTS INFORMING USERS OF ITS CONFIDENTIAL NATURE. THE CONTRACT COULD ALSO REQUIRE THE COMPANY TO CONSULT THE PSYCHOLOGIST BEFORE USING THE INFORMATION TO DETERMINE THE APPROPRIATENESS OF ANY PROPOSED USE.

ANY ETHICAL AND LEGAL GUIDELINES THAT NEED TO BE SPELLED OUT EXPLICITLY CAN BE INCLUDED IN THE CONTRACT AND/OR THE WORK PROPOSAL. EVEN THOUGH THE STANDARDS OF PRACTICE ARE IMPLICITLY INCLUDED IN THE CONTRACT, IT WOULD NOT HURT TO OUTLINE THEM IN THE DOCUMENTATION. THIS COULD PREVENT PROBLEMS AND MISUNDERSTANDINGS DURING THE PERFORMANCE OF THE PROJECT. ANYTHING THAT CAN BE DONE TO PREVENT THE PROJECT FROM STOPPING WILL ULTIMATELY BENEFIT THE CONSULTANT, THE EMPLOYEES, AND THE ENTIRE ORGANIZATION.

References

American Psychological Association. (1985). *Standards for educational and psychological tests*. Washington, DC: Author.

American Psychological Association, Society for Industrial and Organizational Psychology. (1987). *Principles of the validation and use of personnel selection procedures* (3rd ed.). Berkeley, CA: Author.

American Psychological Association. (1990). Ethical principles of psychologists. *American Psychologist, 45*, 390-395.

Equal Employment Opportunity Commission. (1978). *Uniform guidelines on employee selection procedures*. Washington, DC: Government Printing Office.

Golembiewski, R. T. (1990). *Ironies in organizational development*. New Brunswick, USA: Transaction Publisher.

Lowman, R. I. (1985). *Casebook on ethics and standards for the practice of psychology in organizations*. College Park, MD: Society for Industrial and Organizational Psychology, Division 14 of the APA.

Morawetz, V. (1925). *Restatement of the law of contracts.* Washington, DC: American Law Institute.

Privette, M. J. (1985). *Sign here?: All you need to know about contracts.* Garden City, NJ: Doubleday.

Schwitzgebel, R. L., & Schwitzgebel, R. K. (1980). *Law and psychological practice.* New York: John Wiley.

Zelig, M. (1988). Ethical dilemmas in police psychology. *Professional psychology: Research and practice, 19,* 336-338.

8

Using Government Information and Other Archives

JACK McKILLIP
HUGH STEPHENSON

As every independent consultant knows:

Information = Time × Money.

Information and time are what consultants provide. Clients provide the money. The challenge is to maximize information while minimizing required time and money. The good news is that, for many questions, needed information already exists. Allocating alcohol treatment resources, planning health education outreach programming, locating a satellite office or a business, or describing potential markets are more likely to require use of existing government reports and data archives than collection of new data. The task of the consultant is to find and adapt information from reports and archives to answer the question at hand.

This chapter presents sources of government records and other archives, describes strategies for locating this information, and reviews basic estimation techniques. The emphasis is on orientation and starting points. As a consultant becomes more experienced in working with this information, its depth, utility, and limitations will become more apparent. Generating original information will often require spending more

AUTHORS' NOTE: Thanks to Dr. Walter Stubbs of Morris Library, Southern Illinois University at Carbondale, for help in preparing this chapter.

time and money than using techniques presented in this chapter. Whether spending more time and money will produce better information depends on the question and the information already available. For many tasks, use of existing information is appropriate. For others, existing information can provide a guide and context for on-site data gathering. Whether working with business, government, or human services, government reports and other data archives are available to aid need assessment, marketing, program planning, and social policy evaluation.

Finding Government Records and Other Archival Information

The U.S. government is awash in information. It conducts censuses of population and housing on years ending in 0; censuses of governments, transportation, businesses, manufacturers, mineral industries, and construction industries in years ending in 2 and 7; and a census of agriculture in years ending in 4 and 7. The U.S. government also conducts extensive surveys related to economic factors, health, crime, and education. Most of this government-conducted and -supported information is available in report form at one of 1400 depository libraries (A Directory of U.S. Government Depository Libraries, 1987). Much of the original data is available for a relatively low fee from the National Technical Information Service (NTIS).[1] Evinger (1988) and Stratford and Stratford (1987) present compendiums of the government data archives.

University and government-supported groups also maintain vast archives. In addition to government data sets, Inter-University Consortium for Political and Social Research[2] has archived extensive economic and social science research data files for the past 30 years. With funding from the National Institute of Child Health and Human Development, Sociometrics has created an extremely accessible archive of research data sets about families and related issues—the *American Family Data Archive*.[3] Kiecolt and Nathan (1985) and Stewart (1984) provide excellent introductions to secondary data sources both within and outside the government.

Government and other archived data sets usually represent well-designed, large-scale, multivariable studies with adequate to good documentation. Although requiring computer and statistical expertise, they present a source of information on multiple topics at a small fraction of the cost of original data collection. There are drawbacks, however. Archived data sets may no longer be current for the population or topic of interest. Demographic shifts or changes in economic and social factors may make archived information of more historical than current interest. The exact wording of questions used in the archived study may not meet present requirements, and this inconsistency may not be apparent until after several hours of investigation. Sieber (1991) presents a discussion of issues related to use of archived data.

U.S. Census

Because of the extraordinary scope of its geographically based data, most independent consultants will make or have made use of U.S. census information. The just completed 1990 Census is similar in the information gathered and level of problems experienced to 1970 and 1980 censuses (Kaplan & Van Valey, 1980). Table 8.1 presents the information gathered in the 1990 Census of Population and Housing. These questions yield both direct and "derived" characteristics—that is, those based on calculations using two or more questions. For example, income and household size combine to compute the population in poverty.

The Bureau of the Census has gone to extraordinary lengths to make the 1990 Census available and useful. Among the important developments is the topical integrated geographic encoding and referencing system, or TIGER, which maps every inch of the United States. TIGER line files contain codes for census geographical areas, cities, townships, governmental units, voting districts, and Zip codes for streets. In addition, the Bureau of the Census has added the capability to produce data on geographical areas that cross traditional units (e.g., school districts) through its User-Defined Areas Program.[4]

TIGER files are available as maps and in various computer readable formats. TIGER files can be integrated and displayed with the population, social, economic, and housing data from the census providing detailed maps of population, economic and housing characteristics for small areas. Like all computer-based technology, there are hardware, software, and training costs for use of TIGER files.

A number of options have been added for access to census information. Among these are the availability of census data on CD-ROM and on-line,[5] in addition to the more technically demanding computer tapes.

Table 8.1 Question Content From 1990 Census of Population and Housing: Population and Sample Components

Questions to Entire Population

Population	*Housing*
Household relationship	Number of units in structure
Sex	Number of rooms in unit
Race	Tenure—owned or rented
Age	Value of home or monthly rent
Marital status	Congregated housing (meals included
Hispanic origin	in rent)
	Vacancy characteristics

Questions to Sample

Population	*Housing*
Social characteristics	Year moved into residence
Education-enrollment and	Number of bedrooms
attainment	Plumbing and kitchen facilities
Place of birth, citizenship, and	Telephone in unit
year of entry into the U.S.	Vehicles available
Ancestry	Heating fuel
Language spoken at home	Source of water and method of sewage
Migration (residence in 1985)	disposal
Disability	Year structure built
Fertility	Condominium status
Veteran status	Farm residence
Economic characteristics	Shelter costs, including utilities
Labor force	
Occupation, industry, and class	
of worker	
Place of work and journey to work	
Work experience in 1989	
Income in 1989	
Year last worked	

The costs of CD-ROM technology are within the reach of most independent consultants, and, especially in combination with the more expensive TIGER system, open tremendous possibilities for small area analysis. TIGER and summary tape file (STF) CD-ROMs of census information are available for inspection and use at state data centers and at many of the depository libraries. (Two orienting publications are

Census ABCs and *Hidden Treasures: Census Bureau Data and Where to Find It.*[6])

Search Strategies

Many consultants will be less likely to use government information or other records in order to carry out independent analyses, than to have access to descriptions of populations and places. Reports of government information are available and even more extensive than the data sources themselves. The problem is finding the information. An excellent starting point is three census publications that combine census information with that of other government and nongovernment sources:

- *Statistical Abstract of the United States*, 1991
- *State and Metropolitan Area Data Book*, 1991
- *County and City Data Book,* 1988[7]

These are available in book form, on floppy disk, or on CD-ROM. Each volume presents more than 1,000 pages of tables of quantitative information on a wide range of topics for specified geographical areas: from population characteristics to social, government and business indicators. Aside from the wealth of substantive material, all data in these publications are referenced. These references can be consulted when more extensive or detailed information is needed.

A second search strategy uses the *American Statistical Index* (ASI), an extensive guide to quantitative information published by the U.S. government. A key word search yields references to documents that present statistical information on the topic during a specific year. Companion sources to the ASI are the *Statistical Reference Index*, for state and local government and for business organization data, and the *Index to International Statistics*, for statistical information for international organizations. Each of these references is encyclopedic and provides author, title, other bibliographic information, and a short abstract of cited materials.

A search of 1990 and 1991 entries for "homelessness" reveals ten 1991 and eleven 1990 entries, nine in ASI and twelve in SRI. Computerized versions of the ASI allow use of multiple key words. Searching on homelessness and "women" reveals six citations and searching on homelessness and "children" reveals seven citations. The ASI, available at most large libraries, references reports of quantitative information by topic.

These references are particularly useful in a government depository library because the identified reports will also be available.

These search techniques are not substitutes for knowledge of professional literature. An expert can often identify reports that are more timely and appropriate than those published and indexed. However, often it is the role of consultants to be acquainted with many areas but masters of none. Much can be accomplished with the support of a government documents librarian. If all else fails, advertising in the journal *American Demographics* provides listings of data-acquisition consultants.

Working With Published Reports

Among the challenges to using published information or data from archives are (a) adapting statistics on a reference population (e.g., the nation) for the target population, (b) updating information from previous to current time periods, and (c) using correlated or proxy indicators when measures of the construct of interest are not available. There are many ways to develop estimates and approximations that, like analysis of raw data, can be both time consuming and relatively expensive (e.g., trend analysis and regression analysis). Several simpler approximation and estimation techniques will be illustrated: synthetic estimation, the ratio method, symptomatic estimation, and the use of proxy indicators.

Synthetic Estimation

Often information is available on an indicator of interest for a population larger or different from the area or subpopulation of interest. Statistics on a topic can be identified for a reference population but are unavailable for the target group. For example, a consultant may identify pregnancy rates for the nation or a state, but be unable to locate this information for a particular county or university student body (McKillip, 1987). In this case the consultant may estimate the target group statistic based on the reference population information. Difficulties arise because it is not credible to assume that the target group experience is exactly the same as that of the reference population. Adjustment for local characteristics is necessary.

One method of adjusting national or other reference population statistics for use in local estimates is synthetic estimation. This technique

Table 8.2 Synthetic Estimation of Mental Disorders,
Jackson County, Illinois, 1990,
Adjusting for Age and Gender

Age	Jackson County[a] Men (1)	Women (2)	National Rates per 100[b] Men (3)	Women (4)	Estimated Prevalence All Disorders Men (1)/100 × (3)	Women (2)/100 × (4)
18-24	9775	7500	16.5	17.3	1613	1298
25-44	8947	8139	15.4	19.2	1378	1563
45-64	4109	4422	11.9	14.6	489	646
65+	2542	4033	10.5	13.6	267	548
Total	49,467				7801	

NOTE: Numbers in italics are estimated.
a. 1990 Census, STF1.
b. One month prevalence, all disorders (Regier et al., 1988).

was developed by the National Center for Health Statistics (NCHS) to provide estimates of health status for states based on national data (Holtzer, Jackson, & Tweed, 1981; Levy & French, 1977; Schaible, Brock, Casady, & Schnack, 1979). National statistics on the incidence or prevalence of illness and accidents were used to predict the state level experience. The basic assumption of synthetic estimation is that variation between the target and reference population on an indicator to be estimated is due primarily to differences in population characteristics. Except for differences in distribution of population characteristics, rates for the two populations are the same. A county may differ from the nation in the prevalence of a mental disorder because the county's population differs from that of the nation on, for example, gender or age. If differences in population characteristics are adjusted, the reference population rate can be used to estimate the target population rate.

In order to do synthetic estimation, two types of information are needed: demographic characteristics of the target population and reference population indicators for each of the target demographic groups. Table 8.2 provides an example of the use of national estimates of the prevalence of mental disorders to estimate prevalence for a single county. In this example the nation was the reference population and the county was the target population. County population counts were taken from the 1990 Census (STF1) and national prevalence rates were taken from published literature (Eaton & Kessler, 1985; Regier et al., 1988).

The first two columns in Table 8.2 give the 1990 Age × Gender population counts for the county. The next two columns present national, one month prevalence rates for all mental disorders for each demographic subgroup. Notice that the national rates differ by age and gender—younger people and women have a higher prevalence of disorder. The assumption of synthetic estimation is that the rates of mental disorder for the county differ from that for the nation only because of differences in the age and gender distributions. The final two columns of Table 8.2 give synthetic estimates. These subpopulation estimates are summed for the county estimate. The overall synthetic estimate is that 15.8% of the county population, as compared to 15.4% of the national population, experience a mental disorder any month.

The credibility of the synthetic estimate depends on the validity of the assumption that, except for differences on demographic characteristics, the target and reference populations experience the estimated property at the same rate. This assumption is likely to be valid when the national indicator varies as a function of the population characteristics and not because of other factors. Synthetic estimates for larger populations are probably more accurate than those for smaller populations, as are those for heterogeneous rather than homogeneous groups.

Ratio Method and Symptomatic Estimation

A second estimation situation arises when a consultant needs target population indicators that are more current than those available. Unlike the problem described for synthetic estimation, information *is* available on the target population, but it needs to be updated. Such estimation problems often arise when working with census information. Reliable statistics on poverty, fertility, or other derived indicators are only available for many counties, cities, or census tracts every 10 years. During the interim period, revised statistics must be estimated.

The ratio method and symptomatic estimation were designed for updating census population characteristics and together are sometimes called the *vital rates procedure* (Bogue, 1950; Lee & Goldsmith, 1982; Rives & Serow, 1984). The techniques can be combined. First, statistical information or rates must be gathered for both the reference and the target population at some base time, typically a census year. A ratio of

Table 8.3 Example of the Ratio Method and Symptomatic
Estimation (adapted from Rives & Serow, 1984)

	Population	
Steps	*Reference*	*Target*
Ratio Method		
A. Fertility		
Rate in 1990	0.065	0.052
Ratio	0.052/0.065 = 0.80	
B. Fertility		
Rate in 1995	0.060	$0.060 \times 0.80 = 0.048$
Symptomatic Estimation		
C. Births in 1995		824
Women 15-44 in 1995		$824/0.048 = 17,167$
D. Ratio of Men to Women in 1990		1.10
Men 15-44 in 1995		$1.10 \times 17,167 = 18,884$

NOTE: Numbers in italics are estimated.

the statistics is computed, dividing the target statistic by the reference statistic. Unlike the synthetic estimation procedure that assumes that the underlying rates for the target and reference populations are the same, symptomatic estimation assumes that the ratio of these rates is constant over the time of estimation. That is, whatever factors account for differences in rates, these factors do not diverge during the estimation period. Differences in rates are assumed to remain stable.

The second step in the ratio method is to identify the current statistic for the reference population. National and state characteristics are usually available yearly. If the ratio assumption in the first step is accepted, the updated reference statistics can be used with the ratio from the first step to update the target statistic. This updated statistic may then be used as part of a symptomatic estimation of additional target population characteristics.

Table 8.3 presents an example adapted from Rives and Serow (1984) for fertility rates (the number of births per women aged 15-44). If a state (reference population) is found to have a fertility rate of .065 in the 1990 census and the target city has a fertility rate of .052, the method assumes that the ratio of these statistics (.80) will be stable for a number of years (Step A). The ratio can be combined with updated state information to update the target city statistic. In the example, the state's 1995 fertility rate, .060, is multiplied by the ratio of Step A to estimate the 1995 city fertility rate, .048 (Step B). The ratio method does not assume that fertility rates are the same for both populations. It assumes that the factors influencing the state and the city fertility rates are stable over the estimation period.

A third estimation step may now be taken. This step of symptomatic estimation takes advantage of current information that may be available on the target population. This current information, such as vital statistics on births, deaths, or marriages are usually available from county or state health departments on a timely basis. Other local current information includes crime statistics and school enrollments. This current information can be combined with the updated statistics of Step B to develop symptomatic estimates.

In the example of Table 8.3 the updated fertility rate for the city can be combined with the symptomatic indicator of births to estimate the number of women in the target population between the ages 15 and 44. This new indicator can then be used to estimate the number of men in the age group. Births are taken as "symptomatic" of women of fertility age. The number of women is taken as a "symptomatic indicator" of the number of men. Such population estimates by age and gender may not be available for the city until the year 2000.

In Step C of Table 8.3 dividing the number of births to residents of the city (824) by the estimated fertility rate of .048 generates an estimate of 17,167 for women between the ages of 15 and 44. The ratio of men to women can be taken from the 1990 census, or perhaps updated by the ratio method to 1995. If the ratio of men to women age 15-44 in the target population is 1.10 and the number of women 15-44 is 17,167, the symptomatic estimate of the number of men 15-44 in the target population in 1995 is 18,884 (i.e., $17,167 \times 1.10$, Step D).

Symptomatic indicators will be useful to the extent that they correlate with the indicator they are used to estimate. The more estimation steps that are made and the longer the time between the base year and the estimation year, the less credible the estimates. More sophisticated estimation procedures take the correlation between symptomatic and estimated indicators into account.

Table 8.4 Proxy Indicators of Alcohol Abuse for
Five Illinois Counties

	Mortality Rate per 100,000 Motor Vehicles		
County	Cirrhosis	Motor Vehicle Accident	Suicide
Adams	9.6	25.2	10.2
Alexander	6.7	30.0	8.3
Bond	1.2	27.3	6.2
Boone	7.6	18.7	11.1
Jackson	5.9	20.5	5.9

SOURCE: U.S. Alcohol Epidemiologic Data Reference Manual (1991).

Proxy Indicators

A third estimation situation arises when direct measures of the construct of interest are not available. The rational for symptomatic estimation leads to a wide number of estimation procedures based on empirical explorations of the relationships among population, social, and economic indicators (Lee & Goldsmith, 1982). Measures that correlate with the construct of interest can be used as proxies for this construct. Although the logic is straightforward, the use of proxy indicators is much more complex in application than are the other estimation techniques discussed in this chapter.

Because direct measures of alcohol abuse are not available for small areas, the National Institute on Alcohol Abuse and Alcoholism (NIAAA) has produced a manual of proxy indicators for states and counties (*U.S. Alcohol Epidemiologic Data Reference Manual,* 1991). Indicators were selected based on demonstrated relationship to alcohol abuse in the research literature and regular availability. Klosterman, Stephenson, Roe, Lavelle, and Vaux (1989) used these indicators to do a risk analysis for alcohol abuse planning for 34 counties in southern Illinois.

Table 8.4 presents three proxy indicators of alcohol abuse from the *U.S. Alcohol Epidemiologic Data Reference Manual* for 5 Illinois counties. This source estimates that from 41% to 95% of the deaths from cirrhosis involve alcohol, as do from 42% to 53% of the motor vehicle deaths and 20% to 37% of the suicides. Inspection of the table reveals both the strength and weakness of the use of proxy indicators. On the positive side, NIAAA has made a wealth of alcohol abuse-related information easily available for very small areas. On the negative side, none of the information is what is directly needed, incidence of alcohol abuse. Mortality statistics, while available and reliable, are only trailing indicators of abuse. The multiplicity of indicators reveals another aspect of the use of proxy indicators—all indicators do not tell the same story. Among the 5 counties Adams has the highest mortality rate from cirrhosis, Alexander the highest motor vehicle death rate, and Boone the highest suicide rate. Which county has the highest prevalence of alcohol abuse? On the other hand, multiple proxy measures may reflect different facets of a problem so that their convergence may provide a more convincing estimate.

Multiple measures, even those sharing the common mortality metric, require synthesis. McKillip (1987) reviews synthesis techniques of ranking, standardization, and multiattribute utility analysis. Another approach would include the population of the county by translating mortality rates into predicted number of deaths. Use of more sophisticated models requires greater familiarity with the substantive problem area and opens the door to less obvious assumptions about indicators and their relationships. Among the many complexities of using a proxy-indicator approach is the *ecological fallacy* that relationships identified at aggregate levels (e.g., census tract or county) may not hold at individual levels (Milcarek & Link, 1981).

Conclusion

Acquaintance with government reports and data archives can open wide areas for consultation. This information is relatively easy to use, especially for professionals with a general social science background and some computer expertise. Easier access to census information will provide ever-widening information uses, and the increasing practice of archiving research data promises to lessen the cost of answering a wide range of questions.

Like other techniques, use of existing data and the various estimation techniques can be used incorrectly. A sensible approach is to make multiple estimates from multiple sources, where possible. Multiple estimates can provide confidence intervals to guide both the consultant and client. Where more sophisticated techniques are appropriate and affordable, they should be used. However, these sophisticated techniques can also be checked by simple estimates based on existing information.

Wide availability of government reports and other information resources can be a boon to the independent consultant. Given the immense costs and complexities of large-scale studies, skills for finding and working with existing information are likely to be employed as or more often than skills of generating and analyzing data. Time and resources can be invested wisely in developing information from existing data sources.

Notes

1. National Technical Information Service, 5285 Port Royal Road, Springfield, Virginia 22161; (703) 487-4763.

2. ICPSR, Institute for Social Research, P.O. Box 1248, Ann Arbor, Michigan 48106; (313) 763-5010.

3. AFDA, Sociometrics Corporation, 170 State Street, Suite 260, Los Angeles, California 94022; (415) 949-3282.

4. User-Defined Areas Program, Bureau of the Census, Washington, DC 20233; (301) 763-4282.

5. CENDATA can be accessed through DIALOG and CompuServe.

6. Customer Services, Bureau of the Census, Washington DC 20233; (301) 763-4100.

7. Published in years ending in 3 and 8.

References

A directory of U.S. government depository libraries (Y4.P 93/1-10:987). (1987). Washington, DC: Government Printing Office.

Bogue, D. J. (1950). A technique for making extensive population estimates. Journal of the American Statistical Association, 45, 149-163.

Eaton, W. W., & Kessler, L. (Eds.). (1985). Epidemiology field methods in psychiatry: The NIMH epidemiologic catchment area program. New York: Academic Press.

Evinger, W. R. (Ed.). (1988). Federal statistical databases. Phoenix, AZ: Oryx Press.

Holzer, C. E., Jackson, D. J., & Tweed, D. (1981). Horizontal synthetic estimation. Evaluation and Program Planning, 4, 29-34.

Kaplan, C. P., & Van Valey, T. L. (1980). Census 80: Continuing the fact finder tradition. Washington, DC: Superintendent of Public Documents.

Kiecolt, K. J., & Nathan, L. E. (1985). *Secondary analysis of survey data: Quantitative application in the social sciences* (Vol. 53). Beverly Hills, CA: Sage.

Klosterman, B., Stephenson, H., Roe, C., Lavelle, E., & Vaux, A. (1989). *Needs assessment of alcohol/drug abuse services in southern Illinois.* Carbondale: Department of Psychology, Southern Illinois University at Carbondale.

Lee, E. S., & Goldsmith, H. F. (1982). *Population estimates: Methods for small area analysis.* Beverly Hills, CA: Sage.

Levy, P. S., & French, D. W. (1977). *Synthetic estimation of state health characteristics based on the health interview survey* ([PHS]) 78-1349). Hyattsville, MD: National Center for Health Statistics.

McKillip, J. (1987). *Need analysis: Tools for the human services and education.* Newbury Park, CA: Sage.

Milcarek, B. I., & Link, B. G. (1981). Handling problems of ecological fallacy in program planning and evaluation. *Evaluation and Program Planning, 4,* 23-28.

Regier, D. A., Boyd, J. H., Burke, J. D., Rae, D. S., Myers, J. K., Kramer, M., Robins, L. N., George, L. K., Karno, M., & Locke, B. Z. (1988). One-month prevalence of mental disorders in the United States. *Archives of General Psychiatry, 45,* 977-986.

Rives, N. W., & Serow, W. J. (1984). *Introduction to applied demography: Data sources and estimation techniques. Quantitative applications in the social sciences* (Vol. 39). Beverly Hills, CA: Sage.

Schaible, W. L., Brock, D. B., Casady, R. J., & Schnack, G. A. (1979). *Small area estimation: An empirical comparison of conventional and synthetic estimators for states* ([PHS]) 80-1356). Hyattsville, MD: National Center for Health Statistics.

Sieber, J. E. (Ed.). (1991). *Sharing social science data: Advantages and challenges.* Newbury Park, CA: Sage.

Stratford, J., & Stratford, J. S. (1987). *Guide to statistical materials produced governments and associations in the United States.* Alexandria, VA: Chadwyck-Healey.

Stewart, D. W. (1984). *Secondary research: Information sources and methods.* Beverly Hills, CA: Sage.

U.S. alcohol epidemiologic data reference manual (ADM) (3rd ed., 91-1740). (1991). Hyattsville, MD: National Institute on Alcohol Abuse and Alcoholism.

9

Using Graphical Displays to Empower Evaluation Audiences

GARY T. HENRY

In every evaluation, between the data collection and the conclusions, evaluators scrutinize the data, test and retest their assumptions and hypotheses, and construct meaning from what they have found. This process is a "black box," when seemingly, it is necessary for the evaluators to be estranged from the stakeholders and the program they are evaluating. The data analysis and interpretation processes are technical ones: requirements for competent analysis and reasonable conclusions demand that expert judgments dominate the evaluation agenda at this juncture. But we wonder, "How is the evaluation audience to know that the data support our conclusions and recommendations?" or "What other conclusions may have been equally warranted?"

This issue has been discussed by the proponents of stakeholder evaluations and auditors of qualitative evaluations (Greene, Doughty, Marquart, Ray, & Roberts, 1988). However, the issues are just as relevant for those who view evaluations as a scientific activity (Shadish & Epstein, 1987). From this standpoint, evaluators may ask, "How can we avoid as many pitfalls as possible in reaching conclusions?" or "How can we reveal the data to those who seek to understand the program and its implications?" Although replication and secondary analysis, in theory, protect us from these problems, they do not obviate

AUTHOR'S NOTE: The author would like to recognize Kevin Kitchens, Kent Dickey, and Virginia Ginn for their contributions to this chapter.

the need for answers to these questions. Secondary analysis is too rare and too late to reach the primary audience for the information.

The evaluation problem is clear. Quite reasonably, evaluation sponsors expect evaluators to analyze the data and draw conclusions. The usual procedures require technical expertise, computer hardware and software, and perhaps the most scarce resource, time. In undertaking these tasks, the evaluator becomes a filter for the information that goes to the audiences. The consumers' understanding, and "bottom line" from the evaluation, is set by the evaluator. Evaluation consumers cannot be expected to pick up a data disk and do their own analysis. A solution is needed that would reveal the data to its consumers, allow them to do their own analysis, and increase their confidence in the evaluation findings. The essential skill for applied researchers and consultants is to reveal evaluation data in a way that can stimulate analysis and questions about the results by the members of the evaluation audience willing to expend the effort. In this chapter, I argue that evaluators can use graphical analysis and displays to more fully reveal the data to the audiences and empower them with information.

Graphical Displays in Evaluation

Using graphical displays is not a novel idea for evaluators. A casual review of the evaluation journals reveals considerable use of graphical displays. Many fall in the category of graphs not using data, such as depictions of conceptual models, flow charts, and organizational charts. Graphical data displays are more unusual. Feinberg (1979) supports the conclusion that nondata graphics were more prevalent than data graphics in two statistics journals since 1950. In addition, he found that the use of data graphics was declining. Again, a casual review leads me to opine that evaluation reports make greater use of data graphics than the articles in evaluation journals. When we talk to each other we may use a more technical, narrative shorthand than we can use when we share the results with the audiences for our reports.

Intuitively, evaluators have grasped the advantages of using graphics with their report consumers. Graphs communicate quickly and directly. Graphs decorate and entertain. Tufte (1983; 1990), while stressing the substantive importance of graphics, gracefully reminds us not to overlook the elegance with which graphs can carry out these functions. But graphics can do more than illustrate the author's point or enhance a report's aesthetics: the untapped potential of graphics lies in their use for opening up the analysis of data to evaluation audiences.

Feinberg (1979) describes a continuum of purposes for graphics from communication to analysis. On the one end are two categories of graphs described by Tukey (1988): graphs which substitute for tables and graphs that show the results of some other technique. The most popular statistical graph, the trend line (Tufte, 1983), and the bar chart are examples of these graphs. On the other end of the continuum are analytical graphs that "let us see what may be happening over and above what has already been described" (Tukey, 1988, p. 38). Benefits from utilizing analytical graphics are twofold, accruing to both evaluators and audiences. For example, evaluators can glean more from the data and diagnose problems with a particular analysis. Analytical graphs can also serve a purpose with the evaluation audience. Utilizing the capacity to reveal relationships through analytical graphics may enable evaluators to open up the black box that lies between data collection and conclusions and in the process, empower their audiences.

Empowering the Audience

The importance of empowering evaluation audiences relates directly to the philosophical underpinnings of democratic evaluation (MacDonald, 1976). In this type of evaluation, the central value is that of an informed citizenry, and the evaluator takes the role of information broker. The evaluator gives, to those interested, access to information that will allow them to think through the impact of the program and develop their own conclusions. Through graphical data displays, evaluators can "encourage the eye to compare different pieces of data" and "reveal the data at several levels of detail, from a broad overview to the fine structure" (Tufte, 1983, p. 13). Without access to the data, the evaluation audiences are captives of the evaluator's rationale or the reason they have made from their findings. As Liebniz declared, *nihil est sine ratione* ("there is nothing without its reason"). However, other rationale and/or explanations may fit the results just as well as the evaluators'. But unless the data are revealed to the audience in a way they can interpret for themselves, the audience does not have the ability to construct their own explanations for the results. Analytical graphics have the potential to give consumers the option of analyzing the evaluation data for themselves and constructing their own rationale.

To fully appreciate this point, it is important to understand the two traditional methods of reporting evaluation findings. But first, a point must be made that most evaluators consider obvious—evaluation data are complex in most cases. Multiple outcome measures can lead to differences in the assessment of program performance. Initial differences in clients, whether students or parolees, often lead to different levels of and probabilities for success. Thus, an important caution, simple presentation can lead to simplistic and even wrong-headed impressions of the program.

Data Tables

First, we can provide evaluation audiences with tables that display the data for each case or unit and let them ferret out the conclusions through their own analysis. Often, evaluation reports (and reports with evaluative information) include pages of tables. While the intention of providing the consumers with the "actual data" is admirable, their access to the information is limited by the format. If the consumers exhaust their time, energy, and capacity without understanding the relationships or performance of the target/subject of interest, or come to unwarranted or inaccurate conclusions, we may take some comfort that at least we gave accurate data and, perhaps secondarily, we are not responsible for how they use it.

Summary Statistics

A second option is to analyze the data and provide summary conclusions to the consumers. The results of a statistical test of a hypothesis, the interpretation of the direction of a relationship using a regression coefficient, or an estimate of the effect size or confidence interval (Reichart & Gollob, 1989) are methods that summarize data and provide some guidance about the significance and magnitude of relationships.

But the technical artifacts of these relationships do not give as much information to the audience as they may need. In addition, the consumer of the information becomes a captive of the evaluator's analysis and rationale. More sophisticated analysis distances the user of the evaluation further from the evaluative data itself. Yet without a more sophisticated analysis, the consumer can be misled about program success. For example, looking at measures of student achievement without taking the socioeconomic status of their family into account can mislead observers about the impact of schooling.

Finally, these summary analyses do not provide information on specific cases or program sites. For example, analysis of residuals (actual minus predicted outcome measure scores) gives attention to performance of an individual unit after controlling for other variables. However, residual analysis requires some technical sophistication to understand and may imply unwarranted precision in the results.

Graphical Display

Graphical display of evaluation data represents an alternative option. Graphical displays have often been used as a means for presenting data to an evaluation audience simply and concisely. Also, graphical displays can enable the audience to conceptualize the data and its meaning for themselves.

Shapes found in a variety of plots help in drawing comparisons between individual units, groups of units, or a single unit over time. Much graphical innovation in the late 20th century has been in the development of techniques that permit multidimensional displays (Beniger & Robyn, 1978; Feinberg, 1979), despite the fact that we face the physical limitation of the two dimensions of a piece of paper or computer screen. Tufte (1990) terms this problem "escaping flatland." His words are compelling:

> The world is complex, dynamic, multidimensional; paper is static, flat. How are we to represent the rich visual world of experience and measurement on mere flatland? (p. 9)

We cannot expect to overcome the limitations of two-dimensional paper and ink displays in most evaluation reports. The copy machine and the FAX machine impose real constraints on practice that we must live with. However, the graphical arsenal is well stocked despite this constraint.

Our perceptions of the audience and the importance of data inhibit the use of graphics. The "sound bite" mentality inflicted on us by the popular media places a premium on speed at the expense of understanding. We should begin with the presumption that the members of the evaluation audiences are at least as intelligent as ourselves and at least as interested in the program. Their interest in the evaluation data is determined by the relevance of the data being presented to them and other pressures on their time. We can apply what E. B. White has said of writing to graphics: "No one can write decently who is distrustful of the reader's intelligence, or whose attitude is patronizing" (in Strunk & White, 1959, p. 70) Tufte (1983) has shown that some Japanese and German news publications use relatively sophisticated graphics, but no United States publication has reached their level of sophistication. We must consider that we may receive what we give in this regard. If we make evaluation data appear simplistic and obvious, the consumer may regard it as such.

Data show that we can go further. In experiments involving teachers, journalists, and others in the education community, the accuracy of comparisons was 67% for multiple univariate graphics versus 63% for tables (Henry, McMillan, Dickey, & McTaggart, 1991). For a multivariate graphical display, an accuracy rate of 70% was obtained. Thus complex graphics can be used as accurately as tables by typical evaluation audiences. To encourage use, graphical design should provide overview information as quickly as reasonable. This can be aided by clear titles, labels, legends, and some narrative. But they should offer more information for a greater investment of time. Some examples of data displays with these characteristics are presented in the next section.

Examples of Multivariate Graphical Displays for Evaluation

Modern techniques are available that enable evaluators to take advantage of graphics in comparing complex, multidimensional phenomena. Comparisons are at the heart of evaluation: comparisons between groups (e.g., treatment versus control groups, and case studies); comparisons between individuals and a group (e.g., outliers, exceptional cases, and rankings); comparisons of impacts over time (e.g., interrupted time series); and comparisons of a group or individuals with externally derived standards. In this section three examples of data displays that facilitate comparisons will be presented:

a. multiple site, multiple outcome measures,
b. relationships between a dependent variable and two independent variables, and
c. multiple group, multivariate relationships.

Multiple Site, Multiple Outcome Measures

Graphical displays can provide an immediate overview of the performance of each individual, unit, or evaluation site on several outcome

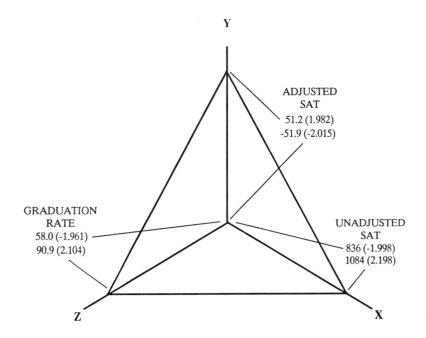

Figure 9.1. The Star Graph Display for Three Educational Outcomes

measures. Analysis becomes a process of comparing shapes of the units or patterns and discrepancies in plots. Well-designed graphical displays focus attention on the outcomes, rather than on the method or form of the graph. Analysis is encouraged because the extent of technical training needed to interpret multivariate analysis is not required to interpret the graphical displays. Consumers must spend time decoding the display, before they can interpret the data presented in the display. However, familiarity with a new type of graphic display develops quickly, allowing rapid understanding of new data.

The STAR icon (see Figure 9.1) is one of the most promising graphical displays for evaluation data (Anderson, 1957, cited in Feinberg, 1979). STARs are not literally stars, but plots that end up as polygons having as many sides as the number of variables to be plotted. Three variables, which will be displayed as triangles, are the minimum.

STARs have several advantages. First, they are relatively easy for a nontechnical audience to decode. The more often these plots are used the quicker the decoding process is for the consumer of the information. Second, these plots require relatively simple mathematical manipulations of the data and in most cases can be developed to allow the audience to read actual values directly from the display. Third, the STAR icons involve two graphical perception tasks—perception of angles and of area—that are capable of being perceived with reasonable accuracy (Cleveland & McGill, 1984; Simkin & Hastie, 1987). Fourth, STARs can be used for comparing the variable values of one unit, or, in the same display, for comparing the values across several units. Fifth, the shape of the graph and its area is interpretable by a quick scan, even in cases in which a member of the audience does not wish to invest the time in using the full analytic potential of the display. The STAR icons can be sorted by an important variable to promote specific comparisons and analysis. Finally, software packages are available in the market that include these displays. All of the data displays in this chapter are done with the SYGRAPH/SYSTAT software package, although some have been enhanced with additional text and drawing.

Each year, the Department of Education has published educational performance data for the fifty states and the District of Columbia in a large table that is called the *Wall Chart* (Ginsburg, Noel, & Plisko, 1988). Using the data obtained from the Wall Chart, published in 1989, student performance indicators: SAT scores and graduation rate, were selected for analysis using graphical displays. In addition, a third outcome measure, a SAT score adjusted for the percentage of students taking the test, is included (Powell & Steelman, 1984; Powell & Steelman, 1987; Wainer, 1986). Figure 9.1 shows the STAR icon using these three outcome variables.

The axes have been drawn in Figure 9.1 for illustrative purposes. In practice, the axes are omitted from the display. The three axes X, Y, and Z correspond to the unadjusted SAT score, adjusted SAT score, and graduation rate, respectively. The triangle has been drawn to correspond to the highest value for each of the three variables. For the 50 states and the District of Columbia (DC), the highest average unadjusted SAT score was 1084 and the lowest was 836. The standardized score is given in parenthesis. The graduation rate ranged from 58.0 percent to 90.9 percent. The adjusted SAT score, which is depicted on the vertical axis, ranged from 51.2 above predictions based on the percentage of students taking the exams to 51.9 below predictions.

In Figure 9.2, the performance of the states in the southeastern region on the three outcome variables discussed above are displayed. Area or

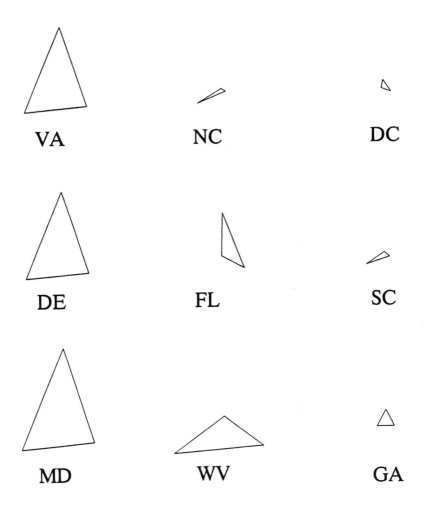

Figure 9.2. Educational Outcomes for the Southeast: An Example of the Star Icon Display

size of the triangle is an indicator of performance on all three variables. Maryland has the largest overall area, indicating the highest cumulative score, defined as the sum of the three variables. However, the relative similarity in shape and size of Delaware and Virginia indicate that the first place designation is a distinction without a difference. In all three cases, the adjusted SAT score seems to register the highest performance in intrastate comparisons. Graduation falls next, as shown by the lower left corner. All three do less well on the unadjusted SAT, suggesting that a high percentage of students took the test. The District or Columbia exhibits the lowest overall performance and its weakest score is the graduation rate on the Z axis, which indicates the area in which improvement is most needed.

North Carolina and South Carolina have similar performance patterns. Their relative strength is in the graduation rate. However, it does not appear to be a strong score when compared with the three states on the left side of the graph. Florida's weakness is the graduation rate when compared with its other outcome measures and the other states. Georgia displays an equilateral pattern indicating no relative strength or weakness among the three measures. Yet at a glance, the size of the Georgia triangle gives an overall indication of weak performance on these three measures. For those interested in a specific state, its internal strengths and weaknesses can be assessed and its performance can be compared with other states using the STAR icon.

Another application using the STAR icon is shown in Figure 9.3, which shows the performance of one school division on four composite indicators of performance. Each of the composite scores is displayed on an axis. The four composite indicators, running from north to east to south to west are graduation rate, college preparation, special education, and work preparation. The endpoints of the axis display the number of variables making up each composite. For example, there are eight variables that make up the graduation rate composite and six for work preparation. The number on which the school district performed at or above expectations is defined by the points of the STAR, which in this case is a box or four-sided figure. The area of the diamond shows the overall performance of the school district. Data for the district plotted in the example show strength in graduation rate, college preparation, and special education. Work preparation appears to need attention. Side-by-side comparisons with similar districts would provide additional useful information for parents, educators, and taxpayers.

The STAR icon is a useful and versatile technique for displaying evaluation results. Its usefulness diminishes when more than six outcomes variables are to be displayed, due to the difficulty in distinguishing the individual axes. To use the STAR icon all data must be standardized or be in the same original metric. This makes the maximum

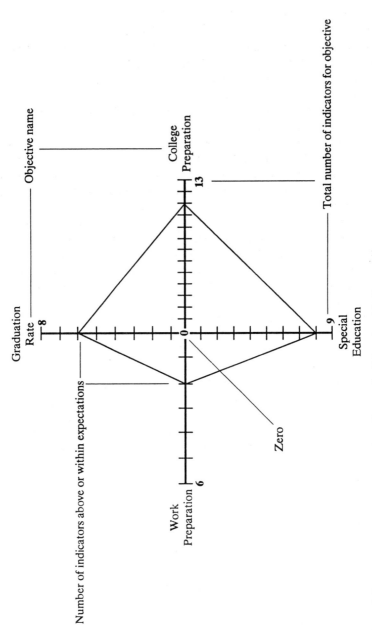

Figure 9.3. The Star Graph Display for Four Composite Educational Indicators

score on each of the axes of approximately equal length. Also, the values for all cases must be positive, which requires a simple additive transformation with standardized scores.

Relationships Between a Dependent and Two Independent Variables

The usefulness of two-variable plots is no news. They allow the viewer to assess the strength and direction of a relationship between two variables as well as showing cases that do not seem to fit the general pattern (outliers). It is interesting that the perception of the amount of correlation decreases as the size of the plot increases (or as the scale decreases) (Cleveland, Diaconis, & McGill, 1982).

Because we are limited to the two dimensions of the paper, adding a third variable has seemed implausible or undesirable. Playing tricks with perspective to simulate the perception of depth is best left to visual artists. (For examples of the distortions that depth perspective can cause, see Tufte, 1983, pp. 53-77.) However, size of the symbol provides a third graphical element that can be varied. In that the third variable is to be represented by area, a two-dimensional construct, some care is needed. For example, the perception of size of square symbols is a function of their area or length multiplied times width ($l \times w$), which is length squared (l^2) in that it is a square. When square symbols are being used as in the example presented here, it may be useful to use the square root of the original variable to avoid distortion ($l^{1/2} \times l^{1/2} = l$). To encourage visual distinction I find that a ratio of 1:7, the ratio of the smallest observation to the largest is preferred. Achieving these objectives can require some creative transformations.

In Figure 9.4, a bivariate plot of the adjusted SAT score, described in the earlier section, and the level of education in each state is shown. Education is measured as the percentage of the population with a college education. The relationship appears to be linear and well summarized by the regression line that is drawn. In Figure 9.5, an additional variable has been added using the size of the symbol, percentage of white population in the state.

First, draw an imaginary horizontal line through the mean of the dependent variable ($Y = 0$). Do the squares above the line appear to be larger, smaller or about the same size as the squares below the line? On average, they are larger. This indicates that there is a relationship between adjusted SAT scores and the percentage of white population. In fact the correlation is .32.

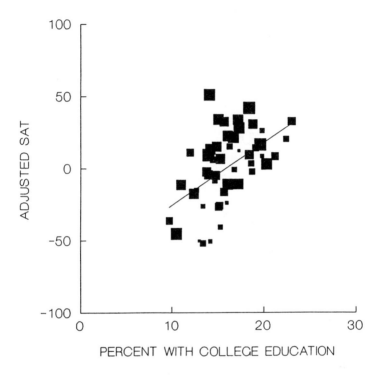

Figure 9.4. Relationship Between Level of Education and Adjusted SAT Score for States

Now observe the difference in the size of boxes above and below the regression line, drawn on Figure 9.5. If the boxes above the line appear to be larger, as they do to me, then there is a relationship between adjusted SAT and race after controlling for education. Thus both variables are important in understanding the adjusted SAT scores.

Of course, these measures leave something to be desired in evaluating state educational performance, but they illustrate the point that comparing performance without taking these variables into account can be misleading. Grasping these patterns may convince skeptical audiences

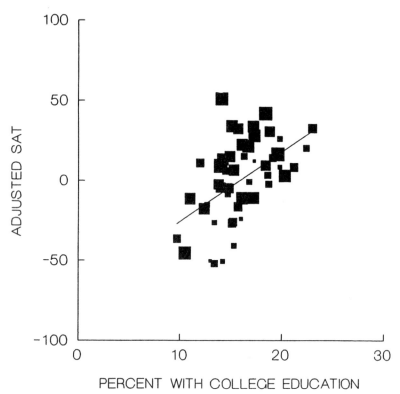

Figure 9.5. Relationship Between Level of Education, Percentage of White Population and Adjusted SAT Scores for States

that educational performance is to some extent dependent on factors that cannot currently be controlled by educators. Or put another way, current educational technology is not producing similar results in states in which educational levels and racial characteristics of the population differ.

Multiple Group, Multivariate Comparisons

It is common in evaluations to examine the responses of different groups on a number of variables. The variables may be impact or outcome measures or they may be attitude measures, such as satisfaction or efficacy. In the experimental to quasi-experimental tradition, groups may be treatment and control or comparison groups. In a less formal setting, they may represent different levels or functions within an organization. In this example, data from stakeholder group representatives is presented (Henry, Dickey, & Areson, 1991). The evaluation is an educational performance monitoring experiment and the stakeholder groups represented are teachers, school district superintendents, school board members, and an education group that included professionals representing higher education, special education, gifted education, NAACP, and principals. In this case, it was expected that the groups would differ on their opinions about the performance monitoring system because their institutional positions—and, therefore, the degree to which they were to be held accountable by the system—were very different. It is often expected that teachers, who have an institutional position at the bottom of the hierarchy, will be the most negative about accountability systems.

The graphical display is a complement to analysis of variance or dummy variable regression. In Figure 9.6, the responses of each participating stakeholder to three questions about the process are given. The three items were selected from a principal components analysis as the items related to quality of the system and commitment to it. For all three items, five represents the most positive response about the system and the development process and one the least positive. The results indicate a relationship between commitment and methodological quality. However, the results do not indicate the direction of the relationship. Did confidence in the methodological quality inspire commitment to the system?

The figure shows that the means for all items were around three, the neutral point on the scale. Also, at a glance the variation for all groups appears to be prominent. The performance system was controversial, but the data show a variety of opinions within the groups. There is no apparent effort to "circle the wagons" against the system as one might have conjectured. This may not have been noticed without the graph.

Contrary to some expectations, the school boards, as the publicly appointed, lay stewards of the education system, were not the most positive and the teachers were not the most negative about a system that would increase accountability. In fact, as the figure shows, teachers were the most positive and the relationship was statistically significant. The most consistently negative group were the superintendents, al-

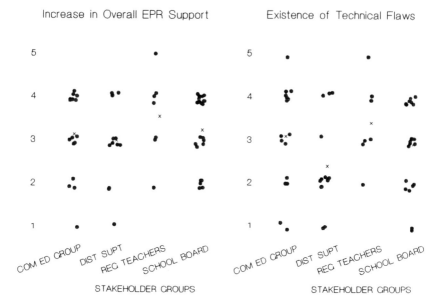

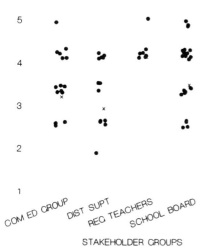

Figure 9.6. Stakeholder Opinions Concerning Outcome Accountability: Three Items by Group
NOTES: x = group mean; • = one observation

though their opinions were not uniform by any means. This is probably attributable to the fact that the system was to report at the school district level and, thus, they would bear the brunt of the added accountability directly.

Figure 9.6 focuses attention on the data directly without the mediating and sometimes confusing language of hypotheses testing. The stakeholders and those interested in the process can look at the data, speculate about the cause for differences and similarities and come to their own conclusions. They can focus on the magnitude of effects and differences before considering the probability of having the differences be due to chance alone. In short, they are empowered by the evaluators to think for themselves.

Conclusions

Statistical graphics are empowering tools for evaluation consumers. The audiences for the evaluation can view the data directly and in a way that facilitates thought and speculation about the results. Evaluators can enhance their role as information brokers called for in democratic evaluations by using graphics to reveal evaluation data to stakeholders and the public. In the role of a management consultant, graphics can make the data accessible to the management without interpretation or "spin." Graphs can become the vehicle for developing plausible interpretations with management and focusing discussion on the issues raised. Graphical displays should be used to a greater extent in evaluation reports and presentations. They are a natural complement to other descriptive and analytic statistics.

There are costs associated with incorporating analytical graphics in evaluations. The obvious costs are the hardware and software, and the evaluators' time in the design, programming and refinement of the graphics. Each of the displays in this chapter took several hours to prepare. None were produced from canned routines on raw data. However, available software can make the process much more efficient. Many packages will import data in a variety of formats and have the statistical routines needed for other analysis.

Another cost is the investment of time in learning and practicing design principles. Some standards have been promulgated, but they are more useful for general guidance than as rules. Listed below are some principles that I have developed or borrowed from others[1] and that I attempt to apply in my work.

- *Make graphs multifaceted.* To the casual observer they should present an overview and to the more interested they should stimulate thought and speculation about the evaluation results and their underlying causes.

- *Make the most important comparisons most obvious.* The most important comparisons should be most proximate, easy for the eye to follow along a horizontal line if possible; use length along a common scale (e.g. simple bar charts) before angle and area (e.g., pie charts and pictograms); and 3-D perspective and hatch patterns that cause optical illusions should be avoided.

- *Make graphic data dense.* Present as much data in as small a space as feasible. Obviously, there are limits to this based on aesthetics and ability to distinguish data points.

- *Use graphs to show relationships and multivariate phenomena.* Too often graphs are overly simplistic and do not attempt to give the audience the richness of the findings.

- *Shadings and color hues are the least effective means to convey quantitative differences.* Choose shading carefully to highlight differences in divided bar charts and pie charts—i.e., have adjacent pie slices displayed with maximum contrast, dark to light to dark; avoid using cross-hatchings that are difficult to distinguish and cause optical illusions.

- *Sweat the details.* Titles, axes labels, legends, scales, symbols, shadings, and size can affect the audience's ability to perform the analytical tasks, print the graph out and see if it can be understood without accompanying text.

- *Decide on the data that are the most important and most in need of analysis.* Graphing every bit of data and every possible comparison can have a numbing effect on the interest of the audience, use your judgment about which data are most important and most interesting.

Another cost is incurred in overcoming the "acquired taste" barrier to graphics. Anecdotal evidence indicates a propensity to be wary of statistical graphics on the part of evaluation audiences. The would-be graphic analyst often finds the first taste of examining a graphic difficult and unfulfilling. Good design can remediate to some extent, but not entirely. To engage them in analysis, this barrier must be overcome. My suggestion is to find a type of display that is useful for a variety of evaluation problems, such as the STAR icon, and use that type of display repeatedly during a presentation. In addition, the discussion should focus on substance of the data before the group, whether in a report or a presentation. Go slowly but make the explanatory points in terms of the displays before them rather than discussing the graphs in abstract terms. Pose evaluative questions and walk them through the analytical process with the actual displays.

Finally, I recommend that you experiment with data graphs, trying different formats and procedures. Be willing to take risks and offer the data in graphical format. Use the graphs to give your analysis and interpretations. Point out anomalies and inconsistencies in particular cases. Modeling these behaviors can foster the analytical approach and refine the audiences' taste for more information, greater understanding of the programs, and more statistical graphics.

Note

1. Ed Tufte introduced me to graphical statistical methods in a graduate seminar in the late 1970s. Since that time my intellectual debt to several scholars in the field has piled up as quickly as the national deficit. Tufte's (1983) *The Visual Display of Quantitative Information* is my first recommendation for anyone with more than a passing interest in graphical display. A most useful practical guide to graphics, in a most unusual source, is in Leland Wilkinson (1988) *SYGRAPH: The System for Graphics*. This is the manual for the graphics package integrated with SYSTAT. For those interested in theory, see Jacques Bertin (1983), *Semiology of Graphics*. If you wish to look for other types of graphs and more guidance in statistical graphics, John Tukey and William Cleveland are two authors with tremendous range and depth in the field. Specifically, I recommend *Exploratory Data Analysis* by Tukey (1977) and his collected works edited by Cleveland. Cleveland is the second author of a text that presents a wide array of statistical graphics and does not require much mathematics, *Graphical Methods for Data Analysis* (Chambers, Cleveland, Kleiner, & Tukey, 1983). Finally, Calvin Schmid's (1983) *Statistical Graphics* provides examples, suggestions, and generally good advice on more standard graphics, such as trends and bar charts.

References

Beniger, J. R., & Robyn, D. L. (1978). Quantitative graphics in statistics: A brief history. *American Statistician*, *32*(1), 1-11.

Bertin, J. (1983). *Semiology of graphics*. Madison, WI: University of Wisconsin Press.

Chambers, J. M., Cleveland, W. S., Kleiner, B., & Tukey, P. (1983). *Graphical methods for data analysis*. Pacific Grove, CA: Brooks/Cole.

Cleveland, W. S., Diaconis, P., & McGill, R. (1982). Variables on scatterplots look more highly correlated when the scales are increased. *Science*, *216*, 1138-1141.

Cleveland, W. S., & McGill, R. (1984). Graphical perception: Theory, experimentation, and application to the development of graphical methods. *Journal of the American Statistical Association, 79,* 531-554.

Feinberg, S. E. (1979). Graphical methods in statistics. *American Statistician, 33*(4), 165-178.

Ginsburg, A. L., Noel, J., & Plisko, V. W. (1988). Lessons from the wall chart. *Education Evaluation and Policy Analysis, 10*(1), 1-12.

Greene, J. C., Doughty, J., Marquart, J. M., Ray, M. L., & Roberts, L. (1988). Qualitative evaluation audits in practice. *Evaluation Review, 12*(4), 352-375.

Henry, G. T., Dickey, K. C., & Areson, J. C. (1991). Stakeholder participation in educational performance monitoring systems. *Educational Evaluation and Policy Analysis, 13*(2), 177-188.

Henry, G. T., McMillan, J. H., Dickey, K. C., & McTaggart, M. J. (1991). *Evaluating graphical displays: An analysis of univariate and multivariate formats.* Paper presented at the American Education Research Association meetings, Chicago, IL.

MacDonald, J. B. (1976). Evaluation and the control of education. In D. Tawney (Ed.), *Curriculum evaluation today: Trends and implications* (pp. 123-136). School Council Research Studies. London: Macmillan.

Powell, B., & Steelman, L. C. (1984). Variations in state SAT performance: Meaningful or misleading? *Harvard Educational Review, 54,* 389-412.

Powell, B., & Steelman, L. C. (1987). On state SAT research: A response to Wainer. *Journal of Educational Measurement, 24*(1), 84-89.

Reichardt, C. S., & Gollob, H. F. (1989). Ruling out threats to validity. *Evaluation Review, 13*(1), 3-17.

Schmid, C. F. (1983). *Statistical graphics.* New York: John Wiley.

Shadish, W. R., & Epstein, R. (1987). Patterns of program evaluation practice among members of the evaluation research society and evaluation network. *Evaluation Review, 11*(5), 555-590.

Simkin, D., & Hastie, R. (1987). An information-processing analysis of graph perception. *Journal of the American Statistical Association, 82*(398), 454-465.

Strunk, W., Jr., & White, E. B. (1959). *The elements of style.* New York: Macmillan.

Tufte, E. R. (1983). *The visual display of quantitative information.* Cheshire, CT: Graphics Press.

Tufte, E. R. (1990). *Envisioning information.* Cheshire, CT: Graphics Press.

Tukey, J. W. (1977). *Exploratory data analysis.* Reading, MA: Addison-Wesley.

Tukey, J. W. (1988). Some graphic and semigraphic displays. In W. S. Cleveland (Ed.), *The collected works of John W. Tukey* (pp. 37-62). Pacific Grove, CA: Wadsworth & Brooks.

Wainer, H. (1986). Five pitfalls encountered while trying to compare states on their SAT scores. *Journal of Educational Measurement, 23*(1), 69-81.

Wilkinson, L. (1988). *Sygraph.* Evanston, IL: SYSTAT.

10

Preparing Reports and Presentations That Strengthen the Link Between Research and Action

CYNTHIA ROBERTS-GRAY

Having the freedom to experiment with innovative and tailored-for-the client reports and presentations is one of the major advantages of being an independent evaluation and applied research consultant. When you work "in house" there almost always is a formal set of guidelines or approved formats and procedures for reports and presentations. But when you are on your own, every new job and every new client gives you a new opportunity to improve methods and formats for communicating results of applied research and evaluation studies. You can shape your reports and presentations to fit clients' preferences and needs for receiving and using research and evaluation data. You can take advantage of word processing and computer graphics capabilities to integrate verbal and visual media to converge on the points you want to make. You can be experimental, creative, and stylish in capturing and holding the attention of your audience.

This freedom to experiment with improved methods for making reports and presentations does not, however, relieve you of responsibility for communicating in ways that gain serious hearing when program or policy decisions are made. The rationale for applied research and evaluation is that it should provide information for action. Even if it succeeds in expanding our knowledge base or in building better theories, applied research and evaluation fails in its purpose if it is not seen and heard when decisions are made (Weiss, 1971). It is, therefore, incumbent upon you, the applied research and evaluation consultant, to take advantage of opportunities to develop, evaluate, and promote improved methods for producing timely, trustworthy, easy-to-use reports and presentations that help link research to action.

As an aid to your pursuit of better methods for making reports and presentations, this chapter is divided into sections that correspond to the three phases of decision making. According to Herbert Simon's *The New Science of Management Decision* (1960) and John Dewey's analysis of *How We Think* (1933), decisions are made by answering the following sequence of problem-solving questions: (a) What is the problem? (b) What are the alternatives? and (c) Which alternative is best? The first section of this chapter explores the problems you face in preparing reports and presentations so that they will gain serious hearing when decisions are made. The second section provides an overview of alternative report formats and presentation styles. The third section summarizes rules of thumb for deciding which alternative is best—that is, it addresses strategies for empowering members of your target audience to use information produced through applied research and evaluation.

What Is the Problem?

If our purpose is to gain serious hearing when decisions are made, then our problem is defined by asking who needs what information to support what kinds of decisions.

Specifying the Audience for the Report or Presentation

There are at least four levels of decision making that may or may not be part of your target audience for a specific report or presentation. A handy mnemonic for remembering the different levels of decision making is to think of them as four P's: practice, program, policy, and public. The most effective reports and presentations will be those that are sensitive to differences in "need to know" at these different levels of decision making.

Practice. First-level managers and staff make daily decisions close to the line where products and services are delivered. Their decisions help translate programs and policies into actual practice. Decision makers at this level need information that helps them adjust or alter their operations so as to contain costs and/or increase benefits or impact line level activity. They want data descriptive of what is working, what is not working, and what can be done to make their operations as effective and efficient as possible. When they receive an evaluation report they expect to see data showing the extent to which activities are being carried out as planned, objectives are being achieved, staff and participants are satisfied with current practices, and expenditures are within budget. This kind of information helps first-level managers decide what accolades should be awarded or adjustments made to maintain high-level performance.

Program. At the next level up the decision hierarchy is the program or division manager. These individuals provide guidance, recruit resources, and enforce sanctions to orchestrate activities and translate policy into programs. In order to make informed decisions, this audience needs information about the extent to which (a) activities of work units or program components are in compliance with performance requirements and outcome expectations, (b) units or individual projects have staff and supplies to implement planned activities, and (c) performance within and across units is timely and effective in addressing program goals and objectives.

Decision makers at this second level usually are very much interested in evaluation reports and presentations that compare performance of different units. These comparisons help to identify strengths and to detect common problems. Program managers can use this kind of information to help them decide where to direct technical assistance, supplemental resources, and guidance to establish conditions that enable all components to perform as well as possible alone and in concert.

Policy. Decision makers at this third level translate ideas and goals into plans and prescriptions for action. They must choose which programs to adopt, expand, or advocate in preference to other programs or action plans. They need data and information that helps them understand the theory or logic of various program models. They also need information about differential effectiveness of program models or policies that might be adopted.

Among the specific things policymakers expect to see in reports and presentation are (a) graphics and testimony that illustrate and clarify the logic or theory supporting the program model, (b) data that compare costs and benefits of the different models or prescriptions for action, and (c) testimony or data to document the extent of need for and the acceptability of adopting a new policy or modifying existing policies. They need hard facts about which they can feel confident. They want to know that there was rigor and objectivity in research that generated facts about costs and benefits of the alternatives so that their choice of the "best" alternative can be relied upon and defended.

Public. A fourth level of decision maker that may be in the target audience for your reports and presentations is the public. People in communities in which policies and programs are implemented or in which products and services are developed or delivered need information about the value of the practices and facilities that are or could be made available to preserve a healthy environment, solve life problems, and promote the common good. Their decisions establish climate, context, and environmental conditions that enable or bar the pursuit of particular ideas and goals. Decision makers at this level are justified in expecting that evaluation and applied research reports and presentations will supply them with information they can use to advocate for adoption or continued support of certain philosophies and/or specific courses of action. Although they may be interested in seeing data that compare benefits and costs of different courses of action or seeing statistics that quantify the magnitude of need or demand for a service or product, they are more likely to respond to expert testimony, compelling examples, and case studies. They desire and need information that is easy to use in persuading themselves and their friends and neighbors that they should contribute their endorsement, time, talent, and money to support a course of action that clearly is the "best" alternative.

Anticipating How the Information Will Be Used

Even if we remain alert to the possibility that our target audience includes decision makers at one or more levels in the decision hierarchy and that their needs to know may be different one from another, we may still fail to solve the problem of how to prepare the best report if we forget that there are a variety of uses for information generated from applied research and evaluation. Data and arguments presented in the report can be used to (a) inform, (b) persuade, (c) reinforce, (d) document, and (e) be proof of project completion. Reports and presentations inform decision processes when they include data and arguments that would not otherwise have been available to members of the target audience. Reports can also be written to persuade—that is, to convince or induce readers to do something. When the report or presentation includes data that can be used to support or commend previous actions or statements of decision makers who are in the target audience, it is useful as a reinforcer. Sometimes reports are useful simply to document or chronicle events so that the information can be retrieved if it is needed at some future date. Finally, a report can serve as tangible evidence that project requirements have been fulfilled.

Sometimes when we are preparing reports and presentations we get lost in the demands of being accurate and timely and forget that we ought to have a clear and specific reason for taking the readers' or listeners' time. More often than we like to admit, we write to fulfill project requirements and fashion the report to provide ample documentation for future reference. But we ascribe our writing to a wish to inform or to the hope that it will reinforce previous action or persuade the audience to take new action. Given that kind of scenario, it is not surprising to find that the report is decried as a "weak link" in the chain of events leading from research to action (DeLoria & Brookins, 1982). If we are to strengthen this weak link, we should make a habit of anticipating and being responsive to the range of uses to which the members of our target audience may put the information they find in our reports and presentations. Having a specific use or set of uses fixed firmly in mind will facilitate selection of methods and data to include or emphasize in your report, help you make decisions about sequence and structure for presenting the information, and direct your choice of words, format, and length.

What Are the Alternatives?

As a spark to your creativity in finding solutions to the problem of making reports and presentations that will gain serious hearing when decisions are made, I offer this survey of five report formats and presentation styles: (a) traditional technical reporting, (b) information design, (c) modular communication, (d) rapid responsive reporting, and (e) chart essay.

Traditional Technical Reporting

The tradition in technical reporting is to begin with an introduction or background section that includes a statement of the problem and the purpose for the research and evaluation study. The methods section then lists the hypotheses that were tested or the evaluation questions that were addressed. This section also describes means that were used to collect and analyze qualitative or quantitative data to measure participation, implementation, outcomes, benefits, costs and/or other variables relevant in testing the hypothesis or answering the evaluation questions. The results section specifies and evaluates the findings. The report usually ends with a discussion or conclusions section that may or may not include recommendations for action. Although this format is regularly accused of being "scientific" or "methods" oriented rather than "policy" oriented (Jones & Mitchell, 1990) and of being written for researchers rather than for executives (Mangano, 1989), it is the most frequent form of evaluation and applied research report.

The traditional technical report format is popular for several reasons. First, it is a familiar and accepted form among researchers and evaluators. Making changes in familiar forms means taking risks and, as I will argue, sometimes requires extra investments of time and energy. When we are pressed for time or uncertain of our audience, it is easier to rely on a proven format than to try something new. Another reason for the popularity of the technical report format is that it lends itself to the purposes of chronicle and of fulfilling project requirements. It also affords the writer ample space and opportunity to document rigor and objectivity of the work and to explore competing explanations of findings so that, at the end, readers can feel confident that the conclusions are trustworthy and defensible.

Among the disadvantages of using the traditional technical report format are that it presents new information somewhere in the middle rather than at the beginning or end of the report and usually leaves it up to the reader to figure out how the information can be used to formulate persuasive arguments or to award commendations. These reports also tend to be very long and appear to be addressed to no one in particular. For these reasons, a number of research and evaluation specialists have invested considerable time and energy in developing and teaching alternative styles for communicating results of applied research and evaluation studies.

Information Design

This format makes it easy for the reader to locate specific pieces of information. Headings and subheadings are placed in the margins to provide a "map" to the text. Information design puts heavy emphasis on avoiding redundancy while building a logical, easy to follow argument. Its principles can be applied in preparing both methods-oriented and decision-oriented reports. The writer can, if it is deemed appropriate, put the results section ahead of the methods section and/or write persuasive arguments or commendations into headings and subheadings. This approach is illustrated in a page from an information design report presented in Figure 10.1.

Among the few disadvantages of the information design approach is that it requires extra work. The writer must think about the sequence in which to present the material rather than relying on the familiar template of the traditional technical report. Information design reports also tend to be text intensive because the format does not easily accommodate liberal use of graphics.

Modular Communication

The modular communication style of reporting relies so heavily on graphics that it is sometimes referred to as graphics-oriented (GO format). Information is presented in modules each consisting of a two-page spread in which one page summarizes the module's thesis in a picture, graphic, or set of information "bullets" and the second page provides narrative to support and elaborate the thesis (see Figure 10.2). This method for making research and evaluation reports was derived from the story board procedure that often is used to develop screenplays. Like information design, modular communication can be used to produce methods-oriented or decision-oriented reports (cf. Figure 10.3).

Modular communication has the advantage of giving the audience both pictures and words to help them understand the points that are being made. It is flexible and, because each point is made both in graphic and in text, it lends itself to disassembly into a set of "slides" and accompanying script for briefings and oral presentations. In one study that asked decision makers at project, program, and policy levels to evaluate the merits of the modular format, there was virtual consensus that this format helped them locate information of special interest,

Analysis of Temporary Emergency Food Assistance Program (TEFAP) Warehouse Data	
Purpose	Information about volume of food distributed, food left in storage, and storage and handling rates were used to project costs for the fiscal year, and to identify factors that may increase efficiency of TEFAP warehousing.
Findings and Conclusions	1. TEFAP cannot afford to handle its current volume of food given current warehousing rates and practices. Charges for the year may exceed the budgeted amount by as much as $200,000.
	2. One explanation of excessive warehouse costs is contractors' requesting more food than they are able to distribute. Only about 80 percent of food requested for August was actually ordered for pickup. Limited supply items, especially flour, honey, and milk, were more likely to be left in the warehouse than were other commodities.
	3. Regression analyses of similar data for three months sampled from the previous fiscal year confirmed that amount of food left in the warehouse helps explain differences in warehousing efficiency (measured in warehouse cents per household served). Amount of butter left in storage accounted for most of the variability from warehouse to warehouse.
	4. Storage and handling rates also were significantly related to warehouse cost per household. Cooler storage rates accounted for most of the variability. In most cases, low rates were reflected in lower costs per household. However, at warehouses where rates were low, large amounts of food could be left in the warehouse and still give the appearance of being efficient. When rates were high, contractors could actually be more efficient in distributing what they ordered but still generate relatively high costs per household served.
Recommendations	1. Contractors should be encouraged to request less and/or take amounts of food closer to their requests. Particular attention should be paid to accuracy of requests for flour, honey, and milk.
	2. Wherever possible, arrangements should be made to use warehouses with lower rates to handle more of the total volume of TEFAP commodities.

Figure 10.1. Sample Page From Evaluation Report Prepared in Information Design Format

Psychosocial Profiles

Homeless clients of JTPA programs appeared to have significantly less self-confidence and less access to social support than a comparison group of non-homeless persons enrolled in regular course work at a local community college, but they did not differ substantially from non-homeless JTPA participants.

| | Average Scores | | |
| | JTPA Clients | | College Students (n = 43) |
Dimension Assessed	Homeless (n = 68)	Non-Homeless (n = 48)	
Locus of Control			
Internal (32)	24	23	23
External (64)	24	26	18
Problem Solving (64)	41	41	42
Perceived Self-Efficacy (100)	64	59	72
Social Relationships (80)	55	56	69

NOTE: Numbers in parentheses are the highest possible scores for that dimension.

RESULTS

The questionnaire that clients completed before they entered JTPA programs at the three service delivery sites— i.e., Texas Employment Commission (TEC), Austin Women's Center (AWC), or Middle Earth (ME)—was divided into four parts.

- *Locus of Control.* Part I included 24 Likert-type items (each worth 0 to 4 points) that can be combined to index the extent to which the individual feels personally in control of events of daily life (internal locus of control) and/or the extent to which they feel that their lives are controlled by powerful others or by luck (external locus of control). When client scores on these dimensions were compared with scores obtained in a comparison group of non-homeless persons attending night classes at a local community college, homeless persons were more often found to have an external locus of control—i.e., to feel that their daily lives are controlled by other people or by luck or chance ($p < .01$). Homeless clients' perceptions of locus of control were not different, however, from those of other economically disadvantaged persons in JTPA programs at TEC, AWC, or ME.
- *Problem Solving.* Part II of the questionnaire was 16 Likert-type items that index the extent to which the person's problem-solving strategies were likely to be productive. There were no differences in obtained values on this scale, indicating that the problem solving capabilities of homeless and non-homeless JTPA participants are comparable to those of college students.

(continued)

Figure 10.2. Sample Page From an Evaluation Report Prepared in Modular Communication Format

- *Perceived Self-Efficacy.* There were 25 Likert-type items that evaluated the individual's perception of their own capabilities for seeking and obtaining employment. The present analysis shows that, before they entered JTPA programs, homeless and non-homeless clients were less confident about their job-getting ability than were college students ($p < .01$). Surprisingly, homeless persons tended to be more confident of their job-getting skills than were non-homeless clients of these JTPA programs ($p = .11$).
- *Social Relationships.* The questionnaire also included a block of 20 questions to indicate the extent to which the individual felt there were people in their naturally occurring social network to give guidance and reassure worth, share social activities, and be a reliable ally in times of stress and joy. Scores obtained by both homeless and non-homeless JTPA clients indicated that they have smaller and/or less dependable social relationships than was common among the non-homeless comparison group of college students ($p < .01$).

These results suggest that economically disadvantaged individuals who seek assistance through JTPA programs have no deficit of problem-solving competencies but do have less self-confidence and less access to social support than may be common in the general population. This profile is consistent with expectations about the strain that adverse events, such as homelessness, places on emotional well-being and social relationships. Mental health interventions should be designed to enable these disadvantaged individuals to benefit from their JTPA program.

Figure 10.2. Continued

made the information easy to use, and reduced the amount of reading time (Stallworth & Roberts-Gray, 1987).

The chief disadvantage of the modular communication format is that it takes extra time. Because there can be no spill over from the bottom of one text page to the top of the next, it often is necessary to reorganize the document and rewrite the modules many times. Modular communication also requires a great deal of skill in merging graphics and text.

Rapid Responsive Reporting

This set of reporting procedures and formats was developed in the office of the Inspector General of the U.S. Department of Health and Human Services (HHS). The guidelines for preparing these reports specify that (a) reports are written for executives, not researchers; (b) they must be short—15 or fewer pages and always with an executive summary; (c) they must be appealing, taking advantage of desktop publishing capabilities to make effective use of graphics; (d) the reports

Data Issues II: Selecting Data Analysis Procedures

The two questions that drive decisions about data analysis procedures are (1) Will this be a quantitative or a qualitative analysis? and (2) What comparisons will be made?

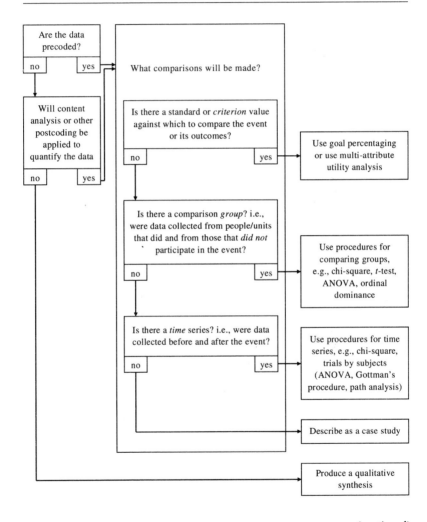

(continued)

Figure 10.3. Sample Page From a Decision-Oriented Report Prepared in Modular Communication Format

DATA ISSUES II: SELECTING DATA ANALYSIS PROCEDURES

For program evaluators, the data analysis phase is the most fun part of the evaluation. It is the place where you discover (or perhaps simply verify) answers to your questions. That's exciting!

Data analysis also is the place where content experts—e.g., health educators, disease prevention practitioners, and program administrators—sometimes become dismayed. Data analysis is that part of the evaluation study that is most heavily dependent on statistical procedures and the plethora of jargon that characterizes the culture of the evaluation expert. Someone else's jargon can be daunting. One need not be dismayed, however. There are many good books and software packages to assist in selecting and applying appropriate statistical tools. If the evaluation has been designed so that the plan is clear about the kinds of comparisons that are needed and about how the data are to used as indicators of program performance, the fun of finding the answers will predominate.

In selecting data analysis procedures, the first question the evaluator must answer is whether or not the data can be used as quantitative indicators of program performance. Sometimes there are features of the project that can easily be represented with numbers— e.g., how many times a cancer prevention coalition met during the quarter—but these numbers may not represent anything meaningful about the impact the project has had. Such numbers are useful, however, in producing a qualitative synthesis that describes how the project was implemented and provides a subjective estimate of its impact.

Answers to the second question that drives the selection of data analysis procedures indicate what kinds of comparisons are to be made.

Even if no other comparisons are planned, it almost always is possible to specify criteria or standards against which to compare actual program performance. In recent years, evaluation researchers have invested considerable energy in finding ways to integrate qualitative and quantitative information about program performance in order to produce evaluation results that are easier to use in decision making. Edwards and Newman's (1982) book on multiattribute evaluation and Nagel's (1986) articles on goal percentaging describe straightforward procedures for establishing standards or criteria for both subjective and objective measures of program performance and then combining or aggregating across the measures to develop an index of overall impact. These procedures are especially fun to use and encourage good communication between content specialists and evaluators.

Chi-square, t-test, and analysis of variance (ANOVA) are procedures that often are used to compare characteristics of those who participated in the treatment with those who did not participate (i.e., the comparison group). Results of such analyses provide some of the most compelling arguments about impact, especially if assignment to groups was random and the group comparison is combined with a time-series (e.g., pre- and post-testing of knowledge of cancer screening resources at worksites where health promotion programs have been established and at those where no programs have been established).

Procedures that are graphics oriented (e.g., ordinal dominance, Gottman's procedure for analyzing time-series data) are not only fun to use but often make it much easier for the user of evaluation results—e.g., the program administrator, legislator, or the general public—to understand the answers that are discovered in the data analysis phase of the evaluation study.

Figure 10.3. Continued

must provide balanced coverage, focusing on the unbiased findings but including comments from program officials; and (e) wide distribution of the written report should be followed up with a personal briefing to a small, select audience so as to create a forum for active discussion of the issues. Each of the reports is "backed up" by sets of working papers that are kept on file so that each finding and conclusion can be traced back to the original data sources.

This framework for making reports is one of several factors named as a contributor to the success and effectiveness of the evaluation unit within HHS (Mangano, 1989). Its advantages are that it is clearly addressed to a defined audience, makes use of text and graphics, accommodates a variety of uses with particular attention to balanced coverage to stimulate action. Its disadvantage is that it demands a larger staff and more routinized procedures for file management than usually are available to the independent research and evaluation consultant.

Chart Essay

This report format uses a separate single page presentation to address each of the research and evaluation questions that are included in a particular study. As is illustrated in Figure 10.4, the research question is showcased at the top of the page. A very brief narrative describing data sources and evaluation methods leads into a chart that summarizes findings relevant to the specific evaluation question. A short essay is added at the bottom of the page to provide a concise explanation of the findings.

Among the many advantages of the chart essay is that it lends itself to use as information, persuasion, and reinforcement. It was designed to be useful to a particular audience—that is, administrators at the policy level—but appears to be equally useful in addressing issues at practice and program levels of decision making. Developers of the chart essay in the Dallas Independent School District report that it is a viable alternative to the traditional technical report. Their experience with this innovative format shows that it improves use of research and evaluation data (Jones & Mitchell, 1990).

The chart essay shares the same disadvantages as other innovative formats. It requires extra time to determine the most compelling sequence for the presentation. And it requires considerable skill in layout and integration of graphics and text.

Question 2: How were data collected to measure outcomes of residential services?

This evaluation uses data provided by residents and by their counselors to compare outcomes for women whose participation in the shelter program is relatively brief with those achieved by women whose engagement with the program is more intense (e.g., those who participate in more hours of counseling or stay for longer periods of time).

Evaluation Question	Data Source	Data Reduction/Analysis
1. Are the women **satisfied** with services and facilities?	*QUESTIONNAIRE* items G-K, M-R, 3, 4 completed by the woman when she exits the shelter	Likert-type scales
2. When they leave, are women positioned to implement **realistic plans for the future?**	*GOALS CHECKSHEET* completed by the woman's counselor when the woman makes her exit	Goal Attainment Scaling
3. Do the women **feel better informed and empowered** to be safe, secure, and in pursuit of happiness?	*QUESTIONNAIRE* items A-F, L completed by the woman when she exits	Likert-type scale

The two data collection formats that were adapted to capture data on immediate outcomes of residential services for women and children for the first phase of this project were used without revision in this second panel of data collection and analysis: (1) The QUESTION-NAIRE that women are asked to complete when they make their exit from the shelter measures the women's satisfaction with services and solicits their self-evaluation of the extent to which they became, during their stay at the shelter, better informed and more empowered to pursue safe, secure, happy futures; and (2) The GOALS CHECKSHEET is completed by the woman's counselor to report which goals the woman pursued during her stay and to measure attainment of goals that position the woman to implement a realistic plan for the future.

To evaluate program impact, the outcome measures (i.e., satisfaction, self-evaluation, and goal attainment) were crosstabulated with two measures of receipt of services: (1) length of stay—measured in days, and (2) amount of counseling—measured in total number of hours the woman was engaged in individual counseling, family counseling, and group education/support sessions. Data on receipt of services were extracted from the service monitoring data base.

Figure 10.4. Sample Page From an Evaluation Report Prepared in Chart Essay Format

Which Alternative Is Best?

Your choice of the best format or style for making any given report or presentation will depend on (a) the levels of decision makers who are in your target audience, (b) how the members of your audience intend to or can use the data you are presenting, and (c) how much time and energy you have to invest in tailoring the report or presentation to match your clients' preferences and needs.

Whether you choose traditional or more innovative formats or develop your own methods for being responsive to your audience, there are several things you can do to increase the probability that results will gain serious hearing when decisions are made.

1. Talk about strengths as well as weaknesses. Applied researchers and evaluators are perceived by many project and program personnel as intruders, sent to find problems and to cut funding of ongoing programs or at the very least, to usurp funding that might otherwise have been spent on direct services or program activities. One way to overcome these negative perceptions is to devote as much time and effort to describing strengths of action plans and programs as you dedicate to discussing detected problems or weaknesses. This advice is based on B. F. Skinner's (1954) observation that the two most powerful reinforcers of human behavior are success and knowledge of progress. By using space in the research or evaluation report to document success and acknowledge progress, the writer not only reinforces positive action but also encourages acceptance of research and evaluation data.

2. Be positive before being critical. Another seldom quoted but sensible rule of thumb is to tell the good before you tell the bad. Technical writers have a tendency to save comments about program strengths and successes for the end of the report so that they can end on a positive note. Communications research indicates, however, that if you have both good and bad things to say about a person (or their project or program or policy), the listener is more likely to believe both parts of the message if it begins with the good comment (Jacobs, Jacobs, Feldman, & Cavior, 1973). Reports and presentations should, therefore, cover success and progress before describing problems and areas in which improvements may be needed.

3. Be brief. Brevity is a feature frequently requested by busy decision makers. One of the reasons that rapid responsive reporting has a 15 page limit is because that is what Joseph Califano demanded when he was secretary of Health, Education, and Welfare (DeLoria & Brookins,

1982). He also stipulated that oral presentations should be limited to 20 minutes with 40 minutes for questions and discussion. Other sources advise that when you make presentations for executive officers you should limit yourself to five briefing slides.

4. Provide the reader with a content map. Even when efforts are made to keep the report as succinct as possible, it is unreasonable to expect that everyone in your target audience will read the whole document. In a study that was conducted to evaluate the modular communication format, only one-fourth of the persons who returned the evaluation questionnaire said they had read the report from cover to cover; the remaining three-fourths said they had read only selected parts of the report (Stallworth & Roberts-Gray, 1987). This finding suggests that it is almost always a good idea to use the rubrics of information design and related techniques to help readers locate sections of your report that may address their particular "need to know."

5. Present statistical information as simply as you can. There are, as is indicated in the "Problem" section of this chapter, many circumstances in which the members of your target audience will want to see evidence of the rigor of the research methods and the statistical reliability of research results. You should know, however, that more often than not the intended users of applied research and evaluation reports are suspicious of statistics, especially the notations of mathematical modeling and inferential statistics. Studies have shown, for example, that teachers and administrative personnel in schools are generally accepting of recommendations emerging from short reports that include no statistics, slightly more accepting if the report includes frequency data and percentages, but rejecting of the same set of recommendations if the report also includes notations for type of statistical analysis and significance levels (Brown & Newman, 1983). In deciding what kind of report format and style is best for reaching your target audience with information that will enable and encourage action, you should carefully consider the kinds of statistics that will have meaning and acceptability within that audience.

6. Be graphics oriented. Pictures can be worth more than a thousand words. Modular communication formats are organized around that principle. You should also be alert to the many ways in which quantitative analyses are being translated into simple graphic formats. You can, for example, use a simple chart to demonstrate ordinal dominance instead of showing the computations for a Mann-Whitney U-Test (Darlington, 1973). Similarly, you can communicate results of quantitative policy

analyses by presenting graphs to portray the relationship between policy options rather than presenting the algebra on which the curves are based (Teasley, 1989). There are today a number of excellent books that can help you decide what kinds of data displays will make your reports and presentations more powerful (see reviews by Hendricks, 1989; 1990).

7. Be timely. The most useful reports and presentations are those that are put into the decision makers' hands early enough to be digested and understood but not so early that they seem outdated by the time the decision is made. Data collection and analysis are time-consuming processes that can cause research and evaluation to proceed at a pace that may seem too slow to be useful in formulating the quick responses that are demanded for practice, program, and policy decisions. One way to guard against bringing your message too soon or too late is to identify at least two or three specific individuals who might use your data and then make a note of the dates on which these individuals will be required to make decisions that could be better informed if they had your report in hand. Having as a goal the delivery of a report for use by a specific individual at a specific time can be a strong cybernetic on timeliness.

8. Link data to action. This, above all, should be the rule that helps you decide how to structure your reports and presentations to enable members of your target audience to hear the voice of applied research and evaluation and use the information it provides. Sometimes applied research is conducted simply to be used as documentation. But that is rare. Research and evaluation activity usually is requested as an aid to decision making. You must be attentive, therefore, to the kinds of action that are contemplated by those who requested that the work be done.

As you contemplate your target audience and how they will use the information you are presenting, you will have to decide whether the data and theory, by themselves, can be depended upon to promote responsible action. In some cases you may agree with Jones & Mitchell (1990) that the evaluator's role ends with presentation of findings and that it is the responsibility of administrators to interpret the data and determine its implications. In other cases you may agree with me that data presented without recommendations can frustrate and immobilize rather than facilitate decision making (Roberts-Gray, 1988; Roberts-Gray, Buller, & Sparkman, 1987). Your choice of whether or not to include recommendations and if so, where to put them, is one of the exciting challenges you face as you experiment with improved methods for communicating applied research and evaluation findings. Whether or not you include your own recommendations, it is essential that the data you present be clearly and easily linked to action. Unless members of your target audience find in your reports and presentations the information they need to help them make better informed decisions, applied research and evaluation will remain vulnerable to the accusation that it is merely "expensive paperwork" (Nagel, 1982, p. 32-36).

Summary

The reader that I envision for this chapter is an independent research and evaluation consultant who already has some degree of experience in making reports and presentations. The chapter, therefore, was designed as an aid in making decisions about the practice of applied research and evaluation.

There are three ways that I anticipate you can use information presented in this chapter. First, I hope that it will help you to become better informed about options and obligations that the independent research and evaluation consultant has when preparing reports and presentations. Second, the chapter was written, at least in part, to reinforce you and your colleagues for investing time and energy in the development of innovative, effective strategies for communicating research and evaluation findings. The final aspiration for this chapter is to persuade you to test and to share improved methods for producing timely, trustworthy, easy-to-use reports and presentations that strengthen the link between research and action.

References

Brown, R., & Newman, D. (1982). An investigation of the effect of different data presentation formats and order of arguments in a simulated adversary evaluation. *Educational Evaluation and Policy Analysis, 4*, 197-203.

Darlington, R. B. (1973). Comparing two groups by simple graphs. *Psychological Bulletin, 79*, 110-116.

DeLoria, D., & Brookins, G. K. (1982). The evaluation report: A weak link to policy. In J. R. Travers & R. J. Light (Eds.), *Learning from early experience: Evaluating early childhood demonstration programs* (pp. 254-271). National Academy Press.

Dewey, J. (1933). *How we think*. Boston: Health Publishers.

Edwards, W., & Newman, J. R. (1982). *Multiattributes evaluation*. Beverly Hills, CA: Sage.

Hendricks, M. (1989). Book reviews. *Evaluation Practice, 10*(2), 68-73.

Hendricks, M. (1990). Book reviews. *Evaluation Practice, 11*(2), 145-147.

Jacobs, M., Jacobs, A., Feldman, G., & Cavior, N. (1973). The "credibility gap": Delivery of positive and negative emotional and behavioral feedback in groups. *Journal of Consulting & Clinical Psychology, 41*(2), 215-223.

Jones, B. K., & Mitchell, N. (1990). Communicating evaluation findings: The use of a chart essay. *Educational Evaluation and Policy Analysis, 12*(4), 449-462.

Mangano, M. F. (1989). *Rapid responsive evaluation for decision makers.* Washington DC: Office of Analysis and Inspections, Office of Inspector General, U.S. Department of Health and Human Services.

Nagel, S. (1982). *Policy evaluation: Making optimum decisions.* New York: Praeger.

Nagel, S. (1986). Microcomputers and improving social science prediction. *Evaluation Review, 10,* 635-660.

Roberts-Gray, C. (1988). On the importance of making recommendations. *Evaluation Practice, 9,* 79-81.

Roberts-Gray, C., Buller, A., & Sparkman, A. (1987). Linking data with action: Procedures for developing recommendations. *Evaluation Review, 11,* 678-683.

Simon, H. (1960). *The new science of management decision.* New York: Harper & Row.

Skinner, B. F. (1954). The science of learning and the art of teaching. *Harvard Educational Review, 24,* 86-97.

Stallworth, Y., & Roberts-Gray, C. (1987). The craft of evaluation: Reporting to the busy decision maker. *Evaluation Practice, 8,* 31-35.

Teasley, C. E. (1989). When a picture is worth more than a thousand words: Graphic versus algebraic sensitivity analysis. *Evaluation Review, 13*(1), 91-103.

Weiss, C. H. (1971). Utilization of evaluation: Toward comparative study. In F. C. Caro (Ed.), *Readings in evaluation research.* Hartford, CN: Russell Sage Foundation.

PART IV

Showing You How: Case Studies of Small Consulting Practices

11

Being Values Driven

A Challenging Way to Do Business

KASS LARSON
ARLENE BROWNELL

The transition from an academic or corporate environment to the private consulting arena can be an eye-opening experience. Familiar rules, clear standards, and predictability are no longer present. Decisions must be based on your beliefs and the risks you are willing to take. Success in an academic or business setting does not necessarily prepare one for the stresses of consulting where your client's job often is on the line and your work determines not only your own company's success or failure but your client's as well. In addition, many decisions in the corporate environment force a confrontation among your company's values, your personal values, and the values of your client.

Our intent in this chapter is to bring to light the importance of "values," both personal and corporate, what it means to be "values driven," and why a consulting firm should be concerned with values. It is our hope that from this chapter you will see a way to conduct business that is neither routinely taught in graduate school nor commonly practiced. We also hope that you will recognize this as a way of doing

AUTHORS' NOTE: The authors are grateful for suggestions from Patricia Kunkel, Gayle Kirkeby, Susan Keaveney, Peggy Steele, and Wayne Smith. Address correspondence regarding this chapter to Kass Larson, International Learning Systems, Inc., 603 Park Point Drive, Suite 200, Golden, CO 80401.

business that enables you to integrate your personal and professional roles, values, and ideals.

The ILS Values

International Learning Systems (ILS) is a values driven company (Howard, 1990; Nelson-Horchler, 1991). What does this mean and how does this set ILS apart from other companies? We define *values* to be the core beliefs people hold that form the foundation for their decision making. In being *values driven* the formally established ILS values provide the parameters for all our activities. Our company values are explicit and visible. The way we accomplish our business objectives is as important as the end result. Our company vision, "A world where people and organizations believe: We must be the change we wish to see in the world," symbolizes our commitment to being personally and professionally guided by values. Stated simply it means: "It begins with us."

ILS founder, Peggy Steele, set out to create a company in which people would be regarded as the most important asset. She repeatedly had seen the brightest people in other organizations become disillusioned by the numerous ways the organizational culture conveyed that people were not respected or valued. Because many either stayed on and were not productive or left frustrated, company time and money was wasted developing those people. Steele believed that ILS employees would continue to be challenged and to find their work rewarding if she could eliminate many of the dehumanizing corporate norms and the bureaucratic posturing. Based on her personal beliefs, a set of values was established as the guidelines for ILS employee behavior and performance. People are encouraged to "be themselves" but vary their behavior on a continuum of formality fitting the situation and client expectations. Energy normally used in maintaining a "work personality" can be refocused on productive efforts. The benefits are that people stay motivated, are more committed to the company and their work, and feel free to express new and creative ideas.

Our five core values provide constants in an ever-changing environment. Identified as the behavioral guidelines most important to us, they serve as the framework for defining problems, identifying solutions, and selecting a course of action. In the absence of other clear guidelines, values provide the boundaries for decision making. Along with profitability, our values serve as standards for measuring our success (Lannon, 1990).

The five established ILS values are:

- Being client focused
- Working with integrity
- Treating people with respect
- Being committed to personal and professional development
- Valuing and maintaining open communication

Based on research and experience, we believe that doing business in accordance with our values provides a sound long-term business strategy. Our goals are: to be profitable; to establish a reputation that attracts and keeps clients; and to create a work environment that promotes learning while stimulating, rewarding, and retaining skilled, dedicated employees. By modeling a values driven business style we strive to demonstrate to our clients and employees that values are important and make good business sense.

ILS is in the business of providing research based, custom-designed training applications for large companies. Like other market-driven companies, we continually seek better ways to meet our clients' changing needs. As we stretch to serve our clients and manage our own company's rapid growth, we do not always act in ways consistent with our values. Yet we have high expectations of ILS and sometimes forget that we are figuring out how to make values-based business decisions as we go. In the process we encounter challenges both internal with employees and external with clients. The remainder of this chapter describes some of the challenges we face as we do business.

Being Client Focused

Success to ILS is determined by how well our clients succeed through the application of our products and services. By focusing all our efforts and resources on understanding and helping our clients, we are able to meet our objective of providing the highest quality product or service possible. We work in partnership with clients by learning about their unique needs and teaching them how to understand and apply our methodologies. Our strategy is not to provide a one-time product but to transfer the skills that allow our clients to develop themselves. ILS benefits from the partnership by observing the different ways our clients apply our products. That knowledge is then turned into product improvements and new ideas to be used on future projects.

Internal Challenges

First among the challenges arising from our internal customer focus is teamwork, not only within ILS, but between ILS and our client. ILS project team members are encouraged to consider clients as "part of the team" versus a traditional "client-vendor" relationship. We actively discourage an "us" and "them" perspective as that attitude undermines working together effectively.

It takes continuous effort to keep people on project teams aware of and focused on our customers' specific needs. With the tight timelines and ongoing changes characteristic of custom research and design projects, it is essential to continually monitor our activities and compare them to client expectations. We make the effort so we do not lose sight of what is to be delivered and how it is to used by the client.

ILS employees must be highly skilled and flexible, in order to continually shift roles to fit current project demands. The success of ILS projects depends on the ability of our team members to work together in a coordinated manner and make mid-course changes based on client concerns and requests. This means that people must be comfortable performing a variety of tasks and willing to learn new skills as the needs arise. The first major ILS project, for example, saw the president of ILS, an ILS director, and the client copying and collating materials for use the next day. Although it is unusual to have a client working in this capacity, it is a good example of the kind of teamwork at ILS and the "do what it takes" attitude prevalent among ILS employees.

External Challenges

We strive to help clients clarify their needs, anticipate potential problems, and view their needs in the context of their entire organization. Clients may see a different set of who's, why's and what's surrounding a problem than ILS perceives. A client may not be familiar with ILS methodologies, so we always explain the reasons for our recommendations. Solutions are derived and refined by mutual agreement only after careful consideration of the client's overall objectives and available resources. During this process, clients often come up with new ideas and needs as they begin to see their organization through different eyes.

Another customer-related challenge is to hit a moving target. Typical of custom-designed training, the project scope may change midstream. Being customer focused means making sure that requested changes are incorporated into our delivery. Consequently, we react quickly and effectively to changes as they occur, by utilizing dedicated project teams and maintaining continual communication with clients. On one client project the initial team consisted of six ILS people and two points of contact within the client organization. As the project progressed, the ILS team had over 20 key players and there were at least 15 points of contact in the client organization. We even had our own phone extensions on the client's phone system, and were linked directly to the client's computer systems. Changes of this magnitude truly test our ability to marshal resources and maintain the level of quality the client expects.

Challenges to Working With Integrity

The traditional way to manage moral principles in an organization is to ignore them and not question how people meet their deadlines and bottom line objectives. At ILS we evaluate our performance within the context of our values because we define success as something more than profitability and market position. We believe that working with integrity is the foundation for the long-term relationships we seek with our clients and our employees.

Internal Challenges

Generally, organizations work with consultants in order to address needs that are better dealt with by an outside person. To protect themselves from undesirable publicity and/or improper use of the information uncovered in the course of the project, clients typically have consultants agree, in writing, not to reveal anything about the project or the client. We willingly sign these agreements because we understand their desire for security, and because ILS needs access to as much relevant information as possible. In this way, working with integrity earns our client's trust and supports a long-term partnership.

One challenge we face is to sensitize ILS employees to the number of ways the proprietary nature of a project might be violated. We try to teach our employees (a) to anticipate the possibility of being overheard when discussing a project with a colleague, (b) to resist describing the specifics of their ILS work to friends, (c) to protect documents when working in public places, and (d) to maintain confidentiality of information when sharing a home office or computer. When employees are aligned with how ILS defines working with integrity, they are more likely to protect the client's interests.

Ongoing change creates demands to demonstrate that we work with integrity. For example, our company's growth has forced us to keep tighter controls in order to effectively manage more people, projects, and budgets. Because ILS does not provide office space for all employees and many work at home, we monitor each employee's performance through self-reported billable hours and through her/his ability to meet deadlines with high-quality work. Some employees, especially those who previously enjoyed our small company informalities, are disappointed by stricter policies and procedures. They feel less trusted because they are asked to be more accountable. In reality, as long as productivity fits the hours turned in, we trust that the reports are accurate. We want employees to understand that more detailed reporting is not a trust issue, but is necessary for us to effectively manage our expanding resources.

External Challenges

On a number of occasions we have been caught in the dilemma of being asked to identify research participants who were promised anonymity. Occasionally, we have resolved this situation simply by reminding the client that we agreed in advance to guarantee anonymity. Other times we have be able to provide alternative information that met the client's need.

There have been instances, however, in which it was not possible to maintain the integrity of our research and satisfy the client. For example, one author was facilitating a computerized, group-input session when the participant's manager demanded copies of each individual's results. He made their receipt a condition for payment. The author was unwilling to violate the condition of anonymity and saw no way to resolve the conflict to everybody's satisfaction. She asked each member of the group to decide whether or not to provide a copy of their results to their manager. We later met with the client and mutually agreed, based on our differences in values, not to continue working together. (He did pay us.)

Experiences like this remind us to evaluate each sale in terms of compatibility with ILS values and capabilities. Every project has potential landmines. Occasionally we decline work that a client wants us to do because we do not think the work will achieve the client's objectives, even though we could do the work and be paid for it. We have yet to regret these decisions. When we fail to recognize, or choose to ignore, differences in values between ILS and a client, we are more likely to encounter problems. However, when our values are aligned with our client, we can generally overcome any difficulties.

Treating People With Respect

ILS was founded with the belief that people are a company's most valuable asset and deserve to be treated as such. People bring the skills, expertise, and dedication that keep organizations alive and growing. Mutual respect for each others' abilities is the foundation of cooperation, trust, open communication, and commitment. It applies to relationships both inside and outside any organization.

Internal Challenges

ILS hires people to fill our need for specific skills and expertise. We respect the competencies of the people we hire. We trust people to keep their own hours, make their own decisions, and take reasonable risks. Management actively seeks and considers their opinions when making decisions that change the company. Their input is valued out of respect for their ability to teach us new ways to serve our customers and to help create a work environment that they themselves find rewarding.

Challenges are created when either ILS, as an organization, or an employee fails to live up to expectations. Problems of this nature may often be a result of miscommunication. Unclear and unmet expectations can dramatically affect a team's productivity in which the synergy of teamwork depends on close cooperation and dependence on each other's output. Prior to any corrective feedback or more serious action, a thorough effort is made to clarify perceptions of the people involved. How problems are dealt with is the key to whether an organization really lives its values. An attitude of respect instead of accusation goes a long way toward keeping teams and people happy and productive.

Direct feedback and coaching are excellent means to improve performance in a manner that shows respect. Both experience and research has shown us that people work better under varying management styles. We have recently implemented a "coaching" feedback system in which each person completes a form identifying ways they wish to be coached, what they do not respond to favorably, and how they most like to be rewarded. The forms are intended to be exchanged between team members and team leaders, as well as the company president and management team. Some pleasant surprises resulted from the effort. First, we learned a great deal about our team members, information that is not normally exchanged. Second, that information has proved very useful as a guide, when encouraging people or giving constructive feedback. It has helped people significantly to see each other as colleagues and opened new avenues of communication.

External Challenges

We cannot profess to know our clients' business as well as they do. They are the experts. Were it not for their abilities, their organizations would not be as successful as they are. It is our job to listen to them, to ask questions, and to work in a nonadversarial partnership to accomplish the client's objectives.

We frequently work with clients whose values are not explicit and have priorities different from ours. To work cooperatively toward a specific goal, both organizations have to find a common ground in which ILS, as the consultant, is comfortable and our client is satisfied with the product they receive. This often requires a compromise of what we think would be the ideal solution and one that best serves our client. We must respect both the limitations and capabilities of the client organization to effectively implement change. The challenge is to produce and deliver what the client needs while maintaining our values and standards.

During the course of a project we occasionally witness a lack of recognition of, or even disapproval of, superior efforts and accomplishments by a person within the client organization who has contributed to our project's success. If possible, we demonstrate respect while in the presence of their manager or supervisors by acknowledging that person for a job well done. Respect for a person's capabilities must be communicated in order to be of benefit. We see organizations that inhibit respectful treatment of individuals, not through malice, but because established communication protocols or barriers prevent people from getting the recognition they deserve. Frequently we interview people at different levels of a client organization, who perform many different functions and who have been identified as subject-matter experts to ILS by others in their organization. They are surprised and pleased when they learn from our interviewers that their expertise and accomplishments are openly respected and recognized by their own organization.

Being Committed to Personal and Professional Development

Successful organizations will be those with the capacity to respond quickly and effectively to worldwide market changes. In these organizations, people at all levels of the company anticipate change, are proactive, and continually learn, adapt, and develop (Brownell, Bache-Wiig, & Steele, 1989; McKnight & Thompson, 1990). Continual skill development for personnel is the best way to ensure long-term survival and leadership in a market-driven environment.

Internal Challenges

ILS is committed to the development of our employees. We believe it is the only way we can be the best in our industry. We strive to create an environment that fosters learning, change, initiative, and experimentation. Our goal is to make the time and resources available for continual learning even though our company growth demands that our efforts be focused on customer projects. One-on-one coaching and group training of team leaders fit best at ILS given our team orientation, tight time frames, budgets, and small staff. The return on development time invested is very high with such focused attention. We all benefit when someone learns new skills and feels good about their new found strengths.

Some people come into ILS with high estimations of their abilities only to be surprised by the demands placed on them. Many are unaccustomed to working under compressed time frames and very high-quality expectations. The most successful employees at ILS are those who are willing to ask for help, find ways to get it, and rebound quickly from mistakes. They also readily learn and apply the lessons gained from experiences on the job. These are the behaviors rewarded at ILS. We want the people at ILS to have fun while being productive and using their talents. Humor at work is important. It is one of the best devices for facilitating self-evaluation, relieving tension, and building open communication. It is much easier to recognize needs for self-improvement if you can laugh at your mistakes, learn from them, and enjoy your accomplishments. We are all challenged to maintain a sense of humor while the company is growing, work is stressful, and meeting deadlines is a primary concern (Lannon, 1990).

External Challenges

ILS was formed by Peggy Steele, because she saw that many organizations sought, and many consultants provided, quick-fix solutions to address human resource training and development needs. She believed that training was only part of the answer to making long-term changes in people's skills and abilities. Work environments not aligned to support training efforts can quickly undo any gains made by teaching people new skills. This wastes valuable training dollars and creates frustration for those who learn new behaviors but are rewarded for old behaviors. Within the client organization rewards such as promotions, raises, or nonmonetary recognition must reinforce the skills and knowledge being trained if the training is to have a long-term impact.

In order to help clients maximize their return on development activities, we identify, through research, the organizational systems that support learning as well as those that hinder learning and performance. With this information, our client knows what exists and works within the organization to help people do the best they can and what systems need to be changed because they prevent people from doing the best they can (Csikszentmihalyi, 1990).

Michael Porter (1985) and others suggest that, in market- or sales-driven organizations, the typical hierarchical organizational chart can be turned upside down. The positions normally depicted at the bottom—that is, those with the most direct interaction with the customers—are now at the top, and the management and supervisory functions exist to support people closest to the customer. This is why it is important for companies to continuously train and develop all their people. Those now at the top of the chart need customer- and product-related skills, and management needs coaching and development skills. ILS actively encourages management in our client companies to act as coaches and development resources, not just as decision makers.

Challenges to Valuing and Maintaining Open Communication

ILS advocates open exchange of information and ideas across organizational functions. Many management decisions are made only after input from employees has been solicited and multiple perspectives taken into account. Employees are free to challenge most decisions and are encouraged to communicate directly with people without regard to role or title.

Internal Challenges

Employees who do well at ILS tend to be assertive and have a strong commitment to the company. Because we value open communication, we want people to suggest ways to improve ILS systems or procedures. It is difficult to be receptive to what sometimes appears to be a continual stream of suggestions about how to do things better: yet, over time, many of the suggestions are implemented and these changes have made us better as a company.

The more information people have regarding ILS and the better their understanding of the way ILS conducts business, the better their ideas for improving our products and services. Also, employees feel more confident about making decisions when they are well informed. Because people are not regularly in the office and because teams reconfigure as projects begin and end, providing timely access to information has been a constant challenge. Project libraries, a weekly ILS newsletter, and cross-functional liaisons on project teams have been well received because they enable us to provide information to those team members who work at remote locations or who are not in the office on a daily basis.

Because of their experiences in other organizations, many employees find it difficult to believe that we are trying to create an organization in which taking reasonable risks is encouraged and learning from mistakes is essential. When people make mistakes because they do not clarify assumptions, ask questions, or express concerns about performing a task, we hold them accountable. When they seek the information they need before they forge ahead on a project, we feel more confident in their ability to do a good job, and we look for opportunities to help them learn and succeed.

External Challenges

Many of the clients we work with are trying to overcome barriers to communication that are typically found in segmented organizations (Kanter, 1983). It is not unusual for our client organizations to be highly structured with hierarchical lines of authority, communication and control, in which only top management knows the long-term business objectives and strategies.

Barriers to open communication in client companies often have an impact on our work. For example, when our requests for critical information and feedback do not reach all of the key client contacts, we may be forced to make decisions without the client's full input. If we receive conflicting information from client contacts who do not communicate among themselves, we are placed in the awkward position of having to resolve their differences. If we continue working to meet a deadline while information we need is delayed by client communication barriers, substantial revisions of our work may be necessary after we receive the information. Delayed or partial communication from a client can create large ripple effects in a project.

Open communication enables us to create better solutions to meet our clients' needs. More and more we seek cooperation with people who would normally view themselves and their organizations as our competitors. It is not unusual for a client to select more than one consultant to work on different aspects of a large project. Although some people are surprised when we suggest working cooperatively, many are pleased and responsive. Working with other consultants who value open communication typically results in a superior product for the client because we learn from each other, build on each other's ideas, integrate our work, and avoid duplication of efforts. In the process, we demonstrate the value of open communication as a strategy to achieve business objectives.

Summary and Conclusions

International Learning Systems is values driven as a long-term business strategy. Our values provide the framework for defining problems, identifying solutions, making decisions, and taking action. Operating within a values framework provides us, we believe, with the best means to support long-term relationships with our employees and clients. By using *values*, in addition to profitability, as standards to measure our performance, we willingly create a new set of business challenges. When combined into one, our five values—being client focused, working with integrity, treating people with respect, being committed to personal and professional development, and valuing and maintaining open communication—say we value people above all else.

References

Brownell, A., Bache-Wiig, T., & Steele, P. (1989). *Adult learning and organizational change.* Unpublished Manuscript. Golden, CO: International Learning Systems.

Csikszentmihalyi, M. (1990). *Flow: The psychology of optimal experience.* New York: Harper & Row.

Howard, R. (1990). Values make the company: An interview with Robert Haas. *Harvard Business Review, 68*(5), 133-144.

Kanter, R. M. (1983). *The change masters.* New York: Simon & Schuster.

Lannon, L. (1990). Giving back: The secret of creating success. *Training & Development Journal, 44*(4), 58-62.

McKnight, R., & Thompson, M. (1990). Navigating organizational change. *Training & Development Journal, 44*(12), 46-49.

Nelson-Horchler, J. (1991). The magic of Herman Miller. *Industry Week, 240*(4), 11-17.

Porter, M. (1985). *Competitive advantage.* New York: Free Press.

12

Applied Research Consultants (ARC)

A Service
and Training Model

ALAN VAUX
MARGARET S. STOCKDALE

Graduate programs in applied psychology and related fields are typically well noted for producing scholarly practitioners adept in the latest theories and research methodologies of their discipline. Practical experience in applying these skills often comes through three- to perhaps twelve-month internships in organizational settings, or through individual practice with local agencies (see chapters by Downey and Kuhnert, and Saal, this volume). The goal of this chapter is not to diminish the merit of these applied experiences but to describe a different model of graduate training in applied research. In this model students become enmeshed in real consulting experiences throughout their graduate-student tenure. In addition to core methodology and content courses, theses, dissertations, and other independent research projects, students are associates in a consulting organization housed within the psychology department. It is this component of our graduate training model that we feel provides students with a unique opportunity to develop and hone comprehensive applied research *and* consulting skills.

This chapter will provide a description of *Applied Research Consultants* (ARC)—a consulting center/graduate course for students in the

Applied Experimental Psychology doctoral program at Southern Illinois University at Carbondale. We will discuss the organization's goals and structure, its procedures for selecting, planning, and implementing projects, as well as for dealing with clients, writing reports, and so forth. In doing so, we hope to highlight features of ARC as a training model for applied psychology graduate programs. We also hope to shed light on the challenges faced by independent or small applied research consultant organizations and some strategies for meeting them.

An Overview of ARC

A Brief History of ARC

ARC was initiated in 1982 as a means to provide practical field experience to students in the applied experimental psychology graduate program. This graduate program was designed to train psychologists to use the principles and research methods of psychology to address a broad range of pragmatic problems in human service, business, and government. ARC was organized as a required course in which students would spend several years of their tenure in the program. It has operated continuously since 1982, comparable in size and function to a small independent applied research consulting firm.

The Training and Service Goals of ARC

ARC has operated with two primary goals: training and service. From an educational perspective, students have an opportunity to take psychological principles and methods learned in the classroom and apply them in real-world situations. This might involve conceptualizing a human problem, developing instructional programs, designing and conducting a survey, designing an evaluation, examining archival data, choosing measurement instruments, conducting statistical analyses, communicating findings, and so forth. Regardless of the principle or method involved, students learn that the opportunities, constraints, and objectives in a field setting may differ dramatically from those in the scientific laboratory or the classroom. In addition, students have an opportunity to learn skills that are unique to field settings or that cannot be taught easily in the classroom. Such skills include planning projects, negotiating contracts and agreements (see Kuhnert & Gore, this volume), working in teams, dealing with clients (see Cristiani, this volume), communicating with individuals from other disciplines or backgrounds (see Barrington, this volume), addressing ethical issues (see Larson & Brownell, and Leong, this volume), and so forth. Many applied researchers receive their formal training in traditional academic programs—applied training occurs on the job. Thus ARC's training goals and experiences are relevant not only to similar graduate programs but also to small firms that need to season new, academically trained employees.

Despite its origin in an educational setting, ARC has always placed great importance on its service goal. It has clearly stated a willingness to provide applied research services to regional agencies and organizations for a modest fee.[1] It has made the availability of its services known, welcomed inquiries, and tried to clarify the nature and extent of its expertise. The importance of this service goal may reflect the fact that ARC functions in a rural, resource-poor, region. ARC staff have the capacity, expertise, knowledge, and technical skills that constitute a significant resource in the local area to help organizations address problems they face. Thus, rhetoric very quickly became reality as ARC recognized the significant service contribution that it could make. Nonetheless, the service goal has consistently complemented the educational goal in the selection and conduct of projects.

Organizational Structure: Roles, Decision-Making Processes, and Teamwork

ARC is a fluid organization with a minimally hierarchical structure. ARC has an executive director, a faculty member who oversees ARC operations and provides supervision on projects. The director is responsible for the academic component of ARC, for the overall coordination of ARC activities, and for ensuring the quality of ARC work. Occasionally, other Applied Experimental faculty, termed senior consultants, provide supervision on projects. The department chairperson serves as fiscal officer, sanctioning and implementing ARC financial decisions. ARC's primary staff are students enrolled in the Applied Experimental graduate program. Staff are termed *ARC associates* generally, *junior associates* in their first year, and *senior associates* after completing 2 years in ARC and leading one or more projects. Sometimes, students from other graduate programs become involve in ARC—they are termed *adjunct associates*.

Status in ARC is nominal, because most operations are organized around projects conducted by teams. Team composition and responsibilities are based on expertise and interest rather than seniority per se. Teams consist of a designated project leader and one or more secondaries. In addition to his or her share of project tasks, the project leader's responsibilities include planning and coordinating the project, maintaining contact with the client, and keeping the director informed of plans, problems, and progress. Other team members are responsible primarily for carrying out tasks assigned to them by the project leader. The ARC director, or other senior consultant, is involved in initial client contact and negotiating the scope of projects. Most importantly, the director is responsible for supervising projects by reviewing plans, progress, and products.

Project progress reports are a routine part of weekly staff meetings. Project leaders often are expected to present plans and decisions to the group. This peer review system is an excellent way of ensuring that the project team has thought through options and has a strong rationale for their plans. Quite often, the entire group becomes involved in generating options and making recommendations both in the initial planning stages and when difficulties arise. Such group problem solving not only serves important educational functions but also often yields a broader range of options. For example, the group generated an array of strategies for efficiently reaching students, staff, and faculty in a sexual harassment survey project that did not allow for formal sampling, the budget for which excluded telephone interviews or noncampus mailing, and which was conducted under time pressure. In another example, ARC members proposed and provided feedback on a variety of methods for the graphic presentation of complicated findings from a university computer user-satisfaction survey.

Whether a consulting organization is part of an academic program or an independent venture, teamwork will probably be a fact, if not a desirable feature of consulting life. Yet, with teamwork comes intergroup conflict. ARC has not been immune to some internal strife. Associates have disagreed over authorship rights, and occasionally a member's commitment to a project is questioned by others. We have not had to yield to bureaucratic rules and procedures, however, for handling personnel conflicts—differences seem to work themselves out. Primarily this has occurred because all team members share a very fundamental superordinate goal—their own personal success as a graduate student depends on ARC success. They know that ARC cannot survive without team-work. In comparison, it is a sad reality that some graduate programs, deliberately or not, build backstabbing competition into their programs.

ARC as an Emulation of an Independent Consulting Firm

Despite its uniqueness as a training and service forum, ARC has had to face many of the same challenges as a group of professional consultants. Therefore, lessons we have learned in starting up, building resources, setting fees, finding and selecting projects, and negotiating with clients can be valuable to the beginning professional as well.

Starting Up

An independent consultant may face many different start-up problems, obstacles, and opportunities than a consulting organization essentially subsidized by an academic department. Independents make a considerable financial investment in both capital expenses and "opportunity costs" (unearned wages from a more predictable income source, e.g., employment in a university or large private or public organization). In addition, private practitioners may become demoralized by the lack of a steady flow of projects during the early months and perhaps years of their consulting venture.

When ARC was created, the psychology department invested a faculty resource, a room for office space, and access to department supplies and commodities (photocopying, mailing, and limited long-distance phone calls). More importantly, however, a few individual faculty members had contacts that they referred to ARC. These referrals provided an initial base on which to build ARC's reputation as a viable consulting organization, producing high-quality applied research at low cost. These clients were willing and happy to work with us knowing that their trusted former consultant, the faculty member, would supervise the project. Although a small, private consulting firm may not be afforded these luxuries that helped us get off to a successful start, academic programs wishing to adopt a similar training model should be able to draw on such resources.

In addition to resources provided by the psychology department, which greatly contributed to ARC's early successes, neither faculty nor the graduate students have depended upon ARC as a source of personal income. Therefore, ARC staff have been less likely to experience the pain of unsteady project flow and low net income in the start-up phase of our organization. Although this may be considered a weakness in our program because it does not expose our students to the harsh realities of independent consulting, we believe that it is really a strength. ARC provides an incubator for students to develop and polish consulting skills. When they graduate from the program, they have a significant edge in establishing their careers as applied researchers and consultants. Because they know *how* to consult, they do not have to begin to develop these skills while trying to eke out a living.

Developing a Base: Skills and Resources

Despite some of the differences between a program like ARC and an independent consulting firm, both types of practices need to assess their skills and resources in order to determine the type of services they are capable of providing. Applied research knowledge and skills are the most important resources needed by the independent consultant. These include technical research competence, management skills, and, of great importance, the ability to communicate effectively. These resources will be discussed in more detail later.

With respect to equipment and support staff, needs are few but important. The personal computer has revolutionized the work of researchers and writers. In that many professionals compose at the keyboard, need for support staff to type is minimal, though such staff may be needed to save professional time on mundane research tasks (e.g., stuffing envelopes for a large mail survey, coding data, and so on). ARC has operated with a small office, an assistant working ten to fifteen hours per week, and a personal computer with printer. We have had access to university resources such as printing, photocopying, an optical scanning machine, and a main-frame computer. However, the independent consulting firm will find that such resources are readily available. Statistical software packages for PCs make mainframe computing unnecessary for all but the most esoteric projects. Desktop publishing software allows a researcher to turn out high quality surveys, reports, and presentations that not long ago required graphic art and typesetting assistance. Indeed, armed with a powerful PC and half a dozen software packages—word processing, spreadsheet, statistical, desktop publishing, database, and project management—a single, skilled professional can be highly productive. Moreover, she or he can have considerable direct control over products, dramatically reducing repetitive tasks and tailoring reports, graphics, and other materials to suit client needs (see chapters by Henry and Roberts-Gray, this volume).

In short, a single professional could operate a small but successful practice from a home office with a personal computer, a telephone, and part-time office assistance. Such an arrangement has a great deal to recommend it—including the opportunity to work in pleasant, informal surroundings, to avoid the time and expense of commuting to work, and to save on rent expenses directly and indirectly through home-office tax reductions (assuming one meets IRS requirements). A group might prefer attractive office space to which they can invite clients, an elaborate computer network system, and a full range of office equipment and support staff. In either case, tools like the PC, telephone, and answering machine greatly facilitate two critical tasks in consulting: to communicate effectively with the client and to create a professional impression. Equipment should be selected and used with this objective clearly in mind.

Finding and Selecting Projects

As noted earlier, ARC differs from a full-time applied research firm on which people are dependent for a living. Clearly, we do not face the urgent need for projects that might characterize such a group. Yet, many individuals provide applied research services on a part-time basis, and others may wish to start up in that fashion, testing the water without giving up a steady source of income. Indeed, the latter strategy has a great deal to recommend it. ARC's experience, though more relevant to part-time applied researchers, is by no means irrelevant to those dependent on such work for a living.

ARC has been in the fortunate position of rarely having to go out and actively seek projects. The group has been involved in conducting a steady flow of projects for about 8 years, including the following:

- An evaluation of an intervention to promote sex equity in vocational education within a school system.
- A content analysis of professional educational materials used by a major accounting firm.
- An item analysis of test materials used by a major accounting firm in their professional curriculum.

- A development of a performance appraisal system for a small city police department.

- A comprehensive survey of utilization and satisfaction with computing facilities and services at a large university.

- A survey of staff, students, and faculty at a large university regarding sexual harassment experiences.

- An assessment of need for alcohol/substance abuse services in a 34-county rural region.

- A survey of the career paths and professional school experiences of law school alumni from a large university.

- An evaluation of a major business ethics intervention program to promote the teaching of ethics in business college programs.

- A survey of the work-related attitudes of personnel in a state university retirement system.

- A focus group study to identify barriers to mammography screening among poor rural women.

- A design of a survey to be distributed to lawyers within a federal court district.

Some of the factors that contributed to this happy state of affairs might be applicable to other groups or individuals. First, our capacity and need for projects grew over time. We were able to develop contacts and a reputation over a period of a few years.

Second, we have not engaged in active marketing of our services, but we have provided information on ARC to interested parties through a simple brochure. Similarly, we have taken advantage of opportunities to make contact with potential clients and to let them know about ARC without actively "networking." It is extremely important to be able to describe what you can do for clients in terms that they can understand.

Third, we have been flexible and have rarely turned down a project, as long as it met the criteria to be discussed below. On a number of occasions, our work on a small project has led a satisfied client to return with a larger and more challenging project.

Fourth, we have built on our strengths and added expertise over time. ARC's initial strengths were in areas such as program evaluation, needs assessment, and survey research, particularly with respect to health and mental health issues. Relying on similar methodologies and gaining new knowledge and skill, we have slowly expanded into personnel and business issues.

Fifth, ARC has begun to familiarize itself with alternative sources of funding and to explore requests for proposals (RFPs). Clearly, this is an important source of funded projects and may be particularly suitable for the specialized group that has established a niche in a well-funded topic area. Our limited experience, however, suggests that a small firm could commit a great deal of time and energy in responding to RFPs without any return.

Finally, ARC has taken advantage of its geographic location. The demand for applied research services undoubtedly is lower in this rural area than in a large metropolitan area, but so too is the supply. Clearly, the supply of and demand for services is an issue that any research firm needs to address.

ARC is quite flexible in the projects undertaken. This reflects our educational goal and the varied knowledge and interests of our staff, and it is facilitated by having access to faculty with diverse expertise. ARC uses several criteria in selecting projects: (a) availability of a project leader with relevant expertise and interest, (b) educational opportunities for ARC staff, and (c) service contributed to the community. Project funding to enhance ARC resources (e.g., conference travel, computer equipment) is secondary to educational and service considerations. ARC sometimes conducts a project for little or nothing beyond direct costs but, generally, an appropriate fee is involved.

Project scope is also relevant. Projects are preferred that can be completed in a semester by a team of two to four staff working about five to ten hours a week—that is, between about 150 and 640 person-hours in total. This preference follows from our goals of providing service to a variety of community organizations and generating diverse educational opportunities for ARC members. Over several years, projects of this scope yield an array of experiences that meet the educational needs of most ARC participants.

Setting Fees: Making a Living?

Professional capacities to plan, conceptualize, examine, generate knowledge, and communicate are somewhat nebulous and intangible compared to building a bridge, removing a tumor, or winning a court case. As a result, many applied researchers and some clients have difficulty viewing these activities as a valuable service worthy of financial reimbursement. This view may be particularly prevalent among those who have worked in academia or whose applied research career rests on strong social, political, or altruistic motives. It is essential that the applied researcher examine his or her attitudes regarding fees for service and adopt an appropriate professional posture. One must learn what service and/or product the client wants, and then expect to be paid for delivering it.

Fee-setting decisions are obvious considerations for independent consultants and may seem less important for an organization whose primary goals are training and service. Yet we follow the same decision-making processes in setting our fees as do independents. The fee-setting process, in fact, is one of the training objectives of ARC.

There are a variety of ways that fees can be set, and therefore, no simple answer to the question, "How much should I charge?" The two major strategies are to request fees by the project or by the hour. The former method may appeal to the client, who knows up front what the project cost will be. The applied researcher, on the other hand, may prefer the latter method in that the risk of underestimating costs is avoided. ARC has found that both parties are best served by a compromise: a project fee based on a thorough plan shared with the client. After initial meetings to discuss the scope and goals of a project, ARC staff prepare a complete project plan with estimated person-hours for each major task, as well as all direct costs for supplies and so forth (see the example in Table 12.1).

This method has a number of advantages. Staff become skilled at analyzing projects and estimating the time required to accomplish tasks: indeed, the budget is the first step in project planning (discussed below). The client knows what the final cost will be and develops an appreciation for the work that goes into a project. Both parties get a sense of how alternative research tactics might affect cost, including how apparently minor changes or additional requests can add substantially to time, effort, or cost. A formal budget also allows for contingency payments (e.g., if additional client questions turn a three-page survey into one of six pages) and for interim payments (e.g., the first of three payments to be made following development of a satisfactory instrument).

Beyond these issues, the best guide in setting fees may be experience, both one's own and that of fellow professionals. One can get a sense of what the going hourly rate is in one's area. Over time, one gets a sense of what clients view as appropriate for different types of project and what they are willing to pay professionals for their work. A final point, clients want a good job and typically are willing to pay for it—low fees are no substitute for quality work.

Table 12.1 Example of an ARC Budget: Test Validation
Proposal and Budget

	I. Personnel Expenses	
	Task	Project Hours
	Job Analysis	40
	Content Analysis	15
	Review of Alternative Tests	10
	Performance Review	20
	Report Writing	30
Total Personnel Hours		115

	II. Supplies and Other Direct Costs	
Item	Description	Unit Cost ($)
Report Writing	Graphs	10.00/ea.
	Final Report	0.05/page
	Binding	2.00/ea.
Tests	Examination Copies and Copyright Charges	Varies
Photocopying	For materials related to the project activities	0.05/page

	III. Total Estimated Costs		
Personnel	$30.00/hr.	115 hours	$3450.00
Supplies[a]	Graphs	4	$40.00
	Final Report	2 (50 pages ea)	$5.00
	Binding	2	$4.00
	Tests	5	$100.00
	Photocopying	400 pages	$20.00
Total Costs			$3619.00

NOTE: a. Actual expenses will be billed directly to client.

Negotiating With Clients: Making Responsibilities Explicit

The first stage of a project involves meeting with the client to achieve several important objectives: (a) to establish a professional working relationship, (b) to communicate what services you can provide (and what you cannot provide), and (c) to establish the scope of the project. The first two objectives may be implicit, but the last should be explicit. Minor misunderstandings at this stage often grow into major problems later in the project. Several meetings may be needed to establish the scope of the project and as a prelude to a formal project plan and budget (see Kuhnert & Gore, and Cristiani chapters).

An important first question that needs to be addressed is, "Who is the client?" Working with a group or committee can be fraught with difficulties if one gets caught in the cross-fire of rivalries or competing priorities and agendas. Within complex organizations, whether a business firm or a human service agency, there are likely to be multiple stakeholders in the wings. These are persons who are quite likely to have an investment in and opinion about the project and how it should be conducted, but who are not directly involved—yet! Even when dealing with an organizational representative who appears to have complete authority regarding the project, it can be very helpful to find out about potential stakeholders and to make explicit their involvement, or lack thereof (see Barrington, this volume).

For example, ARC was involved in a project funded by a national organization. This organization wanted to provide a needed, but expensive service to area residents. ARC was contracted to conduct research to determine potential clients' reactions to the service. At the same time, the national organization had created a team of people in the community who would look into ways of implementing the service. Unbeknownst to ARC, the national organization lead this team to believe that ARC was to report its research progress to them, and that they would channel our findings and recommendations to the national organization. The ARC members on the project did not feel the need to keep this "team" informed of all the details of our progress on the project and were quite perplexed when they kept insisting on monthly reports. The miscommunication was straightened out without creating a rift between these parties, but we learned a valuable lesson in knowing exactly who our client is.

What are the clients goals for the project and how do these fit into broader goals? For example, what kind of information are they seeking and for what purpose? Who will have input on the methodology, such as sample selection, or survey-item content? From whom are data to be collected? What is the time frame for the project? What issues should be addressed in a report? For whom is the report intended? Early discussion of these and similar issues should be the basis for an explicit statement of the scope of a project. The responsibilities of both parties should be set down in a memorandum of agreement or contract, to be signed by both parties, that includes the budget and projected timeline.

The initial agreement need not be set in stone, but it should serve as a clear statement of mutual obligations and responsibilities. One should be willing to consider shifts in the client's goals and accommodate them if possible. Similarly, the client should be willing to consider alternative tactics for meeting project goals, should new opportunities or obstacles arise. However, neither party is obliged to go beyond the initial agreement.

A written agreement or contract signed by both parties goes a long way in preventing client-consultant conflict, but even the best laid plans cannot eliminate the possibility of conflict or tension with clients. Some clients are simply difficult to deal with, and, yes, sometimes we are not perfect! The art of dealing with difficult clients is grounded in the art of dealing with difficult people in general. It is easy to become proud and obstinate and thus build a wall between oneself and the client when they disagree with or misunderstand your methods. After all, who is the expert here? On the other hand, listening, appreciating, and at times, sympathizing with the client can help build a bridge. If the client feels that you really understand her problem or situation, she is much more likely to listen to yours as well. As a training lesson, we do not shield our students from these clients. Sometimes we have treated the difficult client as a case study to give everyone a chance at formulating a response or strategy to deal with the problem.

Conducting Projects: Planning and Timetables

ARC's sense of organization has clearly developed over the years. We have learned that a clearly written plan for project execution has many benefits. Preparing a budget is perhaps the most straightforward rationale for planning. Not only does it help ensure that one will be paid fairly for labor and expenses, but it gives the client a clear idea of what they are paying for. Furthermore, a timetable gives the client an idea of when they can expect to receive preliminary reports. When they understand the stages of your research, they may be less inclined to "look over your shoulder" too early in the project. Also, the client may better understand why apparently small changes may actually cause major problems.

To us, explicit plans and timetables serve two crucial objectives: training and maintaining professionalism. Because ARC is essentially a component of the students' graduate program, they have to schedule ARC activities around their other obligations. Students have found that skills in preparing explicit project plans have generalized to other aspects of their graduate training (e.g., planning their thesis). Similarly, the faculty involved in the program cannot become completely devoted to ARC projects. By articulating project obligations at the outset, students and faculty have a better sense of how to budget their time. The professional consultant also knows the value of explicit planning. For the same reasons, plans and timetables allow the consultant to effectively juggle several projects at one time, or to maintain a sense of sanity if they have multiple commitments (e.g., the professional who does consulting "on the side").

On a few occasions, ARC members have collaborated with professionals outside our organization on joint projects. The success of these collaborations has hinged directly on the degree to which roles, responsibilities and mutual expectations as well as the project execution outline have been specifically articulated. Table 12.2 depicts an example of the type of schedule that was followed on a collaborative project. Although successful collaboration depends on much more than written plans, such planning fosters the necessary conditions for teams to develop good working relationships and mutual goal orientation.

Closing Remarks

There are many models for teaching applied research skills to graduate students. We created a viable consulting firm as a vehicle for this type of training. Just as university counseling and clinical centers serve a training function for students in these disciplines of psychology, and a service function for the university and broader community, our consulting center, ARC, has achieved many objectives. At a recent faculty meeting, others in the experimental psychology program wanted the applied experimental faculty to define the training objectives of ARC in order to establish criteria for (among other things) determining when students could "get out of ARC." Our students responded, "how long can we stay in?" If anything, we have to pull the reins in on their ambitions for ARC.

Table 12.2 Timeline Illustration for an ARC Project

Month/Week		Activity	Description
February	2	Planning	Developing criteria for focus group par-
	4	Planning	ticipation, and developing questioning
March	1	Planning	strategy in coordination with group
	2	Planning	facilitators, community leaders, and client personnel
March	3	Training for Group Facilitators	
March	4	Pilot testing the procedure and revising procedures based on pilot test results	Conduct first focus group session and analyze data to provide additional refinement to the procedure. Data analysis includes videotape transcription and content analysis
April	1	Second Focus Group	A few days between focus group sessions
	2	Third Focus Group	are planned in order to allow time to
	3	Fourth Focus Group	transcribe the facilitator's field notes, to review the videotapes in order to gather meaningful impressions, and to make any further adjustments to the focus group strategy
April	1	Transcribing	Complete transcription of all videotaped
	2	Transcribing	material from the focus group sessions
	3	Transcribing	includes coding key phrases and responses onto index cards for content analysis
April	4	Content Analysis	Using established content analysis tech-
May	1	Content Analysis	niques to uncover important themes,
	2	Content Analysis	ideas, feelings, and perceptions from the focus group discussion. Conducting interrater reliability analysis to determine the accuracy and consistency of the interpretations of the data
May	3	Report writing	Working with all parties to prepare the
	4	and preparation of	report and presentation to meet the expec-
June	1	presentation to the	tations of the form of the final product
	2	client	
	3		

NOTE: June 30 is the target completion date.

In addition to being a key component of a successful graduate program in applied psychology, ARC has become a successful consulting organization in its own right. In this chapter we have tried to relate our experiences as consultants to the kinds of experiences novice professionals are likely to encounter. Our goal has been to inform the reader about ARC as both a training and service program and as a flourishing consulting firm. We hope that the lessons we have learned prove valuable to you as well.

Note

1. Revenue generated by ARC projects is used only to fund education opportunities (e.g., conference travel) and resources (e.g., computer equipment, a library), never for salary.

Index

Adler, T., 40
Alkhafaji, A., 97
American Psychological Association, 107, 113, 115
American Statistical Index, 131
Anderson, 147
APA Committee on Accreditation and Accreditation Office, 4, 6
Applied Research Consultants (ARC), 196
Applied Research Training, 3
Archival Information, 127, 128, 131
Areson, J. C., 155
Audience for report presentation, 162

Bache-Wiig, T., 191
Barriers to Multicultural Success, 86
Beer, M., 38, 47
Bellman, G. M., 55
Beniger, J. R., 145
Benveniste, G., 70
Block, P., 55-56, 61, 66
Bogue, D. J., 134
Boulder Conference, 4
Boyd, J. H., 133, 134
Brayfield, 34

Brock, D. B., 133
Brookins, G. K., 165, 175-176
Brown, R., 176
Brownell, A., 191
Buller, A., 177
Burke, J. D., 133, 134
Burke, W. W., 57
Buxton, V. M., 37, 45

Caplan, 41
Casady, R. J., 133
Cavior, N., 175
Chart Essay, 173
Chelimsky, E., 73, 75
Chicago Conference, 4
Cleveland, W. S., 148, 152
Client/Customer, 53
    Client, 64
    Client-Consultant Relationships, 51
    Client Focused, 185
Collins, E. G. C., 97
Communication, 74
Competence, 59
Confidentiality, 113, 120
Consultant, 53, 54, 57

Consultation, 33
Consulting Skills, 52, 54
Contracting, 60
Contracts, 107-116
County and City Data Book, 131
Credibility, 36, 58, 111, 203
Cristiani, T. S., 58
Cronbach, L., J., 69, 83
Csikszentmihalyi, M., 192
Cummings L. L., 37
Cummings, T. G., 38, 47
Cutts, N., 4

Darlington, R. B., 176
Data Tables, 144
Davis, B. G., 69
DeLoria D., 165, 175-176
Demographics in the Work Force, 86
Dependent Variables, 152
Dertouzos, M. L., 88
Devaluation of Diversity, 87
Devanna, M. A., 97
Dewey, J., 162
Diaconis, P., 152
Dickey, K. C., 146, 155
Directory of U.S. Government
    Depository Libraries, 128
Doughty, J., 141
Downey, R. G., 5, 6

Eaton W. W., 134
Ecological Fallacy, 138
Edwards, 172
Empowering Audiences, 141, 143, 165
Epstein, R., 141
Equal Employment Opportunity
    Commission, 113
Ethical and Professional Guidelines, 38,
    42, 43, 107, 114, 111
Evinger, W. R.,128
Expertise, 36, 54, 203

Fees, Setting, 204
Feinberg, S. E., 142, 143, 145, 147
Feldman, G., 175
Fisher R., 63, 77, 78, 79, 80
Focus on Interests, 78
Ford, S., 41

French, D. W., 133
Frost, P. J., 37

Gaylor, M., 41
George, L. K., 133, 134
George, R. L., 58
Ginsburg, A. L., 148
Goldsmith, H. F., 134, 137
Golembiewski, R. T.,114
Gollub, H. F., 144
Gottfredson G. D., 34
Government Information, 127
Government Records, 128
Graphical Displays, 141, 142, 145, 146
Graystone Conference, 4
Greene, J. C., 141
Greiner L., 70, 81, 83
Gustad, J. W., 4

Hakel, M. D., 36, 38, 46, 47
Hall, E., 100
Hastie, R., 148
Havelock, R., 41
Hendricks, M., 177
Henry, G. T., 146, 155
Hinrichs, J. R., 5
Hoch, E. L., 4
Holland, J. L., 34
Holtzer, C. E., 133
Howard, R., 8, 184
Hudson Institute, 85, 86
Human Participants, 114

Independent Consulting, 85, 200
Independent Variables, 152
Index to International Statistics, 131
Industrial/Organizational, 5
Information Design, 167
Integrity, 115, 187
International Learning Systems (ILS), 184
Internship, 5, 6, 7, 9, 15-20
Invent Options, 79

Jacobs, A., 175
Jacobs, M., 175
Jackson, D. J., 133
Jennings, C. L., 86, 87, 96, 97
Jennings & Jennings, 95

Jones, B. K., 166, 173, 177

Kanter, R. M., 87, 194
Kaplan, C. P., 129
Karno, M., 133, 134
Keep Fit, 81
Kessler, L., 134
Kiecolt, K. J., 128
Klimoski, R., 5
Klosterman, B., 137
Kramer, M., 133, 134
Korman, M., 4
Kuhnert K. W., 5, 6

Lannon, L., 185, 192
Lareau, A., 82
Lavelle, E., 137
Lawler, E. E., 38, 47
Leadership, 88, 199
Ledford, G. E., Jr., 38, 47
Lee, E. S., 134, 137
Leong, F. T. L., 41
Lester, R. K., 88
Levy, P. S., 133
Liebniz, 143
Link, B. G., 138
Locke, B. Z., 133, 134
Lowman, R. I., 113, 114, 115, 116
Lowman, R. L., 43, 47
Luft, J., 94

Mangano, M. F., 166, 173
Marquart, J. M., 141
McGill, R., 148, 152
McKillip, J., 40, 132, 138
McKnight, R., 191
McMillan, J. H., 146
McTaggart, M. J., 146
Metzger, R., 70, 81, 83
Miami Conference, 4
Milcarek, B. I., 138
Miller, G., 39
Misrepresentation, 115
Mitchell, N., 166, 173, 177
Modular Communication, 167
Mohrman, A. M., Jr., 38, 47
Mohrman, S. A., 38, 47
Moore, B. V., 4

Moore, C. M., 79
Morawetz, V., 109
Morrow, A. J., 92
Moses, J. L., 38, 47
Multiculturalism, 85, 88, 92
Multiculturalism in Independent
    Consulting, 85
Multicultural Literacy, 100
Multiple Outcome Measures, 146
Multiple Site Measures, 146
Multivariate Comparisons, 154
Multivariate Graphical Displays, 146
Myers Briggs Type Indicator, 45
Myers, J. K., 133, 134

Nagel, S., 172, 178
Nathan, L. E., 128
National Training Laboratory, 92
Negligence, 112
Negotiating, 62, 63, 206
Negotiation Skills, 76
Nelson-Horchler, J., 184
Newman, D., 178
Noel, J., 148
Nominal Group Technique, 79

Objective Criteria, 80
Open Communication, 57, 58, 193, 207
Organization, 92
Organizational Structure, 198
Organization Development, 85, 92

Parkington, J. J., 37, 45
Partnerships, 67, 68
Personal and Professional Development,
    80-83, 191
Plisko, V. W., 148
Policy Environment, 41, 42, 72
Political Skills, 70-76
Porter, M., 192
Powell, B., 148
Privette, M. J., 109, 110
Process Consultation, 93
Proxy Indicators, 137

Rae, D. S., 133, 134
Rainey, V. C., 4
Ratio Method, 134

Ray, M. L., 141
Realistic Job Previews, 34
Regier, D. A., 133, 134
Reichardt, C. S., 144
Reports, 132, 161
Research, 33, 114
Respect, 189
Responsive Reporting, 170
Rives, N. W., 134, 135
Roberts, L., 141
Roberts-Gray, C., 170, 176, 177
Robins, L. N., 133, 134
Robyn, D. L., 145
Roe, A., 4
Roe, C., 137
Roles,
 Consultants play, 21, 54, 55
 Role Ambiguity, 22-23, 26-27
 Role Conflict, 22-25
 Role Congruence, 27-29
 Role Overload, 22, 23
Ross, A. O., 4
Ross, S., 4
Rossi, P., 83
Rothman, J., 33, 41, 42

Sample Contract, 116
Schaible, W. L., 133
Schein, E. H., 94, 99
Schnack, G. A., 133
Schnieder, B., 35, 36, 37, 45
Schwitzgebel, R. K., 108, 112, 113,
 114, 115
Schwitzgebel, R. L., 108. 112, 113,
 114, 115
Search Strategies, 131
Self-Reflection, 82
Senge, P., 99
Serow, W. J., 134, 135
Shadish, W. R., 141
Shakow, D., 4
Sieber, J. E., 129
Simkin, D., 148
Simon, H., 162
Skinner, B. F., 175
Skodak, M., 4
Smith, F., 52

Society for Industrial/Organizational
 Psychology, 3, 5
Solow, R. M., 88
Sorcher, M., 38, 47
Sparkman, A., 177
Stakeholder, 113, 115
 Analysis, 97
 Players in Evaluations, 70-74
Stallworth, Y., 170, 176
STAR Icon, 147-151
State and Metropolitan Area Date
 Book, 131
Statistical Abstract of the United
 States, 131
Statistical Reference Index, 131
Steele, P., 191
Steelman, L. C., 148
Stephenson, H., 40, 137
Stewart, D. W., 128
Strategic Management, 97
Stress, 22-29, 66
Strunk, W., Jr., 146
Summary Statistics, 144
Super, D. E., 4
Support Systems, 81
Survival Skills, 80
Symptomatic Estimation, 134
Synthetic Estimation, 132, 133

Teasley, C. E., 177
Thayer Conference, 4
Thompson A. S., 4
Thompson, M., 191
TIGER, 129, 130
Timing, 75
Toffler, A., 90
Tokenism, 87
Training for Multiple Professional Roles,
 29-31, 197
Trust, 57, 189
Tufte, E. R., 142, 145, 146, 152
Tukey, J. W., 143
Tweed, D., 133

Ury, W., 63, 77, 78, 79, 80
U.S. Alcohol Epidemiologic Data
 Reference Manual, 137

Vail Conference, 4
Vaill, P. B., 89, 90
Values, 183
Van Valey, T. L., 129
Vaux, A., 137
Vital Rates Procedure, 134

Wainer, H., 148
Wanous, J., 35

Weisbord, M. R., 65
Weiss, C. H., 162
Wells L., Jr., 86, 87, 96, 97
White, E. B., 146
Winder, C. L., 4
Working Relationship, 54, 189-190

Zelig, M., 107

About the Authors

Gail V. Barrington (Ph.D., Educational Administration, University of Alberta) is a Certified Management Consultant and a researcher in the areas of education and training. Her research firm, Gail V. Barrington & Associates, specializes in program planning and evaluation studies and offers seminars in training program effectiveness. Over the past 10 years, she has conducted a number of major research studies for such clients as Employment and Immigration Canada, Athabasca University, Alberta Education, Alberta Career Development and Employment, the Calgary Board of Education, the Calgary Olympic Development Association, the Calgary General Hospital, and the Glenbow Museum. Dr. Barrington has been an educator for more than 20 years and has taught in a variety of settings from elementary school to the community college. She has taught for a number of years at The University of Calgary for the Faculties of Education and Continuing Education. She has written many articles and papers on evaluation topics.

Arlene Brownell (Ph.D.), Director of Research for International Learning Systems, Inc., has consulted extensively in human resource research and development, working in Fortune 1000 companies. Formerly a research psychologist at UCLA and faculty member at Indiana State University, she conducts research to enable organizations to effectively

217

manage current and future organizational performance issues. She recently coauthored, with Kass Larson, a paper titled "Aligning Values and Performance to Strategic Objectives," forthcoming in *Performance Technology—'92: Selected Proceedings of the NSPI Conference.*

Michael F. Cristiani (B.A., Psychology, St. Louis University; M.S. and Ed.D., Counseling Psychology, Indiana University) is Manager, Organizational Development at Storz, a medical specialty division of American Cyanamid, in St. Louis, Missouri. He has extensive experience as both an internal and external consultant with a major aerospace company, an international training and development firm, and many other businesses and organizations. His consulting has focused on organizational effectiveness, total quality management, leadership development, and high performance teams. His publications in professional journals include applying counseling skills in business and industry. He has served as past president of the St. Louis Metropolitan Chapter, American Society for Training and Development, and has been active on a committee of the Private Industry Council.

Ronald G. Downey (Ph.D., Quantitative Psychology, Temple University) is Professor of Industrial/Organizational Psychology and Interim Assistant Provost and Director of Planning and Evaluation Services at Kansas State University. His current research interests include part-time employment, job security, customer service, and organizational commitment.

Barbara A. Gore (B.A., Emory University; M.S., University of Georgia) is a doctoral candidate in the Applied Psychology Program at the University of Georgia. Her consulting experience and research interests include personnel selection, background data, job analysis, assessment center design, and occupational counseling.

Gary T. Henry is the Director of the Center for Urban Policy Research at Georgia State University. His current research interests are graphical analysis of data, performance monitoring systems, and educational policy. Most recently, he has published "Establishing Benchmarks for Outcome Indicators," an article on establishing benchmarks for indicators in *Evaluation Review* and an article on a research and development approach for performance monitoring implementation in *Public Administration Review*. He has been the principal investigator for the educational outcome indicator system project in Virginia. In addition to academic positions, he served as the Deputy Secretary of Education, Deputy Superintendent of Public Instruction, and Chief Methodologist for the Joint Legislative Audit and Review Commission, all in Virginia. He has served as a consultant in more than 10 states and on federal projects and is on the faculty for the National Conference of State Legislatures.

Carl L. Jennings (M.S., City College, CUNY) is an organization and management development specialist. He also received 2 years of interpersonal communications and management development training at the division of Training and Consultation, Yale Medical School department of psychiatry. He holds various certifications. He is interested in the effects of multiculturalism on organizational climate and culture and their resultant impact on qualitative service provision and/or product creation. He is particularly concerned with the creation of high performance multicultural teams for achieving competitive and strategic advantage. He has more than 15 years experience as an organizational consultant with both national and international experience. He is cofounder of the organizational and communications consulting firm of Jennings & Jennings and is a professional member of the NTL Institute for Applied Behavioral Science.

Karl W. Kuhnert (Ph.D., Kansas State University) is Associate Professor in the Applied Psychology Program at the University of Georgia. He has held faculty appointments at Auburn and Ohio State Universities. His publications and research interests include organizational leadership, job stress and job security, and organizational change and development. He has consulted with numerous federal, state, and private organizations.

Kass Larson, Director of Information Technologies, International Learning Systems, Inc., focuses on effectively introducing new technologies into organizations and managing information technologies to support organizational strategies. His work emphasizes the importance of incorporating values, communication, and cross-functional integration into management strategies and business operations.

Frederick T. L. Leong (Ph.D., University of Maryland) is Assistant Professor of Psychology at the Ohio State University. With a double specialty in Counseling and Industrial/Organizational Psychology from the University of Maryland, he currently serves as a faculty member in both the Counseling and Industrial/Organizational Psychology programs at The Ohio State University. His current and past service on editorial boards has included the *Journal of Vocational Behavior*, *Journal of College Student Development* and the *Career Development Quarterly*. He has more than 30 publications in various counseling and psychology journals and 8 book chapters. He was the Guest Editor for the special issue of the *Career Development Quarterly* (March, 1991) on the career development of racial and ethnic minorities. He was also the coeditor of the recently published book *Womanpower: Managing in Times of Demographic Turbulence* (1992) from Sage. He is the current Treasurer of the Association for Multicultural Counseling and Development and also a member of the Board of Directors of the Asian American Psychological Association.

Jack McKillip is Professor of Applied Experimental Psychology at Southern Illinois University at Carbondale. He is author of *Need Analysis: Tools for the Human Services and Education* (Sage, 1987) and numerous papers on needs assessment and applied research methods. He has been head of the Needs Assessment and the Teaching of Evaluation TIGs of the American Evaluation Association. His interests include methodological issues in applied research, especially program evaluation and needs assessment.

Cynthia Roberts-Gray (Ph.D., Experimental Psychology, the University of Texas at Austin) is owner and senior scientist of the Resource Network of Austin, Texas, whose current projects include work to prevent unwanted teenage pregnancies and mitigate problems associated with too early parenting, empower battered women to achieve safe and satisfying futures for themselves and their families and reduce fragmentation in the service system for youth at risk by making it more consumer driven. She has taught research methods and statistics at California State University in Los Angeles and has for the last 12 years been engaged full-time in applied research and evaluation.

Frank (Skip) E. Saal (Ph.D., Psychology, Pennsylvania State University) is Professor and Chair of the Department of Psychology at Kansas State University. He served as the Director of the Industrial and Organizational Psychology program at Kansas State from 1976 to 1989. He has published research articles in performance appraisal, measurement, leadership, and sexual harassment. He is coauthor of several books including *Industrial and Organizational Psychology: Science and*

Practice, with Pat Knight. He consults with local and regional government and with private industry.

Michael J. Schwerin (B.S., Carroll College, Waukesha, Wisconsin; M.A., Southern Illinois University at Carbondale) is a doctoral student in the Applied Experimental Psychology program at Southern Illinois University at Carbondale, Illinois. Research interests include personality testing and measurement, psychosocial aspects of anabolic steroid use, and social perception of anabolic steroid users. He is also a member of Applied Research Consultants (ARC), a consulting firm operating within the Applied Experimental Psychology program at Southern Illinois University.

Hugh Stephenson (B.A., University College, Dublin, Ireland; M.A., Southern Illinois University at Carbondale) is currently completing his Ph.D. at Southern Illinois University. His doctorate is a double major in both applied experimental psychology and clinical psychology. He is a member of Applied Research Consultants and will be completing his clinical internship at Tulane University Medical School.

Margaret (Peggy) S. Stockdale (Ph.D.) is Assistant Professor of Psychology at Southern Illinois University at Carbondale, and Director of Applied Research Consultants. She received her doctoral training at Kansas State University in Industrial and Organizational Psychology and teaches in the Applied Experimental Psychology program at SIUC. Her consulting practices have ranged from conducting salary and job evaluation studies to organizational attitude surveys to focus group studies with economically disadvantaged rural women. Her research interests concern women in the workplace and she has authored several papers on sexual harassment and sexual discrimination against female managers.

Alan Vaux (Ph.D., Psychology, Trinity College, Dublin, Ireland; M.A. and Ph.D., Social Ecology, University of California at Irvine) is Associate Professor of Psychology at Southern Illinois University at Carbondale. He is a Fellow of the American Psychological Association (Community Research and Action Division), author of a book (*Social Support*) and (co-) author of some 40 published articles and book chapters on community psychology. He learned Program Evaluation from Ross Conner at UCI and consultation from being the Director of ARC (1987-1991).